Grand Diplôme
Cooking Course

Index
Glossary

Grand Diplôme Cooking Course

A Danbury Press Book

The Danbury Press

a division of Grolier Enterprises, Inc.

Robert B. Clarke   Publisher

This book has been adapted from the Grand Diplôme Cooking Course, originally published by Purnell Cookery, U.S.A.

Purnell Grand Diplôme Editorial Board

Rosemary Hume and Muriel Downes
Principals, London Cordon Bleu Cookery
School, England

Anne Willan	Editor
Eleanor Noderer	Associate Editor
Sheryl Julian	Assistant Editor
John Paton	Managing Editor
José Northey	Co-ordinating Editor
Peter Leather	Art Editor
Charles F. Turgeon	Wine Consultant

Library of Congress Catalog Card Number: 72-13896
© B.P.C. Publishing, 1971, and
© Phoebus Publishing, 1972.
Filmsetting by Petty and Sons Ltd., Leeds, England.
Printed in the United States of America

23456789987654

All recipes have been tested either at the Cordon Bleu Cookery School in London or in our U.S. test kitchens.

Note: all recipe quantities in this book serve 4 people unless otherwise stated.

Grand Diplôme Cooking Course

Index

*= excellent recipe

A

Abalone **10** 29
Adobo (Philippine chicken and
    pork stew) **11** 89
Adrak (definition) **13**, 82
African cooking **11** 91, 92
Aigrettes **17** 127
Aioli **14** 117
Ajiaco (Cuban pork and vegetable
    stew) **11** 83
Alabama
    dip, with shrimps **10** 31
    sauce **3** 108, **5** 120
Alaska, baked **4** 78
Alfajor de huaura (Peruvian
    pineapple layer cake) **11** 87
Alice salad **15** 63
All Saints' Day fritters **16** 125
Almond(s) **10** 96
    amaretti **10** 92
    apples, baked **5** 104
    balls **10** 94
    blossom dessert (hung gah
        teem choy) **17** 80
    to brown **1** 53
    cake
        angel **6** 64
        meringue **4** 80
        Portuguese **16** 128
        rich **6** 75
    and cheese filling **17** 131
    with chicken **17** 51
    flan, with raspberries **18** 45
    cheesecake **4** 56
    coffeecake, Danish
        (mandelbrød) **12** 29
    croquettes **16** 128
    fillings for Danish pastry **13** 29
    flan
        with apricots **1** 53, **15** 74
        fruit **3** 96

gâteau, meringue and
    chocolate **10** 95
gelatin, with lychees,
    Hong Kong **11** 96
and honey cakes **14** 99
to grind **4** 106
meringue cakes **18** 62
paste **9** 69, **15** 78
    fruits **14** 54
pastry, savory **7** 53
petits fours **16** 132–133
pie, coffee **1** 53
Portuguese cake **16** 128
preparation **10** 90
rocks **16** 132
salted, with smoked cod's roe **7** 50
strudel **9** 33
    with apricot **15** 115
tartlets **14** 99
turquois **10** 95
Alsacienne (definition) **2** 38
Amaretti **10** 92
American tamale pie **11** 73
Ancho chili
    definition **15** 28
    dough **15** 33
Anchovy
    butter **3** 12, **16** 76
    canapés **17** 128
    and chicken liver toasts **14** 45
    diamonds **5** 30, **17** 122
    eggs **5** 30
    fingers **17** 122
    loaf **13** 104
    mayonnaise **5** 49
    relish, with tomato **11** 15
    salad
        with beans **13** 57
        with tomatoes and beans **12** 110
    topping for sandwiches **13** 10
Andouille sausage
    (definition) **12** 123
Andouillette sausage
    (definition) **12** 123

Angel cake with strawberries **1** 97
Angelica **7** 118
Angels on horseback **10** 25
Anglesey speckled bread **14** 46
Anglo-Indian banana and egg **13** 92
Anise, star **17** 75
Anticuchos **17** 134
Apeninno sausages
    (definition) **12** 124
Apfeltorte (meringue apple
    cake) **11** 135
Appetizers
    antipasto **13** 55–61
    cold **15** 117–125
    ginger and grapefruit **17** 36
    seafood and watercress **17** 10

Apple(s) **5** 103–109
    amber **5** 107
    baked **5** 104
        with almonds **5** 104
        with apricots **1** 91, **12** 62
        chocolate **5** 104
    and blackberry jelly **11** 33
    Bristol **5** 107
    brown Betty **5** 106
    butter **11** 33
    cake
        meringue (Apfeltorte) **11** 135
        upside down **9** 65
        Yorkshire **1** 53
    charlotte
        aux pommes **6** 126
        Swedish **5** 104
    chartreuse **11** 47
    chutney, with tomato **11** 34
    compote, with cranberry **6** 100
    crab, spiced **7** 84
    and cranberry jelly **11** 33
    crêpe **9** 106
    crisp **5** 107
    custard **11** 20
    Eve's pudding **5** 106
    filling for
        Danish pastry **13** 29
        strudel **10** 114

Apple(s) *continued*

flan	
ménagère	**3** 29
with orange	**10** 14
spiced	**3** 31
Florentine	**8** 53
fritters	**2** 58
galette	**8** 83
with hazelnuts	**17** 12
jam	
with blackberries	**7** 80
with ginger	**11** 32
jelly	**11** 33
mousse gâtinaise	**6** 14
and pears, with almond	
meringue	**5** 107
pie	**1** 52
and blackberry	**14** 127
latticed	**14** 32
and onion	**14** 42
purée, with potato (himmel und	
erde)	**11** 133
salad, with herring	**10** 70
sauce	**1** 39
cake	**1** 117
with walnuts	**9** 105
slice	**9** 32
Bavarian	**1** 52
snow	**5** 106
soufflé	**8** 96
soup (cream), with apricots,	
iced	**5** 123
spiced	**8** 50
strudel filling	**10** 114
stuffed	
in meringue, with chocolate	
sauce	**7** 92
in salad	**6** 42
stuffing	**8** 49
with pecan and prune	**8** 49
tart tatin	**5** 106
tarte aux pommes à l'orange	**10** 14
topping for coffeecake	**13** 14
whiskey	**10** 131
Apricot(s)	
with baked apples	**1** 91

cheesecake	**4** 22
cup, with orange	**18** 111
flan	**4** 23
with almond	**15** 74
flip	**4** 63, **12** 78
ice cream	**11** 106
jam	**16** 97
glaze	**1** 54, **15** 78
pineapple	**7** 80
moscovite	**14** 123
mousse basque	**15** 22
nut bars	**13** 12
poaching	**4** 17
purée	**11** 106
sauce	
hot and cold	**4** 60
jam	**9** 124
rum	**11** 47
soup (cream), with apple, iced	**5** 123
spiced	**7** 82
strudel, with almonds	**15** 115
stuffing, with celery and pecan	**8** 48
suédoise	**5** 14

Arles sausages	
(definition)	**12** 124
Arni kokkinisto (Greek lamb stew)	**12** 91
Arroz brasileiro (Brazilian rice)	**11** 86
Arroz con leche (Spanish rice	
pudding)	**16** 127
Arroz con leche a la Gallega	
(Galician rice pudding)	**16** 127
Artichoke(s)	
bottoms	**15** 54
garnish	**15** 126
to prepare	**13** 60
à la crème	**3** 123
à la grecque	**4** 115
globe	**7** 34
hearts, to prepare	**6** 32, **16** 72
Jerusalem	
definition	**7** 84
pickled	**7** 84
with mushrooms	**8** 109
Niçoise	**13** 61
potage palestine	**6** 55
salad	
with mushrooms	**6** 32

with tomatoes	**6** 30, **16** 72
stuffed	
Italian	**7** 35
vinaigrette	**16** 10
Asafetida (definition)	**13** 82
Asian cooking, Southeast	**11** 93–97
Asparagus	
with butter, melted	**1** 63
with chicken	**17** 29
and black bean sauce	**17** 80
to cook	**17** 29
with hollandaise sauce	**2** 98
rolls	**15** 23
with scrambled eggs	**5** 29
soup, cream	**17** 54
tartlets	**7** 50
Aspic	**14** 31
basic	**8** 19
beef in	**17** 56
chopped	**8** 18
coating with	**8** 17
mint, lamb chops in	**8** 21
mold, to line	**13** 69
parsley, with smoked trout	**15** 103
poultry in	**7** 124
quick	**8** 18, **16** 42
salmon in	**17** 13
shrimps in	**8** 10
sole, fillets of, in	**8** 23
stocks for	**8** 19
turkey in	**15** 10
Aurore chaudfroid sauce	**18** 95
Australasian cooking	**11** 88–89
Austrian dishes	
boiled beef with horseradish	
sauce	**1** 62
cheese pastries	**15** 92
gâteau	**18** 65–68
rum cake	**16** 39
Avgolemono	**6** 10
sauce	**5** 120
Avocado	**5** 120
ice, with tomato	**5** 125
mousse	**13** 104
salad	**2** 11, **11** 29, **15** 37
with orange and grapefruit	**6** 37
with tomato	**12** 46, **17** 93

Avocado *continued*

sauce	**15**	37
soup	**2** 98, **3**	117
stuffed with cheese	**15**	96
in tarragon cream dressing	**8**	44

B

Baba

definition	**13**	22
ghanouj (eggplant with sesame oil)	**12**	87
au rhum	**13**	24
Baby's ball	**15**	78
Baby's dream	**18**	120
Bacalao a la Vizcaina (Basque salt cod)	**16**	120
Bacalhau Portuguesa (Portuguese salt cod)	**16**	121

Bacon

with frankfurters and sauerkraut	**10**	60
galette, with cheese and potato	**5**	50
omelet		
with croûtons	**1**	79
with potato (bonne femme)	**1**	79
pâte	**7** 25, **9**	48
pie, with leek	**11**	14
rolls	**3**	97
sautéed, with kidneys	**12**	55
and spinach salad	**16**	68
waffles, with cheese	**5**	130
'Bacon and heaven' cake	**16**	128
Bagna cauda	**17**	133
Bake 'blind', to	**1**	55
Baked Alaska	**18**	118
Baked potatoes, orange	**14**	127
Bakewell flan	**3**	28
Baklava (Greek honey and nut pastries)	**12**	95

Ballotine

of chicken with prunes	**16**	106
definition	**2**	13
of duck	**2**	13

Bamboo shoots

definition	**17**	64
garnish	**16**	48
with snow peas and water chestnuts	**17**	80

Banana(s)

	11	22
baked	**12**	77
Brazilian	**11**	22
cake	**6**	105
chartreuse	**8**	26
coconut rolls	**5**	42
coconut sambal	**13**	92
cream roll	**6**	69
egg	**13**	92
flip	**4**	63
fritters	**2**	58
ice cream	**11**	106
with liqueur	**12**	59
milk punch	**11**	84
purée	**11**	106
sauce	**9**	124
spiced	**10**	128
split	**5**	53
Banbury cakes	**2**	29
Banderillas (miniature kebabs)	**16**	112
Bangkok chicken	**16**	30
Bannock, Selkirk	**14**	50
Baps	**7**	70
Barbados guava pie	**11**	84

Barbecue

chicken	**13**	88
party menu	**3**	93–97
sauce		
blender	**3**	81
hot	**3**	81
spare ribs	**7**	25
Barding	**2**	89
fat	**9**	40

Barley

baked	**4**	99
pudding	**4**	61
Barossa chicken	**17**	30
Barquettes italiennes	**18**	62
Bärsoppa (berry soup)	**12**	25
Basket of flowers	**15**	79
Basler leckerli	**18**	70
Basquaise chicken, roast	**1**	18

Basque cooking

definition	**1**	18
fish stew	**16**	120
salad	**17**	85
salt cod	**16**	120

Bass

broiled provençale	**11**	52
caprice	**18**	82
fish couscous	**12**	94
sea, broiled	**3**	80
steamed, duxelles	**1**	65
striped, à la kan	**17**	69
stuffed whole fish, Danish (fylld hel fisk)	**12**	21
Basting	**1**	18
Batarde sauce	**2**	53
Bâteau célestins	**14**	103
Bâteau de miel	**14**	99
Battenburg cake	**15**	78
Batter, for crêpes	**13**	124

Bavarian cooking

apple slice	**1**	52
cream	**2**	95

Bavarois

à la crème	**2**	103
coffee	**15**	51
definition	**2**	95
Baw choy foo yee (spinach with bean cake sauce)	**17**	80
Bean(s), dried	**12**	98–111

black

definition	**17**	64
purée	**12**	109
sauce	**17**	77, 80
soup	**12**	101
Boston baked	**12**	106
cassoulet	**12**	106
chili con carne	**12**	106
to cook	**12**	101
fava	**13**	57
ménagère	**12**	109
soup	**12**	105
frijoles	**14** 18, **15**	36
Galician white soup	**16**	115
kidney, purée	**12**	110
kinds	**12**	100
lentil purée	**12**	109
lima, purée	**12**	109
maître d'hôtel	**12**	109
marrow in cream sauce	**12**	110
navy, with sausages	**12**	106
paste, red	**17**	64

Bean(s) *continued*
pea, in cream sauce	**5** 63
puchero	**12** 105
red, soup	**6** 56
refrid	**15** 37
salad, with anchovy and tomato	**12** 110
to soak	**12** 101
soup, with leeks	**12** 103
succotash	**12** 63
and tomato soup	**9** 120

Bean(s), green
béarnaise ✳	**4** 13
buttered	**1** 35
with chilies	**15** 36
with pine nuts	**2** 38
relish	**7** 85
salad	**6** 30
with anchovy	**13** 57
and tomato	**12** 110
and celery	**8** 64

Bean cake
definition	**17** 64
fermented	**17** 64
sauce	**17** 64
with spinach	**17** 80
sautéed with meat	**17** 77
with stuffed fish	**17** 69

Bean paste bun	**16** 57
Beans, lima	**14** 18
casserole	**4** 95
Marie-Anne	**4** 97
salad	**13** 106, **17** 84
in sour cream	**2** 84
succotash	**4** 114
Bear	**17** 114
ardennaise	**17** 114
Béarnaise	
definition	**5** 87
sauce	**2** 52
Beau monsieur	**17** 125
Béchamel sauce	**2** 45
with vegetables	**7** 43
Beef	
in aspic (medallions de boeuf en gelée)	**17** 56

bitki	**10** 63
boeuf à la mode (braised in wine)	**16** 120
boeuf à la mode (braised in (braised, in gelatin)	**6** 121
boeuf en daube	**6** 121
boiled	
Austrian, with horseradish sauce	**1** 62
corned	**7** 122
with dumplings	**10** 60
New England dinner	**1** 63
braised	
with champagne (boeuf braisé au champagne)	**17** 56
fillet chasseur	**12** 116
Flemish style	**4** 92
provençale	**5** 60
red wine	**5** 68
Roman style	**8** 103
round	**5** 60
short ribs	**10** 63
Brazilian baked meat and beans	**11** 86
carbonade of	**16** 33
casserole	
with rice	**17** 69
smothered	**5** 41
tacos (tacos en cazuela)	**15** 32
cholent	**9** 29
chili con carne	**12** 106
club steak au naturel	**10** 14
corned	
boiled	**7** 122
glazed	**9** 24
cottage (shepherd's) pie	**14** 41
curry, Thai meat	**11** 96
dried, rolls	**3** 41
fermière (farmer's wife-style)	**3** 22
fillet	**13** 102
in aspic	**18** 31
de boeuf en gelée	
bouquetière	**18** 31
Dubarry, roast, italienne	**9** 87
Italienne	**9** 87
steak, papillon	**12** 42

flan	**11** 12
fondue, bourguignonne	**5** 46
fresh, for boiling	**10** 60
fricadelles in tomato sauce	**3** 40
fricassée of, with chestnuts	**14** 127
galette	**11** 72
goulash	
quick	**5** 41
paprika	**3** 19
hash, Danish (labskovs)	**12** 24
hot pot	**9** 120
Indonesian fried beef balls (perkedel daging)	**11** 95
knishes	**9** 22
meat balls with tomato and pepper sauce	**5** 50
meat enchiladen (enchiladen con carne)	**15** 32
meat filling (tamales)	**15** 34
miroton of	**13** 38
à la mode bourgeoise	**7** 124
molded	**13** 38
Niçoise	**13** 102
olives	**11** 72
paupiettes de boeuf braisées à la crème	**5** 60
pie, with grouse	**17** 113
pot-au-feu	**1** 62
pot roast	**2** 24
Diablo	**2** 24
New Orleans	**2** 24
puchero	**12** 105
ragoût	
bourguignonn	**10** 83
with celery and walnuts	**3** 19
with Madeira	**3** 19
Rhineland, marinated	**11** 129
roasting	**1** 28–29
times	**6** 18
roast paysanne	**2** 88
roll	**9** 94
rinderrouladen	**11** 131
roulade	**16** 66
salad	**4** 28
saltenas	**5** 124
sandwich	**14** 114
roast, open-face	**12** 13
sauté	
chasseur	**17** 17
with mushrooms and port	**4** 51
serving, suggestions for	**1** 30–31, **6** 22–23
short ribs, braised	**10** 63
soup, with watercress (sai yong choy yuke gung)	**17** 65
spiced	**7** 122

Beef *continued*

steak	**14** 26
cuts	**3** 72–73
Diane ✳	**5** 126
fillet	
marchand de vin	**16** 61
papillon	**12** 42–43
flan	**16** 109
Garrick	**14** 26
Hawaiian mango	**11** 89
and kidney pie	**7** 91
marinated with piquant sauce	**12** 77
mexicaine	**4** 93
minute	
with madeira	**14** 26
soubise	**14** 26
Morateur	**3** 12
with oyster sauce	**14** 38
pizzaiola	**14** 26
provençale	**14** 26
roulades with celery stuffing	**16** 31
and squab tourtière	**7** 123
strip, Perinette	**12** 42
tartare	**15** 105
stew	**3** 19
Ethiopian	**11** 91
stock for consommé	**8** 20
stroganoff	**12** 57
stufato di manzo alla romana	**8** 103
stuffed	**2** 88
with vine leaves (dolmas)	**12** 86
stuffing (for peppers)	**4** 112
Thai meat curry (Kaeng phet nua)	**11** 96
tournedos	**15** 54–55
Chasseur	**15** 56
Clamart	**15** 54
mâconnaise	**17** 47
Parisienne	**15** 54
Rossini	**15** 106
à la Russe	**10** 72
Seville	**17** 48
tzimmes	**9** 14
Wellington	**15** 19
with wine and prunes	**13** 38
with zucchini and tomato	**13** 37
Beer soup	
cold (bierkaltschale)	**11** 125
hot (biersuppe)	**11** 125
Beet(s)	
bortsch	**9** 21
chrane (morar)	**9** 13
creamed	**14** 22
pickled	
Danish (syltede rødbeder)	**12** 25
with eggs	**7** 85
preparation of	**8** 92
relish	**7** 85, **11** 15

with cabbage	**9** 25
with horseradish	**8** 65
salad	
with celeriac and walnut	**6** 32
gelatin	**8** 27
with green peas	**6** 32
Ukrainian	**7** 116
soup, cream of	**8** 92
Behndi foogath (Okra foogath)	**13** 95

Beignets	**17** 127
cheese	**6** 87
mushroom	**7** 53
soufflés	**6** 87
Belgian endive, braised	**4** 104, **10** 63
Bell pepper	
definition	**15** 28
to peel	**15** 28
to prepare	**16** 114
Belvoir cake	**8** 96
Berry compote with cream, Danish (rødgrød med fløde)	**12** 25
soup (bärsoppa)	**12** 25
Beurre blanc sauce	**2** 52
Beurre manié (kneaded butter)	**7** 29
Bien me sabe (Puerto Rican cake with coconut custard)	**11** 84
Bierkaltschale (cold beer soup)	**11** 125
Biersuppe (hot beer soup)	**11** 125
Bigarade sauce	**13** 71
Bigarde	
definition	**2** 48
sauce	**2** 48
Bigne de cavolfiore	**8** 109
'Bird's nests', Turkish (eash-el-asfoor)	**12** 95
Biscuit(s)	**4** 126
bran	**10** 128
brandy snaps	**1** 41
molasses	**4** 126
soda	**4** 126
whipped cream	**4** 59

Biscuit milanaise	**6** 63
Bishop (definition)	**8** 57
cranberry	**8** 57
Bisques	**3** 118
Bistaela (Moroccan chicken pie)	**12** 94
Bitki	**10** 63
Black beans	**12** 100
definition	**17** 64
purée	**12** 109
sauce	**17** 77, 80
soup	**12** 101
Blackberry(ies)	**3** 57
and apple pie	**14** 127
Bavarian	**3** 57
jam	**7** 80
jelly	**7** 81
with apple	**11** 33
summer pudding	**3** 57
Black-eyed beans	**12** 100
Black Forest cake	**18** 68
Blanche au beurre sauce	**2** 53
Blanquette (definition)	**3** 16
Blenders	**6** 48
Blidahs	**4** 80
Blini	**7** 114
Blintzes	**9** 23
Blood sausage (blutwurst)	**12** 123
Blowfish	**11** 52
Blueberry(ies)	**3** 52–54
cake	**10** 130
compote, Danish with cream (rødgrød med fløde)	**12** 25
conde	**3** 54
crumble	**3** 54
flan, cinnamon	**3** 54
ice cream	**11** 106
jam	**7** 79
muffins	**3** 52
pancakes	**3** 54
pie	**5** 49
purée	**11** 106
soup	**3** 52
bärsoppa	**12** 25
waffles	**5** 130
Bluefish	**11** 52
baked with crab meat	**11** 52

Blue trout (definition)	**11** 125
Forelle-blau	**11** 125
Blutwurst sausage	
with apples	**12** 128
definition	**12** 123
Bockwurst sausage	
definition	**12** 123
to make	**12** 127
Boeuf, see Beef	
Boiled new potatoes	**18** 89
Boiling	**1** 60
Boîte au chocolat	**10** 90
Boîte au chocolat aux fruits	
(chocolate box with fruit)	**12** 118
Bok fon (steamed rice)	**17** 66
Bok opp soong (squab in	
lettuce cups)	**17** 73
Bologna sausage	
(definition)	**12** 123
Bolognese sauce	**5** 93
Bombay duck (definition)	**13** 83
Bombe	
chocolate	**18** 114
coffee	**18** 114
Diane	**17** 41
strawberry	**18** 115
véronique	**18** 115
Bone marrow	**8** 105
Bone stock, white	**2** 19
Bonne femme (definition)	**1** 79
Bordelaise	
definition	**2** 49
sauce	**2** 49
Bortsch	**7** 112–113
beet	**9** 21
spinach (schav bortsch)	**9** 21
Boston baked beans	**12** 106
Boston kisses	**13** 121
Bouchée(s)	**8** 76
case	**8** 75
ham and mushroom	**8** 76
kidney and mushroom	**8** 76
miniature	**17** 125
shrimp and egg	**8** 76

Boudin blanc	
definition	**12** 123
to make	**12** 127
Boudin noir (definition)	**12** 123
Bouillabaisse	**6** 113
Boula boula	**12** 101
Boulangère (definition)	**1** 35
potatoes	**11** 25
Boulettes	
de poisson (jengalese fish balls)	**11** 91
de poulet	**18** 110
Bouquet garni	**1** 45
Brains	**13** 64–65
with black butter (Cervelles au	
beurre noir)	**13** 64
bourguignon	**13** 64
curried	**13** 86
fritot of	**13** 65
to prepare	**8** 107
Braised red cabbage	**17** 105
Braisière (definition)	**5** 56
Braising, see also names of	
various meats	**5** 55–65
Bran biscuits	**10** 128
Brandade de morue	**6** 110
Brandy	
hard sauce	**8** 89, **9** 126
milk punch	**8** 55
snaps	**1** 41
Bran muffins	**4** 124
Brazo de Gitano	**18** 69
Bratwurst sausage	
im biersosse	**11** 128
with chestnuts	**12** 130
definition	**11** 128, **12** 123
Braunschweiger sausage	
(definition)	**12** 123
Brazil nuts	**10** 96
Brazilian dishes	
baked meat and beans	**11** 86
bananas	**11** 22
Brazilian stuffing	**8** 49
Brazo de Gitano (Gipsy's	
arm cake)	**16** 128
Bread	**7** 58–73
anchovy loaf	**13** 104
Anglesey speckled	**14** 46
Arab (pita)	**12** 88
baking temperatures	**7** 60
baps	**7** 70
blini	**7** 114
braided twist, Danish	
(flettbrød)	**12** 29
brown soda	**4** 120
and butter pudding	**4** 60
challah	**9** 29
Christmas saffron buns	
(saffransbrød)	**12** 30

coffee cake	
almond, Danish	
(mandelbrød)	**12** 28–29
Martha's	**7** 64
raisin, Danish	**12** 29
rich	**7** 62
simple	**7** 62
corn	
cakes	**10** 127
dollars	**10** 127
skillet	**4** 123
sticks	**4** 123

cottage loaf	**7** 62
cracked wheat	**7** 70
cranberry orange	**4** 121
croûtes	**7** 12
croûtons	**10** 101
crumbs, fried	**17** 101
Danish	**15** 125
of the dead (pan de Muerto)	**15** 41
flower sandwiches	**9** 116
fly	**4** 120
French	**7** 69
fruit braid	**9** 98
garlic loaf	**5** 46, **9** 120
herb loaf, hot	**4** 11, **6** 103
honey twist	**9** 99
ice cream, wholewheat	**11** 106
Indian and Pakistani cooking	**13** 97
ingredients	**7** 60
kissing crust (definition)	**7** 60
kulich	**7** 119
molasses	**10** 127
muffins, English	**7** 64
nut bread, quick	**6** 101
oatmeal	**14** 46
orange currant	**4** 121
peaked finish (definition)	**7** 67
picnic loaf	**4** 37
pineapple nut	**4** 121
pudding, with butter	**4** 60, **15** 41

Bread *continued*

quick breads	**4** 118–123
rolls	**7** 64
Danish light	**12** 30
roulades of smoked salmon	**7** 46
rye	**7** 69
dark	**7** 69
sweet (limpa)	**12** 29
saffron loaves	**12** 30
Sally Lunn	**7** 70
sandwiches	
flower	**9** 116
open-face, Danish	**12** 8–13
stacked	**7** 49
sauce	**17** 101
Scandinavian	**12** 16–31
skillet corn	**4** 123
soda	**4** 120
sourdough	**7** 72
Spanish sweet	**16** 127
spoon	**4** 121
stages in making	**7** 60–61
stuffed	
French, with omelet	**4** 38
pain farci	**13** 37
toast	
French	**10** 127
French coffee	**5** 42
walnut	**10** 94
turkey and mushroom loaf	**8** 61
walnut and butter rolls	**1** 16
wholewheat	**4** 123
white	**7** 62
stuffed	**7** 69
wholewheat	**7** 67
fine	**7** 67
Grahamsbrød	**12** 30
with yeast	**13** 17–33
Bread of the dead (Pan de muerto)	**15** 41
Bread pudding (capirotada)	**15** 41
Breadcrumbs	
browned	**10** 35
fried	**17** 101
white, fresh	**10** 95
Breton salad	**15** 63
Brinjal Sambal	**3** 65, **5** 79
Brioche	**13** 30–33
grapefruit	**13** 32
loaf	**13** 32
pâté de foie gras en	**13** 32
saucisson	**13** 32
sweet rolls	**13** 32
British cooking	**14** 34–55
Brittany buckwheat crêpes	**9** 107
Broadway chicken pie	**10** 66
Broccoli	
flowers	**17** 72
au gratin	**2** 85

mold	**7** 109
Broiling	**3** 68
see also the names of the various meats	
Broth	
clear (definition)	**2** 19
brown sauce	**2** 47–48
chicken	**7** 107
mushroom	**6** 53
dashi	**16** 49
granny's	**14** 36
Scotch	**14** 36
Brown bone stock	**2** 18
Brown sauce	**12** 65
Brown stock	**4** 90
for aspic	**8** 19
Brownie cake	**12** 80
Brownies	**1** 121
butterscotch	**1** 121
Brunch, ideas for	**10** 116–131
Brunswick stew	**10** 65
definition	**10** 65
Buck's fizz	**18** 111
Buckwheat	
crêpes, Brittany	**9** 107
pancakes	**9** 112
Budin de Mango (mango pudding)	**15** 41
Buffet	
buns, hot cross	**1** 101
drinks	**3** 43
festive	**13** 101–109
menu	**3** 37–43
poolside	**16** 66
winter	**11** 9–17
Bulgur (cracked wheat)	
definition	**12** 84
Bun(s)	
bean paste (Hikichamanju)	**16** 57
Chelsea	**14** 49
with coffee	**13** 15
Bunuelos de viento	**16** 125

jam	**13** 25
revel	**14** 46
Burgundian ham	
with parsley, cold	**10** 83
Butter	
anchovy	**3** 12, **16** 76
black	**13** 64
brandy	**14** 45
for broiled dishes	**3** 80–82
cheese	**6** 57
and cheese hors d'œuvres	**17** 127
chutney	**13** 82
clarified	**3** 80, **12** 37
fondant	**13** 120
frosting	
coffee	**17** 16
cream	**13** 52, **15** 24
fruit	**11** 33–34
garlic	**3** 82
herb	**3** 81
kneaded (beurre manié)	**1** 35
maître d'hôtel	**2** 60, **3** 81, **11** 55
mustard	**3** 82
orange	**3** 81
parsley	**3** 81
sauces, how to make	**2** 50–53
savory	**6** 57
tomato	**3** 82, **5** 25
Buttercream frosting 1 and 2	**18** 53
Buttered noodles	**11** 25
Butterfish	**11** 53
Butterfly cakes	**13** 15
Butternuts	**10** 96
Butterscotch	
brownies	**1** 121
cornflake cookies	**9** 119
cream pies	**1** 53
icebox cookies	**1** 121
sauce	**9** 128
strawberries	**10** 131

Cabbage 1 30
alsacienne 17 44
balls, sweet and sour 9 24
braised green 7 27
crepes (stuffed) 16 33
filling for strudel 10 114
leaves, stuffed 7 40
Lorraine 9 80
red
braised 11 131, 17 105
with duck 10 110
pickled 11 36
salad 9 14
relish 7 85
with beets 9 25
sauerkraut
braised 5 64
stuffed
with chestnuts 6 119, 17 119
lemon 7 41
Cacik (yogurt soup) 12 84, 16 106
Café brûlot 8 57
Cake(s), large, see also Pastry
almond
angel 6 64
coffeecake (mandelbrød) 12 29
rich 6 75

angel, with strawberries 1 97
apple sauce 1 117
apple upside down 9 65
Austrian, rum 16 39
baby's ball 15 78
bake, how to 1 105
banana 6 105
cream roll 6 69
basket of flowers 15 79
Battenburg 15 78
Belvoir 8 96

birthday
maypole 2 76
numeral 2 75
steamship 15 81
biscuit milanaise 6 63
blueberry 10 130
boîte au chocolat 10 90
brownie 12 80
caramel 1 117
cassata siciliana 8 112
cheese cake 9 33
Italian 8 112
pineapple 6 99
cherry
layer 1 115
simple 9 61
and walnut 9 62
chocolate
box with fruit (boîte au
chocolat aux fruits) 12 118
and chestnut 10 91
fudge, quick 5 42
mille feuilles 12 73
roll 6 69
walnut sponge 10 94
Christmas, rich 9 68
decorating 9 69
log 15 83
coconut 1 112
cottage cheese 7 118
Czech torte 10 112
dacquoise 12 50
decorating comb 7 101
decoration 2 78–79
devil's food 1 115
equipment for cake-
making 1 108–109
festive 15 142–145
fruit, fresh 9 63–65
to age 9 68
galette
apple 8 83
peach and hazelnut 15 12
orange caramelized 12 71
strawberry 3 47
gateaux and pastries 14 88–105
alcazar 18 56
Alexandra 18 61
almond meringue
and chocolate 10 95
au café 14 111
aux fruits 6 64
Basic Genoise 18 52
basque 3 31
belle Hélène 9 94
bigarreau 3 52
au chocolat, rich 7 102
Diane 8 67

lyonnaise au chocolat 6 126
Margot 13 109
Mercédès 18 54
mexicaine 18 58
mille feuilles au citron 8 69
moka aux amandes 15 24
mousseline 18 56
nougatine 18 59
Pithiviers 18 54
pistache 18 59
progrès 18 58
réligieuse 18 61
Rivoli 18 64
strawberry 15 17
golden fruit 9 62
hazelnut
coffeecake
(haselnusskuchen) 11 133
meringue 9 91
honey 9 31, 10 95
ingredients, preparation of 9 91
jelly roll 6 68
Madeira 1 112
marble 1 117
meringue 4 80
apple (apfeltorte) 11 135
coffee 13 52
nusskuchen 4 106
orange
raisin 9 96
sponge 6 64
whole 9 63
pans 1 109
Passover
sponge 9 17
wine 9 17
pecan fruit 10 94
pineapple
Hawaiian 11 90
layer 1 115
Peruvian 11 87
upside down 9 63

Cake(s), large *continued*

piping cone	**2** 78–79
Portuguese 'bacon and heaven'	**16** 128
pound	**1** 111
Puerto Rican, with coconut custard (bien me sabe)	**11** 84
raisin	
and cherry cake	**9** 62
coffee cake, Danish	**12** 29
spice	**9** 60
walnut	**1** 112
rum, Austrian	**16** 39
Savarin Chantilly	**4** 41
sour cream	**4** 59
for special occasions	**15** 77–84
sponge	**4** 78, **6** 60–61
crusty top	**6** 62
stencil, cardboard, to make	**7** 100
sticky ginger	**4** 41
strawberry	
cream roll	**6** 69
fresh	**9** 63
galette	**3** 47
gâteau	**7** 98
shortcake	**3** 49
walnut cream	**3** 49
timbale Orta	**6** 67
torta di formaggio	**8** 112
tipsy	**7** 92
porcupine	**7** 128
tub of mushrooms	**15** 78
turquois	**10** 95
Twelfth Night	**11** 17
vatrushka	**7** 118
walnut	
bread	**10** 94
layer	**1** 115
white fruit	**9** 68
Yorkshire parkin	**14** 49
Caldo gallego (Galician white bean soup)	**16** 115
Caldo verde (Portuguese kale soup)	**16** 116

Cake(s), small, see also Cookies

almond and honey	**14** 97
Banbury	**2** 29
'bird's nests', Turkish (eash-el-asfoor)	**12** 95
cannoli	**8** 110
coconut macaroons	**9** 57
for coffee parties	**13** 12–15
Concorde grape kuchen	**4** 40
cream buns	**2** 32
cream pipes	**8** 110
Eccles	**2** 29
English madeleines	**1** 111
Florentines	**7** 101

galettes muscats (oak leaf cookies)	**7** 100
honey and nut pastries, Greek (baklava)	**12** 95
jalousie	**8** 81
ladyfingers	**6** 63
magali	**7** 100
mille feuilles (Napoleons)	**8** 81
palmiers	**8** 83
Passover macaroons	**9** 17
raspberry feuilletées	**8** 83
rock	**4** 123
sacristans	**8** 83
sponge cupcakes	**6** 63
sponge pennies	**6** 63
tayglach (honey balls)	**9** 31
for wedding reception	**15** 24
Cake boards	**9** 69
Calabrese sausage (definition)	**12** 124
Calalou (crab stew with okra and greens)	**11** 83
Calamari al pomodoro	**8** 101
Calamondin preserves	**16** 97
Caldeirada (Portuguese fisherman's stew)	**16** 119
Calves'	
brains	**13** 64–65
feet gelatin	**8** 25
liver molds	**1** 65
tongues, Montmorency	**13** 70
sweetbreads	**13** 65–69
Calzone	**8** 131
Camembert cheese	**15** 89
and gruyère balls	**17** 135
en surprise	**15** 123
Canapés	**17** 128
Canard aux navets (roast duck with turnips)	**17** 30
Candied fruit and nut topping	**13** 14
Candied pineapple	**14** 91
Candy	**13** 111–121
Caucasian walnut	**7** 118
divinity	**13** 115
fondant	**13** 118–121
fudge	**13** 113
glacé	**13** 117
marzipan	**13** 117
dates	**10** 92
pecans	**10** 92
walnuts	**10** 92
nougat	**13** 118
peppermint	**13** 113, 115
taffy	**13** 115
Cane sugar crystals (definition)	**13** 82
Canneloni	**5** 93
basic dough	**8** 118
chicken	**8** 119
verde	**8** 121

Cannoli	**8** 110
Cantaloupe pickle	**7** 84
Caper sauce	**2** 46, 53
Capirotada (bread pudding)	**15** 41
Capon, see also Chicken	
à la crème	**1** 27
cooking times	**8** 45
roast	**8** 46
stuffings for	**8** 48–49
Caramel	
basket	**18** 105
and bavarois, vanilla	**2** 103
cake	**1** 117
cream	**2** 93
with strawberry sauce	**3** 66
custard	**16** 127
ice cream with pecans	**11** 106
icing	**1** 117
mousse	**14** 62
rice, with chocolate	**7** 98
sauce	**9** 128
Caramelized tomatoes	**14** 19
Caraque, chocolate	**7** 96, **10** 75
Caraway seed soup	**10** 108
Carbonade of beef	**16** 33
definition	**16** 33

Carciofi alla barigoule	**8** 109
Cardamoms (definition)	**13** 82
Caribbean cooking	**11** 82–85
Carp	
baked whole	**10** 109
with beer, Polish	**11** 53
Carpetbag steak	**5** 126
Carré d'agneau	**7** 18
Carrot(s)	
in cream and dill	**10** 110
curls	**15** 126
glazed	**2** 87
à la grecque	**4** 115
pickled	**7** 85
preparation of (Japanese cooking)	**16** 57
in salad	**6** 35

Carrot(s) *continued*

with peas	**8** 21
with raisins	**6** 99
soup, cream	**6** 55
Vichy (glazed)	**6** 121, **9** 89
with wine	**2** 85

Carving and carving tools | **16** 18–19
Cartwheels | **13** 27
Cashews | **10** 96
Cassata | **18** 117
   siciliana | **8** 112
Cassava (definition) | **11** 82
   balls (foo foo) | **11** 92
   manioc | **11** 82
Casserole, see also names of the
   various meats
   accompaniments | **4** 98–99
   cauliflower with potato au gratin | **4** 115
   cooking | **4** 83–97
Cassolette
   of cucumber | **15** 125
   fillings | **15** 125
Cassoulet | **12** 106
Catalan shrimp (langostinos a la
   Catalana) | **16** 114
Catfish | **11** 53
Cauliflower
   fritters | **8** 109
   in garlic mayonnaise (coliflor
   con ali-oli) | **16** 114
   mold | **16** 84
   with mushrooms | **7** 41
   with mustard mayonnaise | **6** 32
   soufflé with mornay sauce | **11** 118
Caviar
   canapés | **17** 128
   in consommé | **13** 74, **17** 10
   and salmon checkerboard | **17** 127
   sandwich, open-face, with egg | **12** 10
Cayenne pepper (definition) | **15** 28
Celeriac
   croquettes | **17** 114
   definition | **5** 25
   rémoulade | **6** 32
   salad, with beet and walnut | **6** 32

Celery
   braised | **8** 51, **10** 14
   chartreuse, with green pepper | **15** 11
   curls | **6** 30
   garnish | **15** 126
   green pepper chartreuse | **15** 11
   Julienne of, with potato | **13** 51
   mornay | **9** 55
   pinwheels | **15** 91
   relish, with cheese | **11** 15
   salad
      apple and walnut | **6** 35
      green bean | **8** 64
      with potato and olive | **17** 87
   soup, cream | **7** 10
   stuffing, with apricot
      and pecan | **8** 48
   vinegar | **16** 100
Central European cooking | **10** 106–115
Cervalet salad | **4** 27, **12** 131
Cervelat sausage (definition) | **12** 123
Cervelles au beurre noir | **13** 64
Chafing dish cooking | **12** 52–59
   kinds of cooking dishes | **12** 54
   suggestions for brunch | **10** 130–131
Challah | **9** 29
Chamonix | **10** 90
Champagne
   with braised beef | **17** 56
   cocktail | **18** 111
   cup | **8** 55
   in fondue | **17** 133
   ice | **11** 112
   punch, cardinal's | **8** 57
Champignons sous cloche | **18** 34
Chana dahl (chuck-pea purée) | **13** 92
Chantilly cream | **2** 32, **9** 91, **16** 15
Chapatis (Indian bread) | **13** 97
Chapon demi-deuil
   (capon in half-mourning) | **12** 63

Chard, Chinese
   definition | **17** 64
   with oil and salt | **17** 78
Charlotte
   definition | **6** 126
   aux pommes | **6** 126

   Malakoff | **18** 41
   mexicaine | **7** 100
   peach | **4** 18
   pineapple | **7** 127
   rhubarb | **4** 21
   russe | **7** 118
   strawberry | **16** 36
   Swedish apple | **5** 104
Chartreuse
   apple | **11** 47
   of baby vegetables | **8** 23
   banana | **8** 26
   definition | **8** 23
   tomato | **8** 28
Chasseur
   definition | **15** 56
   sauce | **2** 49
Château potatoes | **7** 109, **9** 55, **12** 66
Chateaubriand | **18** 31

Chaudfroid
   definition | **15** 16
   and galantines | **18** 92–101
   sauce
      aurore | **18** 95
      brown | **18** 95
      white 1 and 2 | **18** 94
Chawan mushi | **16** 52
Checkerboard | **17** 127
Cheddar cheese | **15** 88
   in crêpes | **13** 129
   topping for sandwiches | **13** 10
   with port | **17** 135
Cheese
   and almond filling | **17** 131
   Austrian pastry | **15** 92
   balls | **17** 135
      in syrup | **13** 98
   beignets | **6** 87
   blintzes | **9** 23
   blue-veined | **15** 88
   bread | **15** 96
   with butter (hors d'oeuvre) | **17** 127
   cake, Danish savory | **12** 13
   and celery relish | **11** 12
   and chili (queso y chili) | **15** 31

Cheese *continued*

coeur à la crème	**10** 130
cole slaw	**6** 37
cooking with	**15** 87–99
cottage cheese	**4** 56–57
cream	**15** 92
and smoked salmon rounds	**7** 52
sauce	**10** 67
strudel	**4** 55
and tart jelly rounds	**7** 52
in crêpes	**13** 129
croissants	**6** 57
croûtes	**6** 57
dough for quesadillas	**15** 33
feta (definition)	**12** 88
filling	
with almonds	**17** 131
for strudel	**10** 114
fingers	**17** 122
flan, Swiss (Salé)	**3** 34
fresh	**15** 88
galette, with bacon	
and potato	**5** 50
gougère	**6** 84
Greek pastry	**15** 92
hard	**15** 88
Indian (paneer)	**13** 95
khishes	**9** 22
loaf	**15** 118
mild	**15** 88
omelet, Swiss	**10** 118
palmiers	**15** 119
pancakes	**15** 91
Parmesan	**8** 118
pastry, savory	**7** 49
peppers, stuffed	**5** 122
pie	
Greek (tiropita)	**12** 89
Ricotta	**4** 40
potted	**15** 91
processed	**15** 88
profiteroles	**6** 87
puffs	**6** 57, **13** 48, **14** 69
quiche, with leeks	**10** 118
ramekins	**15** 99
ricotta pie	**4** 40

Roquefort tartlets	**7** 11
sablés	**6** 42, **9** 52
sandwich, open-face	**12** 13
sauce (mornay)	**2** 46
to serve	**15** 89
soft	**15** 89
soufflé	**10** 35
cold	**15** 91
corn	**10** 36
rich	**10** 36
soup, cream of	**13** 48
sticks, pineapple	**9** 116
straws	**7** 47, **16** 70
tacos	**15** 32
tartlets	**7** 11
topping for sandwiches	**13** 10
turnovers, with ham	**8** 131
with veal	**16** 30
waffles, with bacon	**5** 130
Welsh rarebit	**15** 99

Cheesecake	**4** 56, **8** 112, **9** 33
almond	**4** 56
apricot	**4** 22
Danish savory	**12** 13
Lindy's	**4** 55
pineapple	**6** 99
Viennese curd cake	**4** 56
Chelsea buns	**14** 49
Cherry(ies)	**3** 50–52
cake	
layer	**1** 115
walnut	**9** 62
compote	
with port	**17** 33
rich	**3** 50
coupe Française	**10** 105
crêpes	**13** 129
custard	**11** 20
with duck	**17** 32–33
filling for jelly roll	**6** 69
to frost	**17** 57
gâteau Bigarveau	**3** 52
jam, Bing	**7** 79
jubilee	**12** 59
Montmorency	**3** 51
mousse	**3** 50

pie, with praline	**2** 14
pitting	**3** 50
pudding	**3** 12
from Limoges	
(clafoutis Limousin)	**10** 87
sauce	**3** 51
plain	**9** 125
soup (bärsoppa)	**12** 25
spiced	**7** 83
preserves with orange	**7** 80
strudel	**9** 33
Cherry tomato	
pickled	**7** 84
salad	**14** 122
stuffed	**7** 47
Cheshire cheese	**15** 88
Chestnut(s)	**10** 96
boîte au chocolat	**10** 90
with cabbage	**17** 119
cake, with chocolate	**10** 91
chamonix	**10** 90
Chinese (definition)	**17** 64
to cook	**10** 90
crêpes à la cévenole	**9** 107
croquettes	**17** 116
glacé	**7** 128
Mont Blanc	**10** 91
parfait	**16** 35
purée	**4** 98, **12** 128
with meringue rounds	**10** 56
to skin	**12** 65, **13** 67
soup, cream of	**8** 35
stuffing	**8** 48
with sweetbreads	**13** 66
turinois	**10** 92
vacherin aux marrons	**10** 56
water (definition)	**17** 64
Chianti, peaches in	**8** 130
Chicken(s)	
adobo, (pork stew, Philippine)	**11** 89
with almonds	**17** 51
alsacienne	**2** 38
in aspic	**18** 25
baked with mushrooms, peppers	
and zucchini	**8** 104
ballotines of, with prunes	**16** 106

Chicken(s) *continued*

barossa	**17** 30
béarnaise	**4** 87
boiled, with parsley sauce	**1** 62
boning	**1** 81, **12** 64
bonne femme	**4** 88
breasts	
Maintenon	**12** 43
with mushrooms	**11** 29
broiled	**1** 82
with red wine and	
mushrooms	**9** 55
broth	**7** 107
mushroom	**6** 53
to brown	**4** 87
canneloni	**8** 119
capon	
à la crème	**18** 125
in half-mourning	
(chapon demi-deuil)	**12** 63
carving	**1** 21
casserole	**14** 13
italienne	**4** 87
rock cornish game hens	**4** 87
Spanish	**4** 88
with chick-peas	**12** 105
chaudfroid	**18** 97
cocotte grand'mere	**1** 83
coriander	**17** 73
crêpes	**17** 15
with curry	**9** 103
croquettes, with pineapple	**5** 50
cuisses de poulet xérès	**17** 25
curry	**13** 85
mayonnaise	**17** 29
with peaches	**3** 65
in custard (chawan mushi)	**16** 52
cutting up	**1** 82
for sauté	**4** 44
deviled	**3** 94, **11** 12
dijonnaise	**1** 84
in eggs, stuffed (oeufs à la	
Reine)	**17** 16
entrées, classic	**12** 32–43
escabeche de gallina	**5** 124
fat (in Jewish cooking)	**9** 13
fricassée	**3** 17
fried	**2** 100
and ham	
à l'anglaise	**7** 124
or tongue filling	**15** 125
Hong Kong, with lemon	**17** 72
Indienne	**17** 92
Italian	**10** 131
à la kan	**17** 72
Khoreshe	**15** 22
Kiev	**18** 26
with lemon	**10** 85

liver	
and anchovy toasts	**14** 45
knishes	**9** 22
molds	**16** 90
paté	**9** 38
paté, with calves' liver	**9** 45
Majorca	**11** 118
mango	**17** 22
with melon	**17** 78
Mexican	**11** 26
mille feuilles	**17** 30
mock puchero	**5** 38
Mojibi, cold roast	**1** 95
molds	**16** 89
mole	**15** 39
mousse madrilène	**18** 26
mousseline	**16** 91
with mushrooms	**12** 57
with papaya, East African	**11** 92
parisienne	**1** 84
Pascale	**12** 43
with Passover stuffing	**9** 14
paulette	**17** 21
with peanut sauce	
(Ghanian groundnut 'chop')	**11** 92
Persian	**17** 26
petite marmite (stew with	
meat and vegetables)	**6** 114
pie	**2** 32
Broadway	**10** 66
Moroccan (bistaela)	**12** 94
niçoise	**12** 78
tanal	**15** 35
pilaf	**9** 96
pork stew, Philippine (adobo)	**11** 89
Portuguese, with rice	**16** 122
pot roast	**2** 22
poulet	
braisé aux morilles	**5** 59
au chou	**14** 13
à l'estragon (with tarragon)	**17** 22
farcis en gelée	**18** 25
à la Kiev	**18** 26
Marengo	**6** 117

with melon	**17** 78
olivade	**5** 122
pôché au vin blanc	**17** 22
au riz	**6** 115
au romarin (roast with	
rosemary)	**6** 115
Xenia	**18** 26
sauté au citron (sauté of,	
with lemon)	**17** 26
quenelles	**16** 91
with rice, Indonesian (nasi ajau)	**11** 93
with rice and mushrooms	**12** 80
roast, basquaise	**1** 18
rolls, with tongue	**16** 30
Rose Marie	**18** 97
salad	**18** 44
with avocado	**4** 29
with cherry	**4** 29
Chinese (so see gai)	**17** 73
green goddess	**4** 30
Louis	**4** 29
Milanaise	**13** 104
sashi	**16** 52
sauté	**1** 82
mâconnaise	**4** 44
parmesan	**4** 46
rajah (curry)	**4** 45
sesame (gee mah gai)	**17** 71
Spanish, with ham	
and peppers	**16** 122
spezzatino di pollo	
all trasteverina	**8** 104
spiced	**16** 52, **17** 25
with orange	**17** 25
soufflé	**14** 62
soup	**9** 20
cockie-leekie	**6** 51
with matzo balls	**9** 12
splitting	**1** 84
stew	
Brunswick	**10** 65
petite marmite	**6** 114
with pork	**11** 89
stock	**3** 118, **11** 118
Chinese	**17** 65
for consommé	**8** 20

Chicken(s) *continued*
stuffed
alsacienne **10** 72
in aspic **18** 25
stuffing for eggs **17** 16
à la Suisse **16** 12
suprême **10** 72
with cream **15** 107
to cut **12** 43
villeroi **14** 109
terrine of **16** 29
tetrazzini, quick **5** 38
tostadas **15** 31
trois frères **17** 21
trussing **1** 20
with tuna **16** 79
with truffles **18** 27
types **1** 80
veronique **17** 11
Vichy **1** 86
vinaigrette, with asparagus **17** 29
walnut (hop to gai kow) **17** 71
waterzoi **4** 88
Xenia **18** 26
Chicken liver
with eggs, scrambled **10** 130
fingers **17** 122
knishes **9** 22
omelet **1** 76
pâté **9** 38
with calves liver **9** 45
Chick-peas **12** 100
balls (falafel) **12** 88
with chicken **12** 105
paste (hummus bi tahina) **12** 87
with pimiento **15** 36
purée **13** 92
salad **12** 110
Chicory salad **6** 35
Children's party food and drinks **3** 73–79
Children's pussyfoot cocktail **18** 111
Chilean shrimp chowder **5** 124
Chili **15** 28
con carne **12** 106
definition **13** 82
filling **17** 130

with green beans **15** 36
jalapeño **4** 93
peppers, harissa sauce **12** 93
to prepare **11** 82, **15** 28
rellenos (stuffed chilies) **15** 36
sauce **11** 41, **15** 40
hot (môlha de pimenta) **11** 87
vinegar **16** 101
Chilling glass dishes **11** 101
Chinese cooking **17** 61–81
equipment **17** 62
ingredients **17** 64
stir-frying **17** 63
Chips, potato **17** 101
Chitterlings, sautéed **9** 83
Chive pastries **7** 53
Chives
with cream cheese **17** 135
omelet, with sour cream **10** 118
Chocolate
apples, baked **5** 104
beaters (definition) **7** 96
boîte au **10** 90
with fruit **12** 118
bombe **18** 114
cake
chestnut **10** 91
sachertorte **18** 67
walnut sponge **10** 94
candies **18** 110
and caramel torte **18** 70
caraque **4** 61, **18** 68
charlotte mexicaine **7** 100
cookies, iced **2** 74
cooking with **7** 94–103
Florentines **7** 101
fondant **13** 121
fudge **13** 113
fudge cake, quick **5** 42
fudge frosting **1** 115
frosting, rich **4** 59
ganache cream **7** 100
gâteau
and almond meringue **10** 95
au chocolat, rich **7** 102

lyonnaise au **6** 126
strawberry **7** 98
hot **7** 96
ice cream **11** 104
chip **11** 104
log, Christmas **15** 83
magali **7** 100
marshmallow squares **9** 117
Mexicano **15** 43
mille feuilles **12** 73
mousse (au chocolat) **1** 24
macaroon **11** 22
nègre en chemise **7** 103
and orange sauce **7** 97
Peruvian cream **7** 96
pie, meringue **1** 56
praline with cream puffs **17** 94
profiteroles **6** 82
puddings **1** 67
rice, with caramel **7** 98
roll **6** 69
roulade **7** 102
rounds or squares **15** 12
sauces **9** 126, **15** 51
rich **7** 100
snowball **7** 96
soufflé **10** 41
cold **6** 44
pudding, hot **4** 15
squares and rounds **7** 102
suprême de chocolat **7** 98
truffles **18** 128
turinois **10** 92
turquois **10** 95
waffles **5** 130
Chocolatines **14** 100
Cholent **9** 29
Chop frills **6** 115
for other chop references see
separate meat entries
Chopsticks **17** 62
Chorizo sausage
definition **12** 123, **16** 116
with lentil purée **16** 114
salad **12** 131
Choron sauce **2** 52
Choucroûte alsacienne
(sauerkraut with pork and
sausages) **12** 128
Choux
basic **6** 78
à la crème **6** 78
fried **6** 87
pastry **6** 77–87, **14** 85
pralinés au chocolat
(chocolate praline cream
puffs) **17** 94
puffs **8** 45

18

Choux *continued*
miniature 17 125
in salambos 16 132
savory 6 83–87
with fillings 7 55
strawberry tabatières 3 49
sweet 6 78–83

Chow yee peen (fillets of
fish with vegetables) 17 69
Chowder
Chilean shrimp 5 124
clam, Manhattan 6 53
clam, New England 3 106
corn 6 51
definition 1 42
fish 6 51
mussel 1 42
scallop 10 12
Chrane (morar) 9 13
Christmas cooking
cake 9 66–68
rich 9 68
cookies, molded
(springerle) 11 137
crullers, Swedish (Klenäter) 12 15
log, chocolate 15 83
pudding 8 84–87
saffron buns (saffransbrød) 12 30
Chrysanthemum
salad 18 133
turnips 16 57
Churros (Spanish crullers) 16 124
Chutney(s) 11 34–35
apple and tomato 11 34
butter 3 82
fresh 5 79
Indian and Pakistani cooking 13 96
tomato, ripe 11 34
Ciastka miodowe (Polish honey
cookies) 12 70
Cider punch 9 121
hard 8 55
Cigarettes russes 1 25
Cinderella cake 14 15
Cinnamon

flan 3 54
topping for coffeecake 13 14
Cioppino 4 85
Citrus cocktail, fresh 3 43
Citronsovs (Danish lemon sauce) 12 24
Clafoutis Limousin 10 87
Clam(s) 3 104
canapés 17 128
chowder
Manhattan 6 53
New England 3 106
dip 7 53
with eggs, steamed
(sah bok jingdon) 17 78
pizza 8 128
quiche 3 104
sauce, red and white 5 96
soup 8 101
steamed 3 104
stuffed with parmesan 15 121
Clamart (definition) 15 54
Claret
cup 3 43, 8 55
punch 8 57
Clarified butter 12 37
Classic entrées 12 32–43, 15 53–59,
17 42–51
Classic fish dishes 18 75–83
Cleaver, Chinese 17 62
Cloutie dumpling 14 50
Club steak au natural 10 14
Cocado (coconut pudding) 15 43
Cocido Madrileño (Madrid meat,
fowl and vegetable stew) 16 122
Cockie-leekie 6 51
Cocktail(s) 7 57
appetizer 17 10
ginger and grapefruit 17 36
seafood and watercress 17 10
hors d'oeuvres 17 121–135

Cocoa
balls, Maori 11 90
Coconut
cake 1 112
in candy 13 113, 121

chutney 13 96
cocktail 11 85
macaroons 9 57, 15 24
milk 11 82, 16 22
pie, cream 1 55
pudding (cocado) 15 43
sambal, with banana 13 92
soup, Malaysian (sothi) 11 96
Cocottes (definition) 5 22
Cod
broiled, with herbs and garlic 2 112
Cubat 6 72
Danish stuffed whole fish
(fylid hel fisk) 12 21
kebabs 2 112
with paprika 2 112
Portuguese 16 121
roe, smoked, with salted almonds 7 50
salt
alla napolitana 8 101
Basque 16 120
brandade de morue 6 110
à l'espagnole louasardaise 2 114
steaks bretonne 2 112
Coeur à la crème 10 130
definition 10 130
Coffee
almond 1 53
bavarois 15 51
bombe 18 114
buns 13 15
café brûlot 8 57
definition 12 96
frappé, cream 11 113
frosting, butter 6 69, 13 52, 17 16
fudge, nut 13 113
galette, with walnuts 1 102
gelatin 6 102
granité 11 113
ice cream 11 104
iced 4 63
Irish 8 57
to make 2 68–71
meringue cake 13 52
nut slices 17 16

Coffee *continued*

parfait	**18** 118	
party	**13** 9–15	
pots	**2** 71	
sundae	**5** 53	
Turkish (Kahve)	**12** 96	
Coffeecake	**13** 17–33	
almond (mandelbrød)	**12** 29	
babas au rhum	**13** 24	
Danish, almond	**12** 29	
dough, basic	**9** 98, **13** 18	
doughnuts	**13** 24	
Easter braid	**13** 22	
Easter ring	**13** 18	
French fruit braid	**9** 98	
hazelnut	**13** 24	
honey twist	**9** 99	
Hungarian	**13** 22	
jam buns	**13** 25	
kugelhopf	**13** 20	
Martha's	**7** 64	
moka	**14** 89	
quick	**13** 14	
raisin, Danish almond	**12** 29	
rich	**7** 62	
simple	**7** 62	
stollen	**13** 20	
streusel, kuchen	**13** 18	
apple	**13** 20	
Cold beer soup (Bierkaltschale)	**11** 125	
Cold-weather dishes	**10** 58–67	
Coleslaw	**6** 37, 98	
cheese	**6** 37	
country	**5** 51	
with cream	**6** 37	
pineapple	**6** 37	
salad, with fruit	**17** 84	
savoy	**6** 37	
Colettes	**16** 133	
Coliflor con ali-oli (cauliflower in garlic mayonnaise)	**16** 114	
Collée mayonnaise	**17** 30	
Columbines	**18** 15	
Combination salad (salad composée)	**17** 86	

Combs (Danish pastry)	**13** 29	
Compote of dried fruits	**9** 17	
Conch	**10** 29	
Conchiglie		
alla funghi	**5** 87	
all'inferno	**5** 87	
Concord grape kuchen	**4** 40	
Condé (definition)	**3** 54	
Conserve, spiced fig	**7** 80	
Consommé	**8** 20	
basic	**8** 20	
with caviar	**13** 74, **17** 10	
madrilène	**18** 124	
with mushrooms	**9** 93	
quick, hot and cold	**11** 22, **18** 125	
stocks for	**8** 20	

Contrefilet Dubarry	**2** 88	
Cookies		
almond	**5** 80	
balls	**10** 94	
amaretti	**10** 92	
brandy snaps	**1** 41	
brownies	**1** 121	
butterscotch		
brownies	**1** 121	
cornflake	**9** 119	
chocolate, iced	**2** 74	
cigarette russes	**1** 24	
cocoa balls, Maori	**11** 90	
for coffee party	**13** 12, 15	
fruit and nut (mazurki bakaliowe)	**12** 70	
gazelle horns (kaab el ghzal)	**12** 96	
hamantaschen	**9** 35	
honey		
with hazelnuts	**10** 95	
Polish (Uciastka miodowe)	**12** 70	
spiced (melomacarona)	**12** 96	
ice box	**1** 21	
kichlach (drop cookies)	**9** 25	
lemon wine	**1** 21	
ma'amoul	**10** 92	
molded Christmas (springerle)	**11** 137	
party	**12** 68, 71	
peanut balls	**9** 119, **11** 92	

pecan balls	**10** 94	
peppery nuts (pfeffernüsse)	**12** 70	
raisin oatmeal drops	**9** 119	
sesame seed (koulouria)	**12** 95	
spice (speculaas)	**12** 70	
sugar, American	**12** 71	
Venetian	**14** 101	
walnut kisses	**10** 94	
Cooking		
equipment	**1** 124–125	
with flowers	**18** 130–133	
for freezer	**16** 25–39	
outdoors	**16** 59–73	
for two	**11** 19–29	
Copenhagen sandwich	**12** 13	
Coq au vin	**7** 12	
Coquettes au café	**16** 132	
Coquilles St. Jacques		
Armoricaine	**14** 68	
Dugléré	**12** 114	
Coriander chicken salad (so see gai)	**17** 73	
Coriander (definition)	**13** 82	
Corn		
boiled	**4** 114	
bread, skillet	**4** 123	
cakes	**10** 127	
casserole		
Brazilian	**7** 39	
corn (torte de elote)	**15** 36	
with zucchini	**4** 95	
chowder	**6** 51	
creamed	**4** 112	
dollars	**10** 127	
fritters, with shrimp (perkedel djagung)	**11** 93	
kernels, preparation	**4** 114	
mold	**4** 114	
polenta balls	**8** 103	
relish	**7** 85	
roast	**3** 82	
in the husk	**16** 62	
salad	**4** 114	
and pickled onion	**8** 64	
with pimiento and pickled onion	**13** 58	
soufflé, with cheese	**10** 36	
soup, cream of	**8** 44	
sticks	**4** 123	
stuffing (for peppers)	**4** 112	
succotash	**4** 114	
Corned beef salad	**4** 28	
Cornets, ham	**10** 53	
Cornish game hens spatchcock	**1** 83	
Cornish pasties	**14** 39	
Costa Rican onion pie	**10** 121	
Costolette bolognese	**8** 102	

Cotellettes d'agneau
    en cuirasse **18** 34
    Montrouge **18** 34
Cottage pie **14** 41
Coulis
    definition **4** 92
    tomato **10** 65
Country cole slaw **5** 51
Country pizza **8** 130
Coupe française **10** 105

Coupe Jacques **18** 117
    Suzette **18** 118
Couronne of shrimps in aspic **14** 30
Court bouillon **2** 107, **5** 122, **13** 65
    for shellfish **10** 18, **16** 18
Couscous
    definition **12** 84, 93
    fish **12** 94
    lamb **12** 93
Couve à mineira (shredded greens) **11** 87
Crab **3** 109
    armoricaine **16** 21
    cakes, Maryland **3** 109
    and cheese toasts **14** 125
    croquettes **16** 21
    curried, in shell (gah lay hai) **17** 71
    deviled **3** 110
    dip **15** 119, **17** 132
    Dungeness, dressed **3** 110
    with eggplant **9** 53
    filling for sandwiches **13** 11
    legs, broiled, in herb butter **3** 110
    Louis **3** 110
    meat dip **17** 33
    mousse **10** 80
    omelet **1** 79
    ramekins **15** 119
    salad
        green goddess **4** 30
        printanier **12** 84, **18** 86
        with rice **15** 67
    sandwiches **14** 114
    sauce **10** 39
    scalloped **3** 109

soufflé **10** 39
soup **3** 109
stew with okra and
    greens (calalou) **11** 83
Crab apples, spiced **7** 84
Cracked wheat (definition) **12** 84
Crackers, deviled **3** 110, **11** 11
Cranberry
    bread, with orange **4** 121
    compote
        with apples **6** 100
        with raspberries and
        yogurt cream **6** 15
    frappé **11** 113
    ice cream **11** 106
    jelly, with apple **11** 33
    ketchup **11** 40
    poaching **4** 18
    punch **9** 119
    purée **11** 106
    relish, with orange **4** 22
    sauce **11** 132
    sherbet **4** 22
    soup (bärsoppa) **12** 25

Crayfish **10** 31
    with dill (kräftor) **12** 22
Cream, see also Crème
    of asparagus soup **17** 54
    Bavarian **2** 95
    caramel sauce **9** 128
    Chantilly **4** 78, **6** 69, **9** 91
    coeur à la crème **10** 130
    ganache **7** 100
    Grenadian papaya **11** 84
    horns **2** 32
    Mecca **4** 61
    morels with **10** 84
    Norwegian **4** 61
    oatmeal **4** 60
    Peruvian **7** 96
        petits pots de crème (small
        pots of) **2** 95
    pipes **8** 110

puffs, with chocolate praline
    (choux pralinés au chocolat) **17** 94
rice **4** 60
    Tyrolhof **4** 60
sour
    cake **4** 59
    horseradish sauce **7** 112
    mold, with cranberry
        and apple compote **6** 100
    omelet, with chives **10** 118
    pastry **7** 113
    with wild duck **17** 110
    tangerine **2** 95
    whipped cream biscuits **4** 59
    whipped, to pipe **2** 24, 73
Cream cheese
    and chives **17** 135
    dressing **15** 67
    and ham rolls **15** 118
    topping for sandwiches **13** 10
    strudel **4** 76
Creamy mixture, to unmold **10** 80, **14** 58
Crema Danica cheese **15** 89
Crème
    beau rivage **17** 41
    brulée **4** 71
    caramel **2** 93
    Margot **3** 66
    d'or **15** 71
    normande (soup) **3** 117
    St. Germain (soup) **3** 114
    St. Honoré **14** 90
    with strawberry sauce **3** 66
    suisse **3** 55
    à la vanille (vanilla
        custard sauce) **6** 125, **9** 128
Crêpes **9** 101–109, **13** 123–133
    apple **9** 106
    basic batter **9** 102, **13** 124
    Béatrix **9** 104
    à la cévenole
        (chestnut purée) **9** 107
    cheddar or Gruyère **13** 129
    cherry **13** 129
    chicken **17** 15
        with curry **9** 103
    farcies au chou (stuffed
        cabbage) **16** 33
    galetons
        bretonnes (Brittany
        buckwheat) **9** 107
        aux noisettes (hazelnuts) **9** 108
    au Grand Marnier **9** 109
    ham **9** 103
    Hungariana **13** 129
    lobster **13** 124
    normande **9** 104
    Palatschinken **13** 127

Crêpes *continued*
fillings for   **13** 127
pan   **9** 102
peach   **4** 18
praline   **9** 107
savory   **9** 103–104, **18** 33
seafood   **13** 127
spinach   **9** 103
sultane   **9** 104
sweet   **9** 104–109
Crescents   **13** 27
Croissants   **13** 29
de Provence   **14** 104
deviled   **15** 121
Croque   **15** 99
Croquembouche   **18** 106
Croquettes   **13** 43
almond   **16** 128
celeriac   **17** 114
chestnut   **17** 116
chicken
and mushroom   **13** 43
and pineapple   **5** 50
crab   **16** 21
hors d'oeuvres   **17** 127
potato   **15** 59, **17** 57, **8** 107
de riz   **6** 126
turkey   **8** 60
Croûtes   **4** 44
cheese   **6** 57
game   **17** 101
mustard   **6** 57
Croûton(s)   **4** 111, **6** 56, **10** 101
and bacon omelet   **1** 79
potato   **6** 57
Crown roast of pork   **7** 22
Crudités, les   **11** 12
Crumpets   **14** 47
Crust, baked gammon cracker   **1** 58
Crusty top sponge cake   **6** 62, **18** 45
Crystallized mint leaves   **11** 112
Cuban pork and vegetable stew
(ajiaco)   **11** 83
Cucumber
batons   **5** 10
cassolettes of   **15** 125
garnish   **15** 126

with flounder   **7** 106
garnish for egg mousse   **10** 51
mousse, with cheese   **14** 61
pickle
Danish (syltede agurker)   **12** 25
sweet   **11** 39
raita   **5** 79, **13** 95
relish, spiced   **11** 15
salad   **13** 60, **17** 13
with beans   **17** 84
and tomato   **6** 36
gelatin   **8** 27
lettuce   **12** 30
with tomato   **17** 84
soup, iced   **3** 114
twists   **2** 37
Vichy   **8** 12
vinegar   **16** 100
Cuisses de poulet Xérès   **17** 25
Cumberland mutton pies   **14** 44
Cumberland pudding   **11** 49
Cumberland sauce   **1** 45, **9** 125
Cumin (definition)   **13** 82
Cupboard, foods for   **5** 37
Curd (definition)   **13** 82
Currant(s)   **3** 58
cream   **3** 58
jelly, red with pears   **7** 127
pilaf, with pistachios   **12** 91
Curry(ied)   **13** 84–86
accompaniments   **5** 79
brains   **13** 86
chicken   **5** 76, **13** 85, **17** 29
sauté rajah   **4** 45
crab, in shell   **17** 71
definition   **13** 82
egg and lentil   **13** 86
escalopes   **15** 56
hollandaise   **10** 39
lamb   **13** 39
Biriani   **13** 89
methee bhaji   **5** 76
mayonnaise, with chicken   **17** 29
meat balls
kofta kari   **13** 86
shami kebabs   **13** 90

salad   **13** 60
shrimp   **13** 86, **16** 22
pie   **18** 76
soup, iced   **12** 115
Thai meat (kaeng phet nua)   **11** 96
turkey   **8** 60
Czechoslovakian crêpes
(Palatschinken)   **13** 127
Custard(s)   **2** 90–95
apple   **11** 20
bavarois à la crème   **2** 95
caramel and vanilla bavarois   **2** 103
cherry   **11** 20
crème caramel   **2** 93, **3** 66
crème Margot   **3** 66
crème à la vanilla   **2** 92
peach   **11** 20
petits pots de crème   **2** 95
pie   **2** 92
strawberry   **11** 20
pudding   **2** 92
tangerine cream   **2** 95
Czech torte   **10** 112, **17** 112

Dacquoise   **12** 50
Dahi (definition)   **13** 82
Dahl
definition   **13** 82, 92
purée (Chana dahl)   **13** 92
Daikon (white radish)   **16** 57
Dairy foods in Jewish cooking   **9** 25
Damson plum
jam   **11** 32
jelly   **11** 32
Dandelion salad   **18** 132
Danish cooking
bread   **15** 125
pastry   **13** 27–29
basic dough   **13** 27
cartwheels   **13** 27

Danish cooking *continued*

combs		**13** 29
crescents		**13** 27
croissants, French		**13** 29
envelopes		**13** 27
pinwheels		**13** 29
shortcake, raspberry		**1** 73
tartlets		**15** 121
twists		**13** 29
smorrebrød table		**12** 8–15

Dariole molds		**1** 66
Dashi (broth)		**16** 49
Date(s)		
bread		**13** 12
marzipan	**10** 92,	**13** 117
and orange muffins		**4** 124
pudding		**1** 66
en daube (definition)		**6** 14
Day of the dead (definition)		**15** 41
Dead Men's beans		**18** 73
Decorating cone, paper		**7** 46
Deglaze (definition)		**2** 13
Dégorger (definition)	**7** 35,	**11** 70
Délices de sole au parmesan		**15** 46
Délicieuse		**17** 125
Demi-glace sauce	**2** 48, **15** 19,	**16** 90
Dessert, accompaniments		**17** 58
Dessert sour cream sauce		**11** 47
Deviled		
anchovy eggs		**12** 57
chicken	**3** 94,	**11** 12
crackers	**3** 110,	**11** 11
croissants		**15** 121
kidneys	**10** 124	**12** 55
lobster		**10** 21
sardines		**12** 54
tomato sauce		**5** 47
tuna		**4** 26
Devil's food cake		**1** 115
Dhaniya (definition)		**13** 82
Dill		
with carrots and cream		**10** 110
kosher		**11** 39
salad, with herring		**13** 58
and sour cream with summer		
squash		**10** 110
sweet		**11** 39

Dinde braisé au Champagne		**10** 84
Dip(s)		**17** 133
clam		**7** 53
crab meat		**15** 119
devil sauce, with mushrooms		
beignets		**7** 53
for fondue bourguignonne		**5** 47, 49
provençal		**5** 47
Divan, turkey		**8** 60
Doboz torte		**18** 70
Dolmas (stuffed vine leaves)		**12** 86
Don fah tong (egg flower soup)		**17** 66
Doon Doong goo (definition)		**17** 64
Doong gwa		
definition		**17** 64
soup		**17** 65
Dorothea sole, fillets of		**17** 38
Doughnut		**13** 24
Dove		**17** 106
casserole of		**17** 108
Dow foo		
definition		**17** 64
bean cake sautéed with meat		**17** 77
Dow see (definition)		**17** 64
Dressing		
boiled		**3** 108
piquant for cold meats		**8** 122
tarragon cream, with avocado		**8** 44
vinaigrette	**8** 27,	**17** 84
Drinks		
bishop		**8** 57
buffet		**3** 43
café brûlot		**8** 57
for children's party		**2** 77
citrus cocktail, fresh		**3** 43
coconut cocktail		**11** 85
coffee, iced		**4** 63
cold		**8** 55
egg nog		**4** 63
flip		
apricot		**4** 63
banana		**4** 63
peach		**4** 63
German		**11** 124
hot		**8** 57

lamb's wool		**11** 17
lemonade		**4** 41
Mexican		**15** 43
milk		**4** 63
orange and tomato cocktail		**3** 43
picnic		**4** 41
pineapple orangeade		**11** 84
punch		**8** 55–57
banana milk		**11** 84
cider		**9** 121
cold		**4** 63
cranberry		**9** 119
planter's		**11** 85
sangrià		**16** 68
screwdriver		**3** 43
shake		
chocolate		**4** 63
mocha		**4** 63
raspberry		**4** 63
for a smorrebrød party		**12** 15
wassail bowl		**11** 17

Drop scones		**4** 127
Duchesse potatoes	**8** 50,	**12** 63
Duchesses pralinées		**18** 62
Duck		
braised, with olives		**1** 86
canard aux navets (roast duck		
with turnips)		**17** 30
carving		**1** 89
casserole, with apples		**4** 90
cassoulet		**12** 106
chasseur		**1** 86
cutting up	**1** 88,	**17** 72
with lemon compote		**17** 33
lotus stuffed (leen gee opp)		**17** 75
molded with orange		**8** 24
with pâté and cherries		**17** 33
pot roast, with sour cream		**17** 110
preparing		**1** 86
with red cabbage		**10** 110
roast		
with cherries		**17** 32
Chinese		**17** 75
with mint and lemon		**17** 32
with orange		**17** 32
with peaches		**17** 32

Duck *continued*
salmis of, with olives **14** 32
sauté
  with burgundy **6** 13
  with mushrooms **5** 115
soup **6** 51
stock **2** 19, **17** 21
stuffed, cold **18** 105
terrine of **16** 29
wild **17** 108
  roast, with orange gravy **17** 108
Duck liver, Chinese
smoked (definition) **17** 64
Dugléré (definition) **11** 56
Dumplings **11** 125
with boiled beef **10** 60
cloutie **14** 50
herb **4** 99
meat (Königsberger Klopse) **11** 127
plum (Zwetaschgenknödel) **11** 127
potato **11** 127
snow (Schrecklössschen) **11** 125
spätzle **10** 63
Duxelles
definition **2** 88
sauce **16** 84

Eash-el-asfoor (Turkish
  'bird's nests') **12** 95
East African chicken with
  papaya **11** 92
Easter, dishes for
braid **13** 22
eggs **15** 129–131
ring **13** 18
Eccles cakes **2** 29
Eclairs **6** 81

Eel **2** 109
sandwich, open-face, with
  egg **12** 13
Egg(s) (see also Omelet, soufflé) **5** 17–35
anchovy **5** 30
in aspic **8** 21
aurore **4** 27
  with chicken **17** 16
baked **5** 19
  in tomato **12** 76
and bananas **13** 92
basic methods **5** 18–19
barquaise **15** 110
Benedict **5** 22
beurre noir **5** 20
boiled **5** 18
buttered **5** 18
canapés
  with anchovy **17** 128
  with tomato **17** 128
cantalienne **5** 26
Chimay **10** 10
clams, steamed with **17** 78
en cocotte
  with cheese **12** 57
  with smoked salmon **10** 118
coddled **5** 18
in cold dishes **5** 30–34
convent **5** 23
à la crème with mushrooms **5** 25
au cresson **3** 62
curried **13** 86
  Philippine **11** 89
deviled anchovy **12** 57
Dijonnaise **11** 44
flamenco **5** 25
Florentine **11** 26
fried **5** 19
garnishes for mousse **10** 51
gascon **5** 26
en gelée simple **5** 33
glaze **8** 24
à la greque **7** 88
with ham **5** 20
hard-cooked **5** 18, **9** 12
hot dishes **5** 20–29
Hungarian **5** 25
hueon rancheron (country style) **15** 31
Indochine **13** 106
Indonesian spiced (telor
  gembung) **11** 93
Maryland **16** 42
mayonnaise **13** 59
Mexican **5** 22
  baked **10** 121
Mikado **5** 30
mimosa **5** 33
mollets à l'indienne **5** 30

mousse **10** 50
nog **4** 63
oeufs
  d'or **18** 109
  à l'estragon **8** 20
  en gelée **8** 21
  à la neige **1** 25
  Richelieu **18** 20
with olives **17** 127
omelet **15** 102
  Baronte **15** 102
  Germiny **15** 102
oyster purse (ho bow don) **17** 78
pickled, with beets **7** 85
pipérade **5** 29
plum flower **16** 58
poached **5** 19
  Scottish **9** 98
portuguese **5** 25
precious flower (gwai foh don) **17** 67
quiche, with leek and cheese **10** 118
romaine **5** 26
sandwich, open-face
  with caviar **12** 10
  with eel **12** 13
sauces **9** 127–128
Scotch **11** 10
Scotch woodcock **5** 29
scrambled **5** 18
  with asparagus **5** 29
  with chicken livers **10** 130
  with cold ham **12** 78
shirred **5** 29
and shrimp
  bondées **8** 76
  mousse **8** 67
soft-cooked **5** 18
soubise **5** 20

in soy sauce (Malaysian) **11** 95
steamed, with clams (sah bok
  jing don) **17** 78
stuffed, with chicken **17** 16
en surprise **5** 22
suzette **5** 20

Egg(s) *continued*

with tarragon   **8** 20
à la tripe   **5** 26
with tuna   **5** 34
and tuna cream   **5** 37
whites, beating in a copper
   bowl   **10** 35
Xérès   **5** 29

Egg flower soup   **17** 65
Eggplant
   Boston   **7** 35
   casserole   **11** 22
   with crab   **9** 53
   galette   **7** 36
   imam bayeldi (Turkish fainting
     imam)   **12** 91
   with lamb chops   **11** 20
   mold   **16** 84
   moussaka   **11** 70
     classic   **12** 89
   pizza   **8** 127
   poor man's caviar   **4** 113
   provençale   **16** 68
   raita   **13** 95
   in salad   **13** 102
   salpicon   **5** 95
   with sesame oil (baba ghanouj)   **12** 87
   soufflé   **7** 35
   stuffed with kidneys   **11** 70
Eisbein mit erbspuree (pork hocks
   with pea purée)   **11** 128
Ejotes con chiles (green beans with
   chilies)   **15** 36
Elderblossom pancakes   **18** 132
Elderflower syrup   **18** 132
Emmenthal cheese   **15** 89
Empanadillas (miniature
   turnovers)   **16** 112
   fillings for   **16** 112
Emperor's cake   **18** 65
Enchiladas   **15** 32–33
   con carne (meat)   **15** 32
   verdes (green)   **15** 32
Endive
   ardennaise   **6** 122
   braised, Belgian   **4** 104, **10** 63

salad, with orange   **8** 64
Entrée
   accompaniments to   **17** 13
   classic **12** 32–43, **15** 53–59, **17** 42–51
   escalopes   **15** 56–57
   noisettes   **15** 58–59
   tournedos   **15** 54–55
   veal   **15** 58
Envelopes   **13** 27
Escabeche de gallina (Chilean
   pickled chicken)   **5** 124
Escalopes, see also Veal
   curried   **15** 56
   Hongroise   **15** 105
   sauté à l'anglaise   **15** 56
   savoyarde   **17** 48
   tapenade   **15** 105
   Valentino   **18** 89
   de eau provençale   **17** 39
Escarole pizza   **8** 131
Escarole salad   **6** 35
Espagnole sauce   **2** 48, **9** 87, **13** 37
Ethiopian beef stew   **11** 91
Eve's pudding   **5** 106
European gateaux and pastries **18** 51–73

Fainting imam,
   Turkish (imam bayeldi)   **12** 91
Farfalle con piselli   **5** 87
Farfel and prune tzimmes   **9** 25
Farina (definition)   **13** 98
Farmer sausage (definition)   **12** 123
Farofa (toasted manioc meal)   **11** 87
Fats, kinds of   **7** 130–131
Fava beans   **12** 100, **13** 57
   ménagère   **12** 109
   soup   **12** 105
Fave dei morti   **18** 73
Faw opp (Chinese roast duck)   **17** 75
Feast of St. Lucia   **12** 30
Feijoada (Brazilian baked meat
   and beans)   **11** 86
   accompaniments   **11** 86
Fennel   **8** 103
   in béchamel sauce   **8** 103
   sautéed   **14** 22
Fenugreek (definition)   **13** 82
Feta (definition)   **12** 88
Fettucine
   Alfredo   **5** 89
   alla romagnola   **8** 118

basic dough   **8** 116
con prosciutto   **5** 88
Feuilletées   **15** 119
   raspberry   **8** 83
Fidget pie   **14** 43
Field of mushrooms   **2** 74
Fig(s)
   conserve, spiced   **7** 80
   with cream cheese   **14** 118
   spiced   **3** 124
Figues au fromage   **14** 118
Fijian steamed fish with sweet
   potatoes (I'A)   **11** 89
Filberts   **10** 96
Fillet, see Beef
Fillings
   for cassolettes   **15** 125
   for cream puffs   **17** 94
   for crêpes   **13** 127
   Danish pastry   **13** 29
   and decorations   **14** 87–88
   for eggs   **17** 16
   for pastry fingers   **17** 130–131
   for sandwiches   **13** 11
   for tamales   **15** 34
Financières   **18** 63
Finnan haddie, see Haddock
Firni (rice cream with pistachio)   **13** 98
Fish, see also individual names
   alla romana   **8** 102
   balls
     gefilte   **9** 13
     Sengalese (boulettes de
      poisson)   **11** 91
     with tomato sauce   **16** 87
   in batter   **2** 60
   in black sauce   **10** 110
   bouillabaisse (Mediterranean
     fish stew)   **6** 113
   braising   **5** 56
   à la bourguignonne   **5** 57
   broiling   **3** 79–80
   casserole Florentine   **4** 85
   classic dishes (1)   **14** 74–81
   cook, how to   **2** 104–106
   court bouillon   **2** 107, **5** 122
   couscous   **12** 94
   en coquille   **6** 98
   chowder   **6** 51
   in egg and crumbs   **2** 60
   fillets of, with vegetables
     (chow yee peen)   **17** 69
   flan, white   **3** 35
   French names, guide to   **2** 119
   fresh, how to prepare   **2** 118–119
   fritto misto with Alabama
     sauce   **5** 120

Fish *continued*

to fry	**2** 60
Jamaican pickled	**11** 82
matelote mâconnaise (fish stew with red wine)	**6** 110
matelote de poisson (fish stew in white wine)	**6** 110
Mexican, seviche	**15** 35
molds	**16** 85–87
individual	**16** 85
with mushrooms	**18** 23
Newburg	**16** 87
salmon	**16** 85
tomato	**16** 87
Monte Carlo	**5** 37
mousse	**17** 10
mousseline	**16** 91
pie	**10** 123
poaching	**2** 106
potatoes	**11** 65, **12** 48
potted	**10** 123
quenelles	**16** 91
rich	**2** 107–111
roulade	**10** 46–47
in seaweed with vinegared rice (Norimaki sushi)	**16** 50
sliced raw (sashimi)	**16** 51
soufflé	**10** 39
soup	**7** 112
cream of	**2** 10
Norwegian (fisksoppa)	**12** 18
spiced (Garam machli)	**13** 88
steaming	**2** 107
with sweet potatoes (I'A)	**11** 89
stew	**16** 119, 120
bouillabaisse	**6** 113
matelote mâconnaise (with red wine)	**6** 110
matelote de poisson (with white wine)	**6** 110
Nigerian	**11** 91
stock	**2** 19, **11** 56, **16** 22

for aspic	**8** 19
stuffed	**5** 126
in bean cake (yow yeong dow foo)	**17** 69
whole, Danish (fylld hel fisk)	**12** 21

tostadas	**15** 31
white	**2** 112–117
Fisherman's stew, Portuguese	**16** 119
Fisherman's oyster stew	**10** 124
Fisksoppa (Norwegian fish soup)	**12** 18
Flageolets Toulousaine	**14** 71
Flaky pastry	**10** 66
Flambé (flamed)	**13** 130
crêpes Suzette	**13** 130
Flamber	**10** 84, **12** 54, **13** 130
Flan(s)	**3** 27–35
almond	
and apricot	**15** 74
fruit	**3** 96
and raspberry	**18** 45
d'Antilles	**14** 72
apple	
menagere	**3** 29
and orange	**10** 14
spiced	**3** 31
bakewell	**3** 28
beef	**11** 12
caramel custard	**16** 127
case	**8** 76
cinnamon (cannelle)	**3** 54
fish, white	**3** 35
fruit gelatin	**8** 25
gâteau basque	**3** 31
Linzer torte	**3** 55
mushroom	**3** 35
de Naranj a	**16** 127
pastry, French	**14** 84, **18** 52
peach	**3** 29
fresh	**16** 68
pissaladière	**3** 34
prune	**10** 54
quiche	
leek	**3** 32
and cheese	**10** 118
lorraine	**3** 32
onion	**11** 14
smoked salmon	**3** 32
rings, to line	**14** 87
salé (Swiss cheese)	**3** 34
sausage and tomato	**3** 32
savory	**3** 32–35
shrimp	**3** 34
smoked haddock	**3** 34
Spanish orange	**16** 127
steak	**16** 109
strawberry	**3** 47
sweet	**3** 28–31
tarte beauceronne	**3** 31
tarte aux citrons (lemon flan)	**3** 29
tarte aux pommes à l'orange	**10** 14
tarte aux pruneaux	**10** 54
tomato	**11** 14
and sausage	**3** 32

Flapjacks, English	**13** 12
Flettbrød (Danish braided twist)	**12** 29
Floating island	**6** 125
Florentine salad	**17** 87
Florentines	**7** 101
Florettes	**18** 64
Flounder	
broiled	**3** 80
Colbert	**11** 55
with cucumber	**7** 106
Diéppoise	**11** 55
Dugléré	**11** 56
mâconnaise	**18** 80
soup, cream of	**2** 10
véronique	**18** 80

Flour	
rye (definition)	**7** 69
seasoned	**2** 87
semolina	**8** 119
types of	**1** 122–123
Flower petals, garnish	**16** 48
Flower sandwiches	**9** 116
Fly bread	**4** 120
Foie gras	
definition	**15** 106
fingers	**17** 122
Fondant	
candy	**13** 118–121
icing	**7** 102, **14** 88
potatoes	**12** 80
pretzels	**16** 133
Fondue	**17** 133
bourguignonne	**5** 46
simple	**15** 95
Swiss cheese	**15** 95
Foo Foo (cassava balls)	**11** 92
Foo gwa	
bitter melon with chicken	**17** 78
definition	**17** 64
Foo yee (definition)	**17** 64
Forelle-blau (blue trout)	**11** 125
Fortnum and Mason	**17** 125
Fourées au miel	**14** 103
Fours aux amandes	**16** 132, **18** 128
Fowl-in-the-pot	**2** 22
Frangipane	**14** 84

Frankfurter(s)
Frango Portuguêsa (Portuguese
    chicken with rice)   16 122
    definition   12 123
    omelet alsacienne   10 121
    salad, with ham   13 57
    and sauerkraut with bacon   10 60
Frappés   11 112–113
    coffee cream   11 113
    cranberry   11 113
    peach   11 113
    raspberry   11 113
    storing   11 112
    strawberry   11 113
Freezer
    charts   6 92–94
    cooking for   16 25–39
    how to use   6 89–95
    wraps and containers   6 94–95
French bread   7 69
French country cooking   6 107–127
French flan pastry   4 82, 14 84
French fruit braid   9 98
French onion soup   6 109
    simple   6 48
French toast   10 127
    toffee   5 42
Fricadelles in tomato sauce   3 40
Fricandeau

    definition   5 63
    with spinach purée   5 63
Fricassée (definition)   3 16
    of beef with chestnuts   14 127
Fried rice   16 44
Frijoles (beans)   15 36
    refried   15 37
Frikadeller (Danish meat balls)   12 24
Fritot (definition)   13 65
Fritter(s)   9 34
    apple and banana   2 58
    batter   2 58

corn   2 100
cauliflower   8 109
lemon   17 26
oyster   10 25
shrimp and corn, Indonesian
    (perkedel djagung)   11 93
Swedish Christmas crullers
    (klenäter)   12 15
Fritto misto   17 133
    with Alabama sauce   5 120
    definition   8 107
    alla milanese   8 107
Frivolities   17 125
Frogs' legs   11 53
    poulette   11 53
Frosted red currants   14 90
Frosting (see also Icing)
    boiled   1 112, 9 71
    butter cream   14 87, 18 53
    chocolate fudge   1 115
    coffee butter   6 69, 13 52, 17 16
    mocha   1 117
    orange   6 64
    rich chocolate   4 59
Frozen foods, to thaw   16 27
Fruit, see also individual names
    butters   11 33
    cakes   9 59–68
        fresh   9 63–65
        pecan   10 94
    with chocolate box (boîte au
        chocolat aux fruits)   12 118
    compote   8 69
    cookies, with nuts (mazurki
        bakaliowe)   12 70
    dried
        compote   9 17, 111
        filling for hamantaschen   9 35
    flambé   12 59
    flan, with almonds   3 96
    fresh   3 46–59
        with cheese cream   14 130
    gelatin
        flan   8 25
        fresh   11 17
        golden   18 106
        Madeleine   8 26
    glacé   13 117
    ice cream   11 106
    jelly roll gelatine   5 51
    macédoine of   5 80
    marinated   16 44
    muffins   4 124
    peasant girl in a veil   5 123
    poaching   4 16–23
    purée   11 106
        to freeze   16 39
    refraîchis   14 111

salad
    with coleslaw   17 84
    fresh   14 111
    Indonesian, spiced   11 95
    platter   4 30
sauces   6 78, 9 124–125
    spiced   11 40–41
soup (fruktsoppa)   12 25
    with sponge cake   6 64
    in strawberry cream   16 39
tartlets   1 55
trifle   1 103
turnovers   8 79

Fruits de mer
    vol-au-vent aux   8 78
Fruktsoppa (Swedish fruit soup)   12 25
Frying   2 55
    coatings   2 57
    deep fat   2 57
    temperature guide   2 56
    shallow fat   2 56
Fudge   13 113
    cake, quick chocolate   5 42
    sauce   5 53, 9 126
    sundae, hot   5 53
Fuzzy squash (definition)   17 64
Fylld hel fisk (Danish stuffed
    whole fish)   12 21

Gah lay hai (curried crab in shell) 17 71
Galantine
    of duck   18 100
    of pheasant   18 98
    of veal   7 125
    de volaille   18 98
Galetons
    bretonnes   9 107
    aux noisettes   9 108

Galette
apple and hazelnut **17** 12
beef **11** 72
bretonnaise **14** 100
coffee and walnut **1** 102
definition **11** 72, **14** 100
eggplant **7** 36
muscats **7** 100
Nantaise **14** 104
Normande **16** 80
orange caramelized **7** 71
Suisse **14** 104
Galician dishes
rice pudding **16** 127
white bean soup **16** 115
Game **17** 97–117
accompaniments for **17** 101
bear **17** 114
ardennaise **17** 114
braising **5** 56
casserole **4** 90
croûtes **17** 101
duck **17** 108–110
goose, wild **17** 110
roast with mushroom cream
sauce **17** 110
gravy **17** 101
grouse **17** 113
and beef pie **17** 113
mousse **14** 61
partridge **17** 105–106
pheasant **17** 102–103
quail **17** 111
stuffed (en cocotte
alsacienne) **17** 113
rabbit, wild **17** 119
with lentils **17** 119
with red wine **17** 119
roasting **17** 98
squab, pigeon and dove **17** 106–108
terrine **9** 46
trussing **17** 99
turkey **17** 110
braised **17** 110
venison **17** 114
fillets of (poivrade) **17** 116

grenadins **17** 116
woodcock and snipe **17** 113
Ganache cream **7** 100, **16** 133
Gannet (cheese bread) **15** 96
Garam machli (spiced fish) **13** 88
Garam masala **13** 85
definition **13** 82
Garbanzos con pimiento
(chick-peas with pimiento) **15** 36
Garbure paysanne **6** 109
Gardener's omelet **16** 116
Garibaldi (definition) **9** 81
Garlic
butter **5** 29
loaf **5** 46, **9** 120
mayonnaise **14** 117
sausage with potato salad, hot **12** 130
soup **16** 115
Garnishes **15** 126–127
for egg mousse **10** 51
soup **16** 48
Gateau(x), see Cakes
Gaufrettes **5** 131
Viennoise **14** 104
Gaw pay (definition) **17** 64
**Gawn jeen hah look (dry fried
shrimps in shell)** **17** 67
**Gazelle horns, Moroccan (kaabel
ghzal)** **12** 96

Gazpacho **15** 110
alicantina **16** 115
blender **18** 46
definition **16** 115
Gee mah gai (sesame chicken) **17** 71
Gefilte fish balls **9** 13
**Gekochtes sauerkraut (cooked
sauerkraut)** **11** 128
Gelatin(s) savory and sweet **8** 14–26
almond with lychees, Hong
Kong **11** 96
calves' feet **8** 25
chopped **8** 18
clarifying **8** 17

coffee **6** 102
flan, fruit **8** 25
fresh fruit **11** 17
lemon **8** 24
Madeleine, fruit **8** 26
with pineapple **17** 90
port wine **7** 127
powdered **8** 16
salad, molded **8** 27–29
Genevoise sauce **2** 53
Genoa sausage (definition) **12** 124
Genoise, basic **18** 52
German cooking **11** 123–137
drinks **11** 124
potato salad **4** 40
regional specialties **11** 124
German sausage (definition) **12** 124
Germiny (definition) **15** 102
Ghanaian dishes
groundnut 'chop' **11** 92
peanut balls **11** 92
Ghee (definition) **13** 83
Giblet soup (Kleinsuppe) **11** 124

Ginger
cake, sticky **4** 41
cocktail, with grapefruit **17** 36
jam
with melon **7** 80
with rhubarb **16** 96
pancakes **10** 128
root (definition) **13** 82, **17** 64
salad, with peaches **17** 21
soufflé **15** 21
waffles **5** 131
Gingerbread
basic dough **9** 116
house **9** 116
men **9** 116
upside down **10** 67
Ginkgo nuts (definition) **17** 64
Gipsy's arm **16** 128, **18** 69
Girls' festival (definition) **16** 57
Glacé
chestnuts **7** 128
fruits **13** 117
icing **12** 71, **8** 38, **18** 53

Glaze
 apricot jam   **1** 55, **10** 15
 egg   **8** 74
 fruit juice, thickened   **1** 55
 meat   **2** 52
 red currant jelly   **1** 55, **3** 47
Gnocchi   **8** 121–123
 parisienne   **8** 121
 potato   **8** 123
 romana   **8** 123, **9** 87
 small   **8** 123

Gold cake   **18** 107
Golden fruit cake   **9** 62
Golden fruit gelatin   **18** 106
Golden syrup   **5** 106
 definition   **10** 94
Golden wedding anniversary
 ideas   **18** 103–111
Goon yin-yin yang gai (chicken à
 la kan)   **17** 72
Goose
 braised   **12** 65
 carving   **1** 88–89
 cooking times   **8** 45
 cutting up   **1** 88
 deviled   **8** 60
 pie, Yorkshire   **12** 66
 preparing   **1** 86
 roast stuffed   **1** 91, **8** 47
 spiced   **12** 66
 stuffed, Christmas   **12** 64
 stuffings for   **8** 49
 wild   **17** 110
  roast, with mushroom cream
   sauce   **17** 110
Gooseberry(ies)   **3** 58
 cream   **3** 58
 fool   **3** 58
 jam   **7** 79
Göteborg sausage (definition)   **12** 123
Göttinger sausage (definition)   **12** 123
Gougère
 cheese   **6** 84
 chicken livers, game or ham   **6** 84
 shrimp   **6** 83

Goulash
 paprika   **3** 19
 quick   **5** 41
 veal   **11** 25
Graham cracker crusted ham   **7** 30
Grahamsbröd (wholewheat bread)   **12** 30
Granary loaf   **18** 46
Grand Marnier
 crêpes au   **9** 109
 soufflé   **10** 43
Granités   **11** 112–113
 coffee   **11** 113
 grapefruit   **11** 113
 storing   **11** 112
Grape(s)
 butter   **11** 34
 concord, kuchen   **4** 40
 jam, green   **16** 96
 jelly   **11** 33
 to prepare   **5** 80
 salad
  grapefruit   **8** 44
  melon and mint   **17** 87
  molded   **8** 28
 soup, with almond   **3** 117
 stuffed   **7** 46

Grapefruit
 broiled   **8** 34
 cocktail, with ginger   **17** 36
 granité   **11** 113
 marmalade   **16** 96
 mint sherbet   **11** 112
 mousse   **11** 26
 parfait   **9** 99
 salad
  avocado and orange   **6** 37
  with grape   **8** 44
 soufflé   **10** 128
Gratin
 dauphinois   **11** 78
 of seafood   **14** 11
Gravlax (Swedish marinated
 salmon)   **12** 18

Gravy   **1** 31
Great Northern beans   **12** 100
Greek dishes
 cheese pastries (tiropetes)   **15** 92
 lemon soup   **6** 10
 pastry fingers   **17** 130
 stewed lamb with chicory and
  avgolemono sauce   **5** 120
Green Goddess salad   **4** 30
Green mayonnaise   **4** 33, **6** 38, **11** 60
Green pea soup   **12** 103
Green salad   **1** 22
 with fresh pineapple   **2** 100
Green sauce   **8** 104
Green soup (potage vert)   **16** 77

Greens, shredded (couve à
 mineira)   **11** 87
Grenadins
 de veau à l'Hongroise
  (Hungarian grenadins of veal)   **17** 51
 definition   **17** 51
Grenadian papaya cream   **11** 84
Gribiche sauce   **13** 39
Griddle (definition)   **4** 127
 scones   **4** 127
Griestorte with peaches   **3** 40
Grouper   **11** 56
Grouse (definition)   **17** 113
 and beef pie   **17** 113
Gruyère cheese balls, with
 camembert   **17** 135
 crêpes   **13** 129
 definition   **13** 129
 gur (definition)   **13** 82
 and mushroom salad   **15** 64
 and tomato toasts   **15** 47
Gumbo
 definition   **10** 66
 shrimp and oyster   **10** 66
Gwai fah don (precious flower egg)   **17** 67
Guacamole (avocado sauce)   **15** 37
Guava (definition)   **11** 82
 pie, Barbados   **11** 84
Gur (definition)   **13** 82

Hachis (definition) **18** 34
Haddock **2** 114
  baked, niçoise **2** 115
  Finnan haddie, smoked
    cakes **2** 114
  Hong Kong Kedgeree **11** 96
  flan, smoked **3** 34
  au gratin **2** 115
  kedgeree **2** 65
    Hong Kong **11** 96
  mousse **2** 36
  with onions **2** 115
  with paprika and mushrooms **2** 114
  quiche, smoked **6** 103
  sauté, with tomatoes and
    mushrooms **4** 51
  soup, cream of **2** 10
Haldi (definition) **13** 83
Halibut
  casserole **4** 85
  with cider **18** 80
  Dieppoise **18** 80
  with mushrooms and shrimps **11** 56
  with shrimp sauce **11** 22
  steaks, broiled **3** 80
Ham
  baked **1** 45
    maple, with raisin sauce **7** 25
    stuffed **12** 63
  and beef, potted **14** 44
  boiled, with carrots and onions **1** 102
  braised
    with Burgundy **7** 29
    with Madeira sauce **7** 31
  Burgundian, cold, with parsley **10** 83
  canapé **17** 128
  carving **7** 24
  and cheese turnovers **8** 131
  with chicken
    à l'anglaise **7** 124
    filling **15** 125

  and peppers **16** 122
  chili filling (tamale) **15** 34
  cold, with scrambled eggs **12** 78
  cooking with **7** 25–31
  cornets **10** 53
  country **7** 25
  à la crème **7** 29
  crêpes **9** 103
  crescents **17** 122
  graham cracker crusted **7** 30
  hash, Danish (labskovs) **12** 24
  jambon bourguignonne **7** 29
  maple baked, with raisin sauce **7** 25
  in marsala **18** 46
  mold **16** 88
  mousse **14** 61
    cold **7** 31
  and mushroom
    bouchées **8** 65
    stuffed **17** 130
  omelet, Swiss **10** 118
  with orange **4** 93
  pâté **9** 42
    with turkey **9** 46
  and pease pudding **10** 64
  pie, with veal **2** 28
  pilaf **13** 39
  pizza **8** 128
  and pork loaf, glazed **4** 38
  rarebit **10** 124
  rolls, with cream cheese **15** 118
  roulades **8** 21
  salad, with frankfurter **13** 57
  sandwiches
    and cream cheese **14** 114
    topping for **13** 10
  sautéed, with bean cake **17** 77
  serraño **16** 115
  soufflé, cold **13** 39
  spread **17** 135
  steaks, broiled **3** 77
  sweet and sour **10** 131
  véronique **7** 30

Hamantaschen **9** 35
Hamburgers and accompaniments **5** 53
Hans Christian Anderson
  open-face sandwich **12** 10
Hard sauces **9** 126–127
Harira (Moroccan soup with
  lentils) **12** 84
Harissa sauce **12** 93
Harlequin salad **15** 64
Haselnusskuchen (hazelnut coffee
  cake) **11** 133
Hash
  Danish (labskovs) **12** 24
  Mexican meat **15** 34
Hawaiian dishes
  mango steak **11** 89
  pineapple cake **11** 90
Hazelnuss küchlein **18** 68
Hazelnut(s) **10** 96
  to brown and grind **11** 133, **15** 12
  cake
    coffee (haselnusskuchen) **11** 133
    meringue **9** 91
  cookies **13** 12, **18** 68
    with honey **10** 95
  galetons aux noisettes
    (crêpes) **9** 108
  galette
    with apple **17** 12
    with peach **15** 12
Heavenly cakes **14** 103
Hello to snaps open-face
  sandwich **12** 10
Herb(s) **3** 84–89
  butter **3** 81
  dumplings **4** 99
  loaf, hot **4** 11, **6** 103
  omelet (omelet fines herbes) **1** 76
  and onion stuffing **2** 85
  tomato soup **4** 37
Herring(s) **2** 108
  calaisienne with mustard sauce **2** 109
  casserole **10** 108
  pie, with potato (sill pudding) **12** 22
  pie, Stargazy **14** 43

Herring(s) *continued*
pudding (sillgratin) **12** 22
quick, chopped **9** 23
salad **10** 108
with apple **10** 70
with dill pickle **13** 58
Swedish pickled **5** 123
soused **2** 108
topping for sandwiches **13** 10
High altitude cooking **12** 132–133
Hikichamanju (bean paste bun) **16** 57
Himmel und erde (apple and
potato purée) **11** 128
Ho bow don (oyster purse eggs) **17** 78
Ho lon dow (definition) **17** 64
Hollandaise sauce **2** 51
blender **2** 52

Hominy squares, broiled **17** 102
Honey
balls **9** 31
cake **9** 31
cookies **14** 103, **18** 70
Greek spiced
(melomacarona) **12** 96
with hazelnuts **10** 95
Polish (ciastka miodowe) **12** 70
and nut pastries (baklava) **12** 95
sauce **10** 128
twist **9** 99
Hong Kong dishes
almond gelatin with lychees **11** 96
chicken, with lemon **17** 72
kedgeree **11** 96
Hontaka chili (definition) **15** 28
Hop to gai kow (walnut chicken) **17** 71
Hors d'œuvres **17** 121–135
cocktail **16** 130
cold **7** 46–52, **15** 117–125
hot **7** 53–55
zakouski **7** 112
informal **17** 130–131
Spanish and Portuguese
cooking **16** 112

Horseradish
and beet relish **8** 65
cream **1** 30
sauce **5** 49
with Austrian boiled beef **1** 62
Danish (peberrodssvors) **12** 21
morar **9** 13
sour cream **7** 112
vinegar **16** 101
Hot beer soup (Biersuppe) **11** 125
Hot pot **10** 64
Hot savory molds **16** 83–91
Ho yow
definition **17** 64
oyster sauce beef **17** 75
Hubert, St. **17** 106
Hueros rancheron **15** 31
Hummus bi tahina (chick-peas
with sesame paste) **12** 87
Hung gah teem choy (almond
blossom dessert) **17** 80
Hungariana crêpes **13** 129
Hungarian dishes
coffeecake **13** 22
crêpes **13** 129
grenadins of veal **17** 51
Hungarian sausage (definition) **12** 124
Hymettus (definition) **4** 13

I'A (Fijian steamed fish with sweet
potatoes) **11** 89
Icebox cookies **1** 121
butterscotch **1** 121
vanilla **1** 121
variations **1** 121
Ice cream, see also Frappés,
Granités, Ices and
Sherbets **11** 99–113
apricot **11** 106
banana **11** 106
blueberry **11** 106
caramel pecan **11** 106
chocolate **11** 104
chip **11** 104
churn freezers **11** 100
coffee **11** 104
cranberry **11** 106
frappé(s) **11** 112–113
to freeze
in a churn freezer **11** 101
in ice trays **11** 101

fruit **11** 106
granité(s) **11** 112–113
ice for churning **11** 100
ice(s) **11** 112
peach **11** 106
peppermint **16** 35
pistachio **11** 104
points to remember **11** 103
praline **11** 104
raspberry **11** 106
to serve **11** 101
sherbet(s) **11** 108–112
to store **11** 101
strawberry **11** 106
sugar content **11** 103
sundaes **5** 53
tutti frutti **11** 106
vanilla
custard base **11** 103
egg mousse base **11** 104
wholewheat bread **11** 106
Ice(s) **11** 112
Champagne **11** 112
lime **11** 112
mango **11** 79
storing **11** 112
Iced caramel pecan mousse **16** 72
Iced strawberry mousse **11** 121
Icing (see also Frosting)
boiled **9** 71
caramel **1** 117
color and flavoring **9** 69
fondant **7** 102, **14** 88, **18** 52
glacé **3** 47, **12** 71, **18** 53
milk **9** 71
royal **9** 71, **14** 87, **18** 53
Ikokore (Nigerian fish stew) **11** 91
Ile flottante **6** 125
Illaichi (definition) **13** 82
Imam bayeldi (Turkish fainting
imam) **12** 91
Imli (definition) **13** 83
Indian cooking **13** 81–99
bread **13** 97
curry **13** 84–86
kebab **13** 90
pickle and chutney **13** 96
raita **13** 95
sambal **13** 92–93
spiced dishes **13** 88
sweet dishes **13** 98–99
Indienne, à l' (definition) **5** 30
Indonesian dishes **11** 93–95
Informal menus **14** 112–131
Insalati di legumi **8** 104
Involtini alla milanese **8** 103
Irish coffee **8** 57
Irish stew **3** 17

Italian brigidini	**5** 132
Italian cooking	**8** 98–113
boats	**18** 62
chicken	**10** 131
relish	**11** 15
salad	**13** 59
turkey	**14** 122
soufflé	**10** 38
Italian sausage	
with chicory	**12** 128
definition	**12** 124

Japanese cooking	**16** 47–58
ingredients	**16** 48
soup garnishes	**16** 48–49
Japonaise	
meringue	**18** 58
salad	**15** 67
strawberry	**8** 38
Jaggery	**13** 82
Jalapeno chili	**4** 93, **15** 28
Jalousie	**8** 81
Jam(s) (see also Conserve; Jelly;	
Preserves)	**7** 76–80, **11** 32
apple ginger	**11** 32
apricot, glaze	**8** 69, **10** 15
Bing cherry	**7** 79
blackberry and apple	**7** 80
blueberry	**7** 79
buns	**13** 25
causes of failure	**7** 76
damson plum	**11** 32
equipment for making	**7** 76
glaze, apricot	**10** 15
green grape	**16** 96
gooseberry	**7** 79
melon and ginger	**7** 80
omelet	**10** 43
pear and lime	**11** 32

pineapple	**16** 96
pineapple apricot	**7** 80
plum	**11** 32
raspberry	**7** 79
rhubarb and ginger	**16** 96
rhubarb and orange	**7** 80
sauce	**9** 125
hot	**6** 87
strawberry 1 and 2	**7** 77
sun-cooked	**7** 77
to test for jell point	**11** 32
Jamaican pickled fish	**11** 82
Jambalaya	**2** 64
Jambon bourguignonne	**7** 29
Janssons frestelse (Jansson's	
temptation)	**12** 21
Japanese cooking	**16** 47–58
Japonaise salad	**15** 67
Jardinière platter	**18** 12
Jeanette, tartlets	**17** 124
Jeera (definition)	**13** 82
Jelabis	**13** 98
Jell point	**16** 94
Jelly(ies)	**7** 81–82, **11** 33
apple	**7** 82
bag	**8** 16
blackberry	**7** 81
and apple	**11** 33
cranberry and apple	**11** 33
damson plum	**11** 32
grape	**11** 33
lemon verbena	**7** 82
lime	**16** 97
orange lemon	**16** 97
red currant	**7** 81
rose geranium	**7** 82
tart, and cream cheese rounds	**7** 52
to test for jell point	**11** 32
Jelly roll	**6** 68
banana cream	**6** 69
case, to make	**6** 68
chocolate	**6** 69
gelatine, fruit	**5** 51
strawberry cream	**6** 69
Jewish cooking	**9** 8–35
Jing lo yee (striped bass	
à la kan)	**17** 69
Jow yeong dow foo (fish stuffed	
in bean cake)	**17** 69
Julglögg (Scandinavian hot punch)	**12** 27
Julienne (definition)	**1** 22

K

Kaab el ghzal (Moroccan gazelle	
horns)	**12** 96
Kachoomber	**13** 93
Kaeng phet nua (Thai meat curry)	**11** 96
Kahve (Turkish coffee)	**12** 96
Kaisertorte	**18** 65
Kakimiso (oyster soup)	**16** 49
Kale soup	**16** 116
Kantonese salt (definition)	**17** 64
Kartoffelpuffer (potato pancakes)	**11** 125
Kartoffelstangen	**15** 121
Kasha	**4** 99, **7** 116
Kebabs	**3** 75
in Indian and Pakistani cooking	**13** 90
Indonesian barbecued pork	
(saté babi manis)	**11** 95
miniature	**17** 134
banderillas	**16** 112
sausage	**12** 130
shashlik	**7** 116
shrimp	**10** 80
en brochette	**10** 29
turkey, deviled	**4** 38
Kedgeree	**2** 65
Hong Kong	**11** 96
Kesar (definition)	**13** 83
Key lime pie	**7** 127
Khaskas (definition)	**13** 83

Kibbeh (definition)	**12** 87
bi sanieh (baked)	**12** 87
broiled	**12** 87
fried	**12** 87
nayya (ground lamb with bulgur)	**12** 87
Kichlach	**9** 25
Kidney(s)	
brochettes of	**3** 96
chausseur	**15** 107
deviled	**10** 124, **12** 55
eggplant stuffed with	**11** 70

Kidney(s) *continued*

lambs' 3 75
  Garibaldi 9 81
  with herb stuffing 9 83
  with rice 9 81
  Turbigo 9 83
  and mushroom bouchées 8 76
  potatoes 11 20
  rognons, sauté au vin blanc 10 81
  sautéed
    with bacon 12 55
    with Madeira 4 48
    in white wine 10 81
  soup 10 81
  with steak pie 7 91
  veal, broiled 3 77
  Robert 12 80
Kidney beans, red 12 100
  purée 12 110
Kielbasa
  with cabbage 12 130
  definition 12 123
Kingfish 11 56
Kipper pâté 11 11
Kissing crust (definition) 7 60

Kleinsuppe (giblet soup) 11 124
Klenäter (Swedish Christmas
  crullers) 12 15
Knackwurst
  definition 12 123
  to make 12 127
Knaidlech 9 20
Knishes 9 22
Knives, sharpening 6 19
Kofta kari (curried meatballs) 13 86
Kolbascy sausage
  (definition) 12 123
Königsberger Klopse (meat
  dumplings) 11 127
Korma (spiced lamb) 13 88
Kosher dill pickles 11 39
Köttbullar (Swedish meatballs) 17 135
Koulouria (Greek sesame seed
  cookies) 12 95
Kraftor (Swedish crayfish with dill) 12 22

Kreplach 9 20
Kromeskis 13 43
  chicken or veal 13 45
  shrimp 13 45
Krumkaces 5 131
Krupuk (Indonesian shrimp puffs) 11 93
Kugel, lockshen 9 25
  potato 9 21
Kugelhopf 13 20
Kulebiaka 7 116
Kulich 7 119
Kumquat preserves 16 97

Labskovs (Danish hash) 12 24
Ladyfingers 6 63, 15 84
Lamb 7 16–19
  ballotine 2 87
  banyuls 10 81
  braised
    with pineapple 5 64
    spiced leg of 14 71
  breast of
    fallette 8 95
    stuffed, Dundee 10 65
  for broiling 3 75
  carré d'agneau 7 18
  carving 7 16, 18
  casserole
    with potato 10 64
    with tomato 4 91
  chops
    alsacienne 17 44
    barbecued 3 96
    with cheese 12 38
    with corn and tomatoes 12 78
    with eggplant 11 20
    with herbs 17 46
    loin, broiled 3 75

  in mint aspic 8 21
  Montrouge 18 34
  with mushroom stuffing 16 62
  Niçoise 12 38
  in pastry 18 36
  quality of 11 20
  reform 17 44
  rib, broiled 3 75
  soubise 17 46
  volnay 17 46
  with walnuts 12 37
  cooking and serving
    suggestions 7 17
  couscous 12 93
  curry 13 39
    methee bhaji 5 76
  cuts 7 16
  ground, with bulgur (kibbeh
    nayya) 12 87
  hot pot 10 64
  kebabs, broiled 3 75, 17 134
  kidneys, broiled 3 75
  leg
    braised, stuffed 7 107
    bretonne braised 5 63
    duxelles 2 88
    pot roast
      provençale 2 23
      with spring vegetables 1 72
    ragoût, with savory rice 3 17
    spiced 5 13
  loin
    bretonne 2 87
    Doria with orange and
      red currant sauce 5 73
    portugaise 4 70
  moussaka 11 70
    classic 12 89
  neck
    navarin 3 17
    Irish stew 3 17
  noisettes of 12 40, 15 58–59
    Henri IV 15 58
    mililanaise 15 59
  rack
    Conti 12 42
    provençale 12 40
  ragoût, with savory rice 3 16
  riblets, navarin 3 17
  with rice (Biriani) 13 89
  roast
    gratiné 5 115
    saddle of 18 12
  for roasting 1 32–33
    to serve with roasts 1 35
    times 7 20
  saddle of, roast 18 12
  shashlik 7 116

Lamb *continued*
shoulder, broiled | **3** 75
  ballotine | **2** 87
  Caucasian | **7** 114
  pot roast | **2** 22
  stuffed | **13** 76
  à la Turque | **10** 103
spiced (korma) | **13** 88
stew
  with chicory and avgolemono
    sauce | **5** 120
  Greek (arni kokkinisto) | **12** 91
stuffed vine leaves (dolmas) | **12** 86
sweetbreads | **13** 76
with yogurt | **10** 112
Lambs' wool (definition) | **11** 17
Landjäger sausage (definition) | **12** 123
Langosta a la Barcelonesa
  (spiny lobster from
  Barcelona) | **16** 119
Langostinos a la Catalana
  (Catalan shrimps) | **16** 114
Laranjas (orange salad) | **11** 86
Larding | **11** 129
Lardons (definition) | **14** 13

Lasagne
  basic dough | **8** 118
  bolognese | **8** 118
  rustica | **8** 119
  with sausage | **11** 73
Latkes, potato | **9** 34
Leaves (vegetable), as a garnish | **16** 48
Leberwurst sausage
  (definition) | **12** 123
Leckerli (definition) | **18** 70
Leek(s)
  braised | **1** 39
  pie | **14** 41
    with bacon | **11** 14
  quiche, with cheese | **10** 118
  soup
    and bean | **12** 103
    with rice | **16** 104
  vinaigrette | **10** 70
Leen gee
  definition | **17** 64

stuffed duck | **17** 75
Legumes (definition) | **13** 82
Lemon(s)
  chiffon pie | **1** 58
  with chicken | **10** 85, **17** 72
  compote | **17** 33
  dressing | **13** 57
  duck, roast | **17** 32
  fritters | **17** 26
  garnish | **15** 126–127
  gelatin | **8** 24
  hard sauce | **9** 127, **8** 96, **1** 66
  krumkakes | **5** 131
  meringue pie | **1** 58
  orange jelly | **16** 97
  pickle | **13** 96
  pie | **11** 25
  pie sherbet | **11** 108
  sauce (citronsovs) | **12** 24
  soufflé | **10** 41
    cold | **7** 12
  stuffed cabbage | **7** 41
  syllabub | **10** 87
  verbena jelly | **7** 82
Lemon pine needles, garnish | **16** 48
Lentil(s) | **12** 100
  curry | **13** 86
  purée | **7** 27, **12** 109
    with chorizo sausage | **16** 114
    masur dahl | **13** 93
  soup | **12** 101
    Moroccan (harira) | **12** 84
Leo soon gai kow (fresh asparagus
  chicken with black bean
  sauce) | **17** 80
Lettuce
  braised | **5** 64
  hearts, garnish for egg
    mousse | **10** 51
  salad, with cucumber | **10** 80, **12** 80
  soup, cream of | **3** 63
Liaison(s) | **1** 83, **2** 44

Light bread | **7** 67
Lima beans | **12** 101, **14** 18
  casserole | **4** 95
  Marie-Anne | **4** 97, **14** 18
  purée | **12** 109

salad | **13** 106, **17** 84
  with rice | **17** 84
Lime
  garnish | **15** 126–127
    Japanese | **16** 48
  ice | **11** 112
  jelly | **16** 97
  and pear jam | **11** 32
  pickle | **13** 96
  pie, key | **7** 127
Limpa (Swedish sweet rye bread) | **12** 29
Linguica sausage | **16** 116
Linguine tutto mare | **5** 88
Lion's snack open-face
  sandwich | **12** 10
Liptaur cheese | **15** 118
Lisettes | **18** 64
Liver(s)
  and bacon | **9** 79
  braised with mushrooms | **9** 80
  chicken | **9** 38
    anchovy toast | **14** 45
    and calves' | **9** 45
    fingers | **17** 122
    knishes | **9** 22
    with scrambled eggs | **10** 130
  chopped | **9** 21
  fried, with orange | **9** 78
  mold, calves' | **1** 65
  omelet | **16** 116
  pâté | **9** 40
    chicken liver | **9** 38
    Danish | **12** 10
  sandwich, with sausage and
    chutney | **14** 114
  sausage
    leberwurst | **12** 123
    salad | **12** 131
  sauté of Italienne | **10** 81
Loaf
  anchovy, hot | **13** 104
  cheese | **15** 118
  turkey and mushroom | **8** 61
Lobster | **10** 18–21
  Americaine | **16** 21
  Andalouse | **10** 21
  boats | **7** 50

34

Lobster *continued*

bordelaise	**18** 25
boréale	**16** 19
coral	**10** 20
crêpes	**13** 124
deviled	**10** 21
to dress	**10** 18
to flame	**10** 20
gratiné	**10** 20
a l'Hongroise	**17** 125
to kill	**10** 18
margareta	**16** 18
mousse	**14** 58
Newburg	**10** 20
Parisienne	**10** 21
pilaf	**16** 18
preparation	**10** 18
salad, Valencia	**5** 22
sauce	**10** 39
Spanish	**12** 54
spiny	**16** 119
tails, stuffed (yeong loong hah mei)	**17** 67
thermidor	**10** 19
Lockshen	**9** 20
kugel	**9** 25
Lon dow jook soon ma tai (snow peas with water chestnuts and bamboo shoots)	**17** 80
Lop cheong	
definition	**17** 64
steamed pork patty with Chinese sausage	**17** 77
Lotus nuts (definition)	**17** 64
Lotus stuffed duck (leen gee opp)	**17** 75
Lucia, Feast of St.	**12** 30
Luting paste	**9** 42, **16** 29
Lychee(s)	
with almond gelatin, Hong Kong	**11** 96
baw law goo lo yuke (lychee pineapple pork sweet and sour)	**17** 77
Lyon sausage (definition)	**12** 123
Lyonnaise salad	**17** 86

M

Ma'amoul	**10** 92
Macaroni	
con acciughe (with anchovies)	**5** 87
and cheese	**5** 84
pastitso	**5** 41
pie	**13** 41
Macaroon(s)	
almond	**15** 24
and chocolate mousse	**11** 22
coconut	**9** 57
with orange	**15** 107
small (à l'orange)	**17** 58
syllabub	**13** 52
Passover	**9** 17
Mace (definition)	**13** 82
Macédoine of fresh fruit	**5** 80
Mackerel	
broiled	**3** 80
with mushrooms and tomatoes	**2** 111
à la provençale	**2** 111
with Venetian sauce	**2** 111
Mâconnaise (definition)	**4** 44
Madeira cake	**1** 112
Madeira sauce, with braised ham	**7** 31
Madeleines	**14** 98
English	**1** 112
Madère sauce	**2** 49, **15** 41, **16** 90
Madrid meat, fowl and vegetable stew	**16** 122
Madrilène soup, simple	**12** 80
Magali	**7** 100
Maids of honor	**4** 57
Maître d'hôtel butter	**3** 81, **11** 55
Maître d'hôtel potatoes	**14** 13
Malakoff (definition)	**18** 41
Malaysian dishes	
coconut soup (sothi)	**11** 96
eggs in soy sauce	**11** 95
Maltaise sauce	**2** 52
Mancha vegetable stew	**16** 119
Mandarin orange peel, dried	**17** 64
Mandelbrød (Danish almond coffeecake)	**12** 29
Mandoline (definition)	**6** 73, **11** 78
Mango(es)	
chicken	**17** 22
chutney	**13** 96
ice	**11** 79
pudding	**15** 41
steak, Hawaiian	**11** 89
Manhattan clam chowder	**6** 53
Manicotti con fegato	**5** 88

Manioc meal, toasted	**11** 87
Maori cocoa balls	**11** 90
Maple	
divinity (candy)	**13** 115
mousse	**12** 73
parfait	**18** 120
Marble cake	**1** 117
Marchand de vin (fillet beef)	**16** 61
Marinade	
for beef	**5** 68
fruit	**16** 44
game	**5** 71
quick	**5** 70
piquant	**5** 70
saté	**5** 70
spiced	**5** 70
Marinate, how to	**5** 67–73
Marineret stegt svinekam (Danish marinated roast pork)	**12** 24
Marjolaine tartlets	**6** 84
Marmalade	
orange 1 and 2	**16** 94
pineapple and grapefruit	**16** 96
purée	**8** 81
sauce	**9** 124
tangerine	**16** 95
three fruit	**16** 95
topping for coffeecake	**13** 14
Marquise Alice	**18** 39
Marrow, bone	**8** 105
Marrow beans	**12** 100
in cream sauce	**12** 110
Marshmallow chocolate squares	**9** 117
Martha's coffeecake	**7** 64
Marzipan	
candies	**13** 117
dates	**10** 92, **13** 117
for decorations	**15** 81
walnuts	**10** 92, **13** 117
Masa de quesadilla	
con chili ancho (chili dough)	**15** 33
con quesco (cheese dough)	**15** 33
Masur dahl (lentil purée)	**13** 93
Matelote (definition)	**6** 110
mâconnaise	**6** 110
de poisson	**6** 110

35

Mattar paneer (Indian
    cheese with peas) **13** 95
Mayonnaise **5** 112, **6** 38, **11** 45
  anchovy **5** 49
  blender **4** 32
  collée **17** 30
  curry **13** 106, **17** 29
  egg **13** 59
  garlic **14** 117, **16** 114
  green **6** 38, **11** 60
  nantua **17** 13
  tomato **6** 38, **11** 60
Maypole birthday cake **2** 76
Mazagrans **13** 37
Mazurki bakaliowe
    (Polish fruit and nut cookies) **12** 70
Measuring and measurement
    1 126, **2** 130, **3** 128, **10** 132
Meat(s), see also individual names
  barding **2** 89
  blintzes **9** 23
  braising **5** 56
  broiling **3** 68–77
  carving and carving tools **6** 18–19
  classic entrées **12** 32–43
  cold cooked, platter of **10** 53
  curry Thai (kaeng phet nua) **11** 96
  dishes, unusual **11** 69–73
  dumplings (königsberger klopse) **11** 127
  glaze, mock and true **7** 122, **9** 94
  grades of **1** 27
  hash (labskovs) **12** 24
  larding **2** 89
  mixed grill **3** 76
  potted **10** 123, **14** 44
  roasting **1** 26–27
    rotisserie **9** 130–133
    slow oven **9** 130–133
    for special occasions **2** 86–89
    times, regular **1** 26
  stew **3** 15–25
  variety **9** 77–83
  veal, how to roast **2** 80–84
Meatballs
  curried **13** 86, 90

frikadeller **12** 24
leftovers **13** 34–45
Swedish **17** 135
  with tomato and pepper sauce **5** 50
Mecca cream **4** 61
Meeta pilau (sweet saffron rice) **13** 98
Mei jing (definition) **17** 64
Mejillones gratinados
    (browned mussel) **16** 114
Melba sauce **9** 124
Melba toast **17** 54
Melomacarona (Greek spiced
    honey cakes) **12** 96
Melon
  bitter
    definition **17** 64
    with chicken **17** 78
  compote **11** 26
  cup, with strawberries **10** 130
  jam, with ginger **7** 80
  pickle, with cantaloupe **7** 84
  salad **4** 10
    with cream cheese dressing **15** 67
    with mint **17** 87
  storing **11** 26
  en surprise **17** 57
  winter **17** 64
    soup **17** 65
Menudo (tripe soup) **15** 35

Meringue(s) **4** 72–82
  Alaska, baked **4** 78
  almond, with apples and pears **5** 107
  basket **4** 77
  Blidahs **4** 80
  cake
    almond **4** 80
    apple (Apfeltorte) **11** 135
    coffee **13** 52
  Chantilly **4** 78
  cuite **16** 132
  dacquoise **12** 50
  field of mushrooms **2** 74
  gâteau, almonds and chocolate **10** 95
  glacé maison **18** 117

ile flottant (floating island) **6** 125
Italienne **4** 76, **18** 53
Japonais **18** 58
leftover **5** 15
milk flan **4** 82
Mont Blanc **10** 91
oeufs à la neige (snow eggs) **6** 125
Pavlova **5** 127
petits mont blancs **4** 82
pie
  chocolate **1** 58
  coconut cream **1** 55
  lemon **1** 58
rounds with chestnut purée **10** 56
suisse **4** 75
topping **4** 75
turquois **10** 95
vacherin aux marrons **10** 56
Methee bhaji (mild lamb curry) **5** 76
Methi (definition) **13** 82
Mexican cooking **15** 27–43
  chicken **11** 26
  eggs, baked **10** 121
Middle Eastern cooking **12** 83–97
Milano sausage (definition) **12** 124
Milk
  coconut **11** 82
  cooking with **4** 52–65
  drinks **4** 63
  forms of **4** 64–65
  icing **8** 38, **9** 71
  puddings **4** 60–61
  punch **8** 55–56
    cold **4** 63
Mille feuilles **8** 81
  chicken **17** 30
  chocolate **12** 73
  gâteau au citron **8** 69
  strawberry **18** 90
Mince **14** 39
Mince pies **8** 89
Mincemeat
  pie **7** 109
  simple **8** 89
  traditional **8** 89

Minerves 18 15
Minestra 6 53
Minestrone 6 53
Mint
  with duck, roast 17 32
  with grape and melon salad 17 87
  with grapefruit sherbet 11 112
  leaves, crystallized 11 112
  sauce 1 35
  vinegar 16 100
Minute steak with Madeira 14 26
Mirasol colorados 15 28
Mirlitons 14 100
Miroton of beef 13 38
Misoshiru (soybean paste soup) 16 49
Mocha
  frosting 1 117
  shake 4 63
Mo gwa bok opp tong
    (fuzzy squash and
    pigeon soup) 17 65
Moka pralin soufflé 14 64
Molasses
  biscuits 4 126
  bread 10 127
  definition 4 126
  taffy 13 115
  toffee 13 113

Mold(s) 8 30–31
  beef 13 38
  broccoli 7 109
  cookies, Christmas (Springerle) 11 137
  fillings 8 18
  kulich and paskha 7 119
  to line, with aspic 13 69
  moulé à manqué 8 24
  raised pie 9 48
  savory, hot 16 83–91
  small, to turn out 5 33
  spinach 7 39
  to steam 16 84
  tartlet pans, to line 14 86
  terrine 9 42
  turning out 8 18
  in a water bath 16 84

Mole
  chicken 15 39
  green 15 39
  pork 15 39
  turkey (poblano) 15 39
Môlho de pimento (hot pepper
    sauce) 11 87
Monosodium glutamate
    (definition) 17 64
Mont Blanc 10 91
Monts blancs, petits 4 82
Montmorency (definition) 3 51
Morels
  with cream
    (morilles à la crème) 10 84, 17 57
  definition 17 57
Morilles à la crème 10 84
Mornay sauce 7 39
  with cauliflower soufflé 11 118
Mortadella sausage
    (definition) 12 123
Moselle wine cup 18 47
Moule à manqué 8 24, 18 56
Moules marinière 10 26
Moussaka 11 70
  classic 12 89
Mousse(s) 14 56–65
  apple, gâtinaise 6 14
  avocado 13 104
  basic mixture for bombes 18 114
  basque, apricot 15 22
  brown bread caramel,
    with plum sauce 14 63
  caramel 14 62
    pecan, iced 16 72
  cherry 3 50
  chocolate 1 24
    and macaroon 11 22
  cucumber and cheese 14 61
  crab 10 80
  egg 10 50
    and shrimp 8 67
  game 14 61
  grapefruit 11 26
  haddock 2 36

ham 14 61
  cold 7 31
  of liver pâté 3 124
  lobster 14 61
  maple 12 73
  Marie-Christina 8 28
  orange 4 106
    with lychees 15 17
  pineapple, en surprise 14 64
  de poulet madrilène 18 26
  roquefort 15 92
  salmon 1 70
  de saumon à la Nantua 18 22
  strawberry 14 62
    iced 11 121
  tangerine 16 104
  tongue 14 61
  trout, smoked or finnan haddie 14 61
  turkey 8 61
Mousseline
  definition 16 91
  of fish, chicken, rabbit or veal 16 91
  sauce 2 52
  of sole 18 104
  stuffing 14 77, 18 77
Mousses and soufflés 14 56–65
  savory 14 58–62
  sweet 14 62–65
Muffins 4 123–124, 14 47
  blue berry 3 52
  English 7 64
Mulato chili (definition) 15 28
Mullet 11 56
  Fijian steamed, with sweet
    potatoes (I'A) 11 89
  fish couscous 12 94
  en papillote 11 57
Mulligatawny soup 6 56
Muscadins 17 58
Mushroom(s)
  beignets with devil sauce dip 7 53
  bouchées
    ham 8 65
  and brandy butter 14 45
  canapés 17 128
  casserole, with potatoes 5 13
  and cauliflower 7 41
  Chinese (definition) 17 64
  croquettes, with chicken 13 43
  deviled 8 93
  duxelles 11 57
  filling for cassolettes 15 125
  flan 3 35
  garnish 16 48
  under glass 18 34
  au gratin 17 36
  kidney 8 76
  mold, spiced 8 27

Mushroom(s) *continued*

morels, with cream	**5** 59, **10** 84
morilles à la crème	**10** 84
omelet	**1** 76
and onions à la greque	**4** 115
Philippe	**12** 46
pickled	**11** 36
pizza	**8** 130
salad	
with artichokes	**6** 32
with gruyère cheese	**15** 64
sauce	**2** 45
cream	**16** 91
with snails	**17** 130
soufflé	**10** 36
soup	**3** 10, **3** 117
with oysters	**10** 23
with watercress	**17** 15
stems	**3** 76
stuffed	
with anchovy	**4** 115
with ham	**17** 130
stuffing	
with lamb chops	**16** 62
with rice (for peppers)	**4** 112
and turkey loaf	**8** 61
types of	**11** 132
in wine (white)	**16** 76
Mushroom cake, tub of	**15** 84
Mussels	**10** 26–27
baked stuffed	**6** 113
browned (Mejillones gratinados)	**16** 114
chowder	**1** 42
moules marinière	**10** 26
preparation	**10** 26
with rice	**10** 26
Mustard	
butter	**3** 82
Chinese hot (definition)	**17** 65
cream	**5** 47
croûtes	**6** 57
Dijon-style	**1** 85

Mustard sauce	**2** 46, 53
cream	**16** 30
simple	**16** 21
Swedish (sennepssovs)	**12** 18
sweet and sour	**7** 30
Mutton pies, Cumberland	**14** 44

N

Nantua	
mayonnaise	**17** 13
sauce	**18** 20
Ngow yuke fon (beef casserole with rice)	**17** 69
Napoleons	**8** 81
Napolitana sauce	**5** 95
Nasi ajam (Indonesian chicken with rice)	**11** 93
Nasturtium seeds, pickled	**18** 132
Navarin (definition)	**3** 16–17
Navets braisés	**6** 122
Navy beans	**12** 100
with sausages	**12** 106
Neapolitan fondants	**13** 121
Nectarine(s)	
butter	**11** 33
spiced	**7** 82
Nègre en chemise	**7** 103
Nesselrode (definition)	**7** 128
pudding	**7** 128
Newburg, fish mold	**16** 87
New England dishes	
clam chowder	**3** 106
boiled dinner	**1** 63
New Orleans pot roast beef	**2** 24
New potatoes	**14** 19
New Year (Japanese)	**16** 58
Nigerian fish stew (ikokore)	**11** 91
Nockerin	**9** 111
Noisettes of lamb	**15** 58
Nom moong gai (Hong Kong lemon chicken)	**17** 71

Noodles	
buttered	**11** 25, **12** 116
lockshen	**9** 20
lockshen kugel (noodle pudding)	**9** 25
in salad	**15** 64
Norimaki sushi (vinegard rice and fish in seaweed)	**16** 50
Normande (definition)	**4** 46
Normande galette	**16** 80
Normandy pear pie (le poirat)	**11** 121
Norwegian cream	**4** 61
Norwegian goro	**5** 132
Nougat	**13** 118
cake	**18** 59
Numeral birthday cake	**2** 75
Nusskuchen	**4** 106
Nusstorte	**18** 67
Nut(s), see also individual names	
bars, apricot	**13** 12
blanched	**10** 90
bread, quick	**6** 101
cake	**18** 67
in candy	**13** 118
cooking with	**10** 88–95
deep fat fried	**10** 90
to freeze	**10** 90
ground or grated	**10** 90
kinds of	**10** 96–97
milk	**3** 65, **10** 90
muffins, spiced	**4** 124
pastries, with honey (baklava)	**12** 95
preparation of	**10** 90
roasted	**10** 90
salted	**10** 90
shredded	**10** 90
slices, coffee	**17** 16
slivered	**10** 90
toasted	**10** 90
waffles	**5** 130

Oak leaf cookies **7** 100
Oatcakes, Scottish **14** 53
Oatmeal bread **14** 46
Oatmeal cream **4** 60
Oeufs, see Eggs
Oil, Chinese cooking (definition) **17** 64
Okra
  definition **5** 77
  pilaf **4** 111
Olives
  black, with partridge **17** 106
  with eggs **17** 127
  to pit and reshape **10** 73
  pizza **8** 128
  salad, with rice and tomato **13** 58
  with salamis of duck **14** 32
  with stuffed eggplant **14** 22

Omelet **1** 74–79, **15** 102
  alsacienne **10** 121
  Arnold Bennett **5** 34
  bacon and croûton **1** 79
  barante **15** 102
  bonne femme (with potato
    and bacon) **1** 79
  cheese **1** 76
  chicken liver **1** 76
  Clamart **10** 121
  crab meat **1** 79
  fine herbs **1** 76
  Germiny **15** 102
  Grimaldi **1** 79
  jam **5** 42, **10** 43
  Lyonnaise **10** 121
  mushroom **1** 76
  oyster **1** 79
  peperoni **5** 34
  plain **1** 76, **10** 118
  potato **1** 76
  provençale **10** 121

  rum **10** 43
  shredded **16** 51
    Indonesian spiced **11** 93
  soufflé **10** 43–44
  sour cream and chives **10** 118
  Spanish **5** 34
  stuffed **1** 76
    French bread **4** 38
  Swiss **10** 118
  tomato **1** 76
  tortilla **16** 116
  truffle **1** 79
  zucchini **1** 79
Onigari-yaki (broiled shrimps in
  soy sauce) **16** 57
Onion(s)
  and apple pie **14** 42
  braised, in wine **5** 64
  broiled **16** 62
  canapé, with tomato **17** 128
  casserole, with potato **15** 113
  in cream **8** 51
  fried **17** 46, **3** 82
  glazed **1** 39
    and chestnuts **8** 51
  à la greque with mushrooms **4** 115
  juice **13** 125, **14** 58
  kinds of **6** 128–129
  omelet Lyonnaise **10** 121
  pickled, salad and corn **8** 64
  pie, Costa Rican **10** 121
  preparation **3** 82
  quiche **11** 14
  ragoût **4** 98
  relish **11** 15
  rings, fried **2** 117
    with eggs soubise **5** 20
  salad
    with corn and pimiento **13** 58
    with orange **7** 31
  sauce (soubise) **2** 46
  soup
    cream of (le Thourin) **13** 74
    French **6** 109
    simple **6** 48
  spiced **13** 60

  stuffed **7** 39
  stuffing **12** 62
    with herbs **2** 85
    with sage **1** 39
  sweet pickled **11** 37
  with turnips **1** 91, **14** 19
Opera fondants **13** 121
Opp geok bow (definition) **17** 64
Orange
  baked potatoes **14** 127
  baskets **2** 74
  butter **13** 130
  cake
    whole **9** 63
    mousseline **18** 56
    raisin **9** 96
    sponge **6** 64
  in caramel **1** 46
  caramel nuts **13** 118
  cocktail, with tomato **3** 43
  cream **16** 132
    sauce **9** 124
  currant bread **4** 121
  duck, roast **17** 32
  flan **16** 127
  flower water (definition) **12** 84
  frosting **6** 64
  galette, caramelized **12** 71
  garnish **15** 126–127
  gravy, with roast wild duck **17** 108
  jam, with rhubarb **7** 80
  jelly, with lemons **16** 97
  macaroons **15** 107, **17** 58
  macaroon syllabub **13** 52
  marmalade 1 and 2 **16** 94
  mousse **4** 106
    with lychees **15** 17
  muffins, with date **4** 124
  pastry cream **9** 112
  peel, dried mandarin (definition) **17** 64
  potato, baked **14** 127
  salad **17** 102, **11** 86
    with avocado and grapefruit **6** 37
    with celery and chestnut
      17 87, **18** 100
    and endive **8** 64
    with onion **5** 13
    with pineapple **6** 36
    with shrimp **10** 124
    with tomato **9** 89, **17** 87
  sauce
    with chocolate **7** 97, **9** 126
    with red currant **6** 73, **9** 125
  sherbet **11** 109
  slices for decoration **9** 112
  soufflé **10** 41
    nantaise **15** 51
  soup, with tomato **5** 11

Orange *continued*

spiced	**7** 83
sundae, with strawberry	**5** 53
en surprise	**5** 116
sweet potatoes	**10** 101
and tomato cocktail	**3** 43
Orangines	**16** 133
Osso buco	**8** 105
Outdoor entertaining	**16** 59–73
Oven temperatures and shelf positions	**1** 127, **14** 133
Oxtail, braised	**9** 80
Oyster(s)	**10** 22–25
angels on horseback	**10** 25
beef (ho yow ngow yuke)	**17** 75
broiled	**10** 25
casino	**10** 23
creamed	**10** 25
fritters	**10** 25
kakimiso (soup)	**16** 49
marinated	**13** 60
omelet	**1** 79
Rockefeller	**10** 23
definition	**10** 23
sauce (definition)	**17** 64
scalloped	**8** 51
and shrimp gumbo	**10** 66
smoked, à l'indienne	**17** 125
soup, with mushroom	**10** 23
stew	**10** 23
fisherman's	**10** 124
stuffing, with roast turkey	**10** 101
Oyster purse eggs	**17** 78

P

Pacific Island cooking	**11** 88–90
Paella	**16** 120
barcelonesa	**2** 67
catalan	**2** 67
definition	**16** 120
how to cook	**2** 67

Paella (definition)	**16** 120
Valenciana	**16** 120
Pain farci (stuffed bread)	**13** 37
Pains de seigle	**14** 125
Pakistani cooking	**13** 81–99
bread	**13** 97
curry	**13** 84–86
kebab	**13** 90
pickles and chutney	**13** 96
raita	**13** 95
sambal	**13** 92–93
spiced dishes	**13** 88
sweet dishes	**13** 98–99
Palatschinken crêpes	**13** 127
Palmiers	**8** 83, **15** 119
Pan(s), how to choose and care for	**2** 120–123
Pancake(s)	**9** 110–113
buckwheat	**9** 112
cheese	**15** 91
corn cakes	**10** 127
corn dollars	**10** 127
à la crème	**15** 107
deep-fried	**9** 112
ginger	**10** 128
nockerin	**9** 111
pfannkuchen	**9** 111
potato	
kartoffelpuffer	**11** 126
latkes	**9** 34
regular	**9** 111
saucer	**10** 67
savory, with fillings	**7** 54–55
Welsh	**14** 50
Pandolce	**13** 33
Pan dulce (Spanish sweet bread)	**16** 127
Panada	**16** 87
Pan de muerto	**15** 41
Paneer (Indian cheese)	**13** 95
Pannequets soufflés	**18** 36
Papas con aji	**5** 125
Papaya (definition)	**11** 82
with chicken, East African	**11** 92
cream, Grenadian	**11** 84
Paprika	
definition	**10** 112
goulash	**3** 19
rice	**15** 56
veal	**10** 112
Parathas (Indian bread)	**13** 97
Parfait	
bombe and iced desserts	**18** 113–121
chestnut	**16** 35
layered	**2** 41
pecan, with peaches	**17** 15
raspberry	**2** 41
Parisienne	
definition	**15** 54

potatoes	**10** 73, **12** 40
Parkin, Yorkshire	**14** 49
Parmesan cheese	**8** 118, **15** 89
Parsee cooking	
definition	**13** 90
eggs	**13** 90
khichri, with shrimps	**13** 90
shrimp pickle	**13** 96
Parsley	
aspic	**15** 103
with Burgundian ham, cold	**10** 83
butter	**3** 81, **14** 27
with snails	**10** 29
Chinese (definition)	**17** 64
fried	**10** 10, **13** 43
sauce	**15** 40
Partridge	
with black olives	**17** 106
casserole of	**17** 105
in chocolate sauce	**16** 124
in cream with grapes (Rebhuhner in sahne mit weintrauben)	**11** 131

Party entertaining	
desserts and cookies	**12** 68–73
meal	**17** 89–95
picnic	**18** 43
treats	**9** 114–119
for parents	**9** 120–121
Pasilla chili (definition)	**15** 28
Paskha	**7** 119
Passover	
macaroons	**9** 17

Seder table	**9** 8–17	
sponge cake	**9** 17	
stuffing	**9** 14	
wine cake	**9** 17	

Pasta	**5** 83–101, **8** 114–123	
(see also individual names)		
sauces	**5** 93–97	
types	**5** 98–101	
Paste, luting	**16** 29	
Pasties, Cornish	**14** 39	
Pastitso	**5** 41	
Pastry		
almond, savory	**7** 53	
apple slice	**9** 32	
baking 'blind'	**1** 55	
beignets soufflés	**6** 87	
boats and		
tartlet shells	**7** 50, **17** 124–125	
cheese		
beignets	**6** 87	
croissants	**6** 57	
gougère	**6** 84	
profiteroles	**6** 87	
sablès	**6** 42	
savory	**7** 49	
choux	**6** 78–83, **14** 85	
(see also choux entry)		
cream	**18** 71	
Danish	**13** 27–29	
shortcake	**16** 80	
éclairs	**6** 81	
finishes	**1** 50	
flaky	**7** 91	
flan	**18** 52	
frangipane	**14** 84	
French	**14** 84	
gâteau Paris-Brest	**6** 79	
gougère	**6** 83–84	
Greek fingers	**17** 130	
for hors d'œuvres	**17** 122	
marjolaine tartlets	**6** 84	
nut and honey (baklava)	**12** 95	
pâté en croûte	**9** 48	
petits Paris-Brest	**6** 79	

pie	**1** 49	
rich	**11** 12, **13** 43	
profiteroles	**6** 82	
puff	**8** 70–83, **15** 15, **18** 90	
rough	**2** 27	
raised pie, simple	**14** 44	
rose, to make	**11** 14	
salambos	**6** 81	
sour cream	**7** 113	
strawberry swans	**6** 79	
strudel, rolled	**9** 32	
tartlets	**7** 50, **17** 124	
Pastry cream	**14** 88	
Pâté	**9** 37–49	
in aspic	**18** 48	
bacon	**9** 48	
de campagne	**9** 40, 42	
en croûte	**9** 48	
with duck	**17** 33	
ham	**9** 42	
and turkey	**9** 46	
kipper	**11** 11	
liver	**9** 40	
chicken	**9** 38	
and calves'	**9** 45	
Danish	**12** 10	
rillettes	**9** 38	
shrimp	**15** 123	
tongue, smoked	**16** 66	
trout, smoked	**11** 65	
Paulette chicken	**17** 21	
Paupiettes		
de boeuf braisées à la crème	**5** 60	
de veau Bayonne	**15** 58	
Pavlova	**5** 127	
Pea(s)		
beans	**12** 100	
with cream sauce	**5** 63	
bonne femme	**14** 19	
boula boula	**12** 101	
chick-pea(s)		
balls (falafel)	**12** 88	
with chicken	**12** 105	
salad	**12** 110	
with sesame paste		
(hummus bi tahina)	**12** 87	
Chinese (definition)	**17** 64	
dried	**12** 98–111	
Flamande	**4** 51	
omelet clamart	**10** 121	
petits pois à la française	**1** 35, **17** 47	
purée with pork hocks (eisbein		
mit erbspurée)	**11** 128	
in raita	**13** 95	
salad		
with beet	**6** 98	
with carrot	**8** 21	
split, with vegetables	**13** 93	

Peach(es)		
alsacienne	**4** 18	
butter	**11** 33	
caramelized	**17** 32	
cardinal	**3** 124	
charlotte	**4** 18	
in Chianti	**8** 130	
crêpes	**4** 18	
custard	**11** 20	
with duck, roast	**17** 32	
flambé	**4** 19	
flan	**3** 29, **16** 68	
flip	**4** 63, **12** 78	
frappé	**11** 113	
galette, with hazelnuts	**15** 12	
with griestorte	**3** 40	
ice cream	**11** 106	
with liqueur	**12** 59	

melba	**16** 15	
definition	**16** 15	
parfait	**18** 118	
with pecans	**17** 15	
pie	**5** 49	
cream	**5** 42	
poaching	**4** 17	
preserves	**7** 80	
purée	**11** 106	
salad, with ginger	**17** 21	
soufflé	**14** 64	
spiced	**7** 82	
stuffed		
pêches farcies	**15** 107	
pickled	**7** 83	
in wine, spiced	**3** 123	
Peaked finish (definition)	**7** 67	
Peanut(s)	**10** 97	
balls	**9** 119	
Ghanaian	**11** 92	
saté sauce, Indonesian		
(saos saté katjang)	**11** 95	
Pear(s)		
belle Hélène	**7** 97	
butter	**11** 33	
charcot	**8** 13	
en douillon (pears in a sleeve)	**16** 36	
in ginger	**5** 109	

Pear(s) *continued*

and lime jam	**11** 32
meringue (almond), with apples	**5** 107
in orange cream	**5** 109
pickled	**11** 39
pie, Normandy (le poirat)	**11** 121
pralinées	**11** 78
in red currant jelly	**7** 127, **16** 64
salad, with walnuts	**9** 52
in wine	
red	**5** 109
spiced	**3** 123

Pearled tartlets	**18** 62
Peasant girl in a veil	**5** 123
Pease pudding and ham	**10** 64
definition	**10** 64
Peberrodssvors (Danish	
horseradish sauce)	**12** 21
Pecan(s)	**10** 97
balls	**10** 94
caramel ice cream	**11** 106
fruit cake	**10** 94
marzipan	**10** 92
in mousse, iced caramel	**16** 72
parfait, with peaches	**17** 15
pie	**8** 52
stuffing	**2** 85
with apple and prune	**8** 49
Pectin (definition)	**7** 76, **16** 96
to test for	**7** 76
Pennsylvania dandelion salad	**18** 132
Peperoni	**5** 34
Pepper(s)	**15** 28
bell, to prepare	**16** 114
with chicken and ham	**16** 122
green and celery chartreuse	**15** 11
peperoni	**5** 34
peperonata	**4** 117
pickled	**11** 37
to prepare	**11** 82, **15** 28
salad, with veal	**15** 64
sauce, hot	**11** 87
soup, sweet red	**11** 82
stuffed	**4** 112
with cheese	**5** 122

Peppermint	
creams (candy)	**13** 113
cushions (candy)	**13** 115
ice cream	**16** 35
Peppers	
bell, to prepare	**16** 114
with chicken and ham	**16** 122
Pepperonata	**4** 117
Pepperoni sausage (definition)	**12** 124
Peppery nuts (pfeffernüsse)	**12** 70
Perch (ocean)	
Alphonse XIII	**2** 117
croquettes vert-pré	**2** 117
diable	**2** 115
Perdiz con chocolate (Spanish partridge	
in chocolate sauce)	**16** 124
Périgueux sauce	**2** 49
Perkedel	
daging (Indonesian fried	
beef balls)	**11** 95
djagung (Indonesian shrimp	
and corn fritters)	**11** 93
Persian chicken	**17** 26
Peruvian dishes	
cream	**7** 96
pineapple layer cake (Alfajor	
de huaura)	**11** 87
Pesto sauce	**5** 96
Petite marmite	**6** 114
Petits fours	**16** 130–133
basic mixture	**17** 58
definition	**16** 133
Petits Japonais	**12** 62, **18** 62
Petits mont blanc	**4** 82
Petits pois à la française	**1** 35, **17** 47
Petits pots de crème	**2** 95
Petits Paris-Brest	, **6** 79
Pfannkuchen	**9** 111
Pfeffernüsse (German peppery	
nuts)	**12** 70
Pheasant	**17** 102
to bone	**10** 12
braised (vallée d'Auge)	**17** 103
pot roast	**2** 22
smetana	**8** 36
stuffed, en cocotte	**10** 12
with truffles	**17** 102
viroflay	**18** 27
Philippine dishes	
chicken and pork stew (Adobo)	**11** 89
curried eggs	**11** 89
Phulkas (Indian bread)	**13** 97
Phyllo	
definition	**12** 84
pastry (to use)	**12** 89
Picadillo (Mexican meat hash)	**15** 34
Piccalilli	**11** 36

Pickle(d)(s), see also	
Relishes	**7** 82–85, **11** 36–40
artichokes, Jerusalem	**7** 84
beets	
Danish (syltede rødbeder)	**12** 25
and eggs	**7** 85
cantaloupe	**7** 84
carrots	**7** 85
cherry tomatoes	**7** 84
cucumber	
Danish (syltede agurker)	**12** 25
sweet	**11** 39
dill	
kosher	**11** 39
sweet	**11** 39
garnish	**15** 127
Indian and Pakistani	**13** 96
mushrooms	**11** 36
mustard	**11** 37
onions, sweet	**11** 37
peaches, stuffed	**7** 83
pears	**11** 39
peppers	**11** 37
piccalilli	**11** 36
plums, spiced	**11** 37
red cabbage	**11** 36
in salad with herring	**13** 58
tomato, sweet green	**11** 40
ripe	**11** 40
topping with cheese	**13** 10
walnuts	**11** 39
watermelon rind	**11** 37
Pickled nasturtium seeds	**18** 132
Pickling spice	**2** 109, **11** 36
salt	**11** 36
Picnic	
drinks	**18** 47
loaf	**4** 37
menu	**4** 35
party	**18** 43–49
Pie(s)	
apple	
American	**1** 52
latticed	**14** 32
and onion	**14** 42
and blackberry	**14** 127

Pie(s) *continued*

English	**1** 52
Florentine	**8** 53
latticed	**14** 32
and onion	**14** 43
blueberry	**5** 49
butterscotch cream	**1** 53
cheese (tiropita)	**12** 89
cherry and praline	**2** 14
chicken	**2** 32
Moroccan (bistaela)	**12** 94
chocolate meringue	**1** 58
coffee almond	**1** 53
coconut cream	**1** 55
cottage (shepherd's)	**14** 41
Cumberland mutton	**14** 44
custard	**2** 92
dish, English (note)	**2** 28
fidget	**14** 43
fish	**10** 123
funnels	**7** 91
guava, Barbados	**11** 84
key lime	**7** 127
leek	**14** 41
leek and bacon	**11** 14
lemon	**11** 25
chiffon	**1** 58
meringue	**1** 58
lime	**7** 127
macaroni	**13** 41
mince	**8** 89
mincemeat, fresh	**7** 109
onion, Costa Rican	**10** 121
party	**8** 52–53
pastry, rich	**11** 12, **13** 43
peach	**5** 49
cream	**5** 42
pear, Normandy (le poirat)	**11** 121
pecan	**8** 52
pumpkin	**8** 53
Ricotta	**4** 40
rum	**8** 52
sausage	**12** 130
seafood	**16** 21
spinach (spanakopita)	**12** 89
stargazy	**14** 43

steak and kidney	**7** 91
tamale, American	**11** 73
veal and ham	**2** 28
Yorkshire	**12** 66
applecake	**1** 53
Pigeon, see also Squab	**17** 106
casserole of	**17** 108
with apple rings (en cocotte normande)	**6** 118
farci St. Cyr	**18** 29
soup, with squash	**17** 65
Pigs' feet, deviled	**9** 80
Pigs in a blanket	**5** 38
Pike	**11** 57
Danish stuffed whole fish (fylld hel fisk)	**12** 21
roast	**14** 38
Pilaf	
chicken	**9** 96
cooking of	**2** 64
definition	**13** 84
ham	**13** 39
lobster	**16** 18
pistachio and currant	**12** 91
with raisins	**15** 22
and pistachios	**7** 115
seafood	**9** 95
with squab, roast	**17** 106
tuna	**3** 124
Pilau	
definition	**13** 84
Meeta, sweet saffron rice	**13** 98
vegetables (Sabzika chaval)	**13** 89
Pimiento	
to prepare	**11** 82
salad, with corn and pickled onion	**13** 58
sauce	**15** 40
soup, iced, with zucchini	**14** 120
topping for sandwiches	**13** 10
Pineapple	
Anna	**9** 57
bread, with nuts	**4** 121
cake	**14** 90
Hawaiian	**11** 90
layer	**1** 115
Peruvian layer (Alfajor de huaura)	**11** 87
upside down	**9** 63
candied	**14** 91
charlotte	**7** 127
cheesecake	**6** 99
and cheese sticks	**9** 116
cole slaw	**6** 37
flambe	**12** 59
gelatin	**17** 90
jam	**16** 96
with apricot	**7** 80

Japonaise	**15** 18
marmalade, with grapefruit	**16** 96
mousse, en surprise	**14** 64
Ninon	**18** 36
orangeade	**11** 84
to peel and cut fresh	**11** 29
with pork, sweet and sour	**17** 77
with rice cream	**14** 14
with rum and sugar	**11** 29
salad	**2** 100
with orange	**6** 36
sauce	**9** 124, **11** 49, **18** 40
sherbet	**11** 109
en surprise	**18** 15
topping for coffeecake	**13** 14
Pine nuts	**10** 97
with green beans	**15** 49
Pinto beans	**12** 100
Pinwheel salad	**9** 120
Pinwheels	**13** 29
celery	**15** 91
Piped decorations for cakes	**9** 74–75
Pipérade	**5** 29
Piquant sauce	**1** 65, **3** 108
Piroshki, with fillings	**7** 113
Pissaladière	**3** 34
Pistachio nuts	**10** 97
cake	**18** 59
ice cream	**11** 104
Pistachio	
cake	**18** 59
pilaf, with currants	**12** 91
and raisins with pilaf	**7** 115
and rice stuffing	**12** 62
salad, with rice	**1** 95
Pisto	**16** 119
definition	**16** 119

Manchego (la manga vegetable stew)	**16** 119
Pita (Arab bread)	**12** 88
Pizza(s)	
basic dough	**8** 127
calzone	**8** 131
cheese and ham turnovers	**8** 131

Pizza(s) *continued*

clam	**8**	128
country	**8**	130
definition	**8**	128
eggplant	**8**	127
escarole	**8**	131
al funghi	**8**	130
ham	**8**	128
individual	**8**	127
al melanzane	**8**	127
mushroom	**8**	130
napolitana	**8**	129
olive	**8**	129
con olive	**8**	129
party	**8**	124–131
al proscuitto	**8**	128
rustica	**8**	130
alle salsicce	**8**	130
sausage	**8**	130
di scammero	**8**	131
with shrimps	**8**	127
alle vongole	**8**	128
Plantain (definition)	**11**	82
Planter's punch	**11**	85

Plum(s)

butter	**11**	34
compote	**6**	75
Condé	**4**	22
dumplings		
(Zwetschgenknödel)	**11**	127
filling for hamantaschen	**9**	35
hamantaschen	**9**	35
jam	**11**	32
peasant girl in a veil	**5**	123
poaching	**4**	17
sauce		
definition	**17**	64
spiced	**11**	40
spiced	**11**	37
suédoise	**4**	21
Plum flower egg	**16**	58
Poblano chili	**15**	28
Poetic salad	**18**	132
Poirat, le (Normandy pear pie)	**11**	121
Poivrons niçoise	**14**	118

Pojarski cotleti	**7**	115
Polenta		
balls	**8**	103
cakes	**4**	99
Polish carp with beer	**11**	53
Polish sausage (kielbasa)		
definition	**12**	123
Pollo chilindrón (Spanish chicken with ham and peppers)	**16**	122
Pompano		
stuffed with shellfish	**11**	59
in white wine	**11**	59
Poolside buffet	**16**	66
Poor man's caviar	**4**	112
Poppadums (Indian bread)	**13**	97
Poppy seeds		
definition	**13**	83
filling		
for hamantaschen	**9**	35
for strudel	**10**	114
Porco alentejana (Portuguese pork with clams)	**16**	124
Porcupine tipsy cake	**7**	128
Porgy	**11**	59

Pork	**7**	20–27
American, tamale pie	**11**	73
for broiling		
carving	**7**	20
casserole, with beef	**4**	93
dijonnaise	**15**	113
chops		
broiled	**3**	77
casseroled	**4**	95
dijonnaise	**7**	27
with ham (côtes de porc ardennaise)	**6**	118
with tomato sauce	**16**	30
cooking and serving suggestions	**7**	21, 25–27
crown roast	**7**	22
cured	**7**	23–24
cuts	**7**	20
fat, savory	**12**	10
glazed ham and pork loaf	**4**	38
hash (labskovs)	**12**	24

hocks with pea purée (eisbein mit erbspuree)	**11**	128
involtini alla milanese	**8**	103
kebabs	**11**	95
loin		
alsacienne	**2**	89
braised, chestnuts	**5**	71
marinated roast (marineret stegt svinekam)	**12**	24
mole	**15**	39
pâté, with bacon	**7**	27
patty with Chinese sausage	**17**	77
pot roast, Marielle	**2**	24
puchero	**12**	105
roast sucking pig	**12**	62
accompaniments	**12**	62
roasting	**1**	36–37
to serve with roasts	**1**	39
times	**7**	20
salad	**4**	28
sausage	**12**	124
definition	**12**	124
to make	**12**	124
with sauerkraut (choucroûte alsacienne)	**12**	128
sautéed, with bean cake	**17**	77
spareribs	**3**	77
barbecued	**7**	25
sweet and sour	**4**	38
stew, with chicken (Philippine)	**11**	89
sweet and sour, with lychee pineapple	**17**	77
tenderloin		
with celery and onion fondue	**6**	118
with cider	**7**	27
with prunes	**13**	51
sauté normande	**4**	46
spiced	**16**	44
stuffed	**12**	48
terrine	**9**	46
vegetable stew, Cuban (ajiaco)	**11**	83
Portugaise (definition)	**4**	46
Portuguese cooking	**16**	111–129
Port wine gelatin	**7**	127
Pot roast	**2**	20–25
see also names of the various meats		
Potage fréneuse	**14**	68

Potage, see soup

Potato(es) **14** 11
- Anna **6** 73
- au gratin, with cauliflower **4** 115
- aurore **2** 84
- baked **3** 83
  - with sour cream and chives **12** 77
- balls **9** 21
- boiled, new **2** 13
- boulangère **11** 25
- cake, julienne **1** 22
- casserole
  - with lamb **10** 64
  - with mushrooms **5** 13
  - with onions **15** 113
- and celery, julienne **13** 51
- château **9** 55, **12** 66
- chips **17** 101
- creamed **1** 102
- croquettes **8** 107, **15** 59, **17** 57
- croûtons **6** 57
- duchesse **8** 50, **12** 63
- dumplings **11** 137
- duxelles **14** 19
- filling for quesadillas **15** 33
- fish **11** 65, **12** 48
- fondant **2** 84, **12** 80
- French fried **2** 60
- galette, with cheese and bacon **5** 50
- gnocchi **8** 123
- goulash **9** 99
- gratin Dauphinois **11** 78
- Jansson's temptation
  - (Janssons frestelse) **12** 21
- kartofflstangen **15** 121
- kidney **11** 20
- knishes **9** 22
- kugel **9** 21
- latkes **9** 34
- lyonnaise **3** 83
- maître d'hôtel **13** 38, **14** 13
- mashed, for piping **3** 100, **4** 48
- new **14** 19
- omelet **16** 116
  - with bacon (bonne femme) **1** 79

- orange baked **14** 127
- pancakes (Kartoffelpuffer) **11** 125
- papas con aji (in hot sauce) **5** 125
- parisienne **12** 40, **15** 54
- pie, with herring
  - (sill pudding) **12** 22
- purée with apple (Himmel
  - und erde) **11** 128
- refrigerator rolls **16** 39
- roast **1** 31
- salad **6** 35, **14** 122
  - with celery and apple **6** 35
  - with celery and olive **17** 87
  - curried **13** 60
  - German **6** 103
  - with hot garlic sausage **12** 130
  - spicy **3** 96
  - with white wine **14** 19
- sautéed **3** 83, **17** 93
- savoyarde **12** 48
- Scandinavian **8** 95
- scones **4** 127
- Sicilian **6** 13
- soup, cream **6** 55
- spätzle **10** 63
- spiced **13** 95
- straw **1** 83
- stuffed, baked **5** 41
- stuffing, with apple **8** 49
- à la Suisse **16** 62
- sweet
  - candied **1** 39
  - casserole **4** 99
  - glazed **8** 50
  - with orange **10** 101
  - with steamed fish **11** 89
  - stuffing with celery **1** 91
- with white wine **14** 19

Pot-au-feu **1** 62

Potted ham and beef **14** 44
- tongue **14** 45

Poulade truffée **18** 27

Poulet, see Chicken

Poultry, see also individual names
- boning **1** 81

- braising **5** 56
- carving **1** 21, 89
- chaudfroid **18** 95
- cooking times **8** 45
- cutting up **1** 81–82
- leftovers **8** 58–61
- shears **1** 88
- splitting **1** 84
- trussing **1** 20

Poulet au chou **14** 13

Pound cake **15** 81

Poussins farcis en gelée **18** 25

Praline **2** 14, **3** 51
- candies **18** 110
- chocolate, with cream puffs **17** 94
- cookies **18** 62
- cream **16** 107
- crêpes **9** 107
- duchesses **18** 62
- ice cream **11** 104
- petits fours **14** 125
- powder **9** 107, **14** 123, **18** 53

Precious flower egg **17** 67

Preparation of vegetables **16** 57

Preserves **7** 74–85, **11** 31–41, **16** 93–97
- to skim and store **16** 94
- to test for jell **16** 94

Pretzels, fondant **16** 133

Princess cake **18** 72

Prinsesstarta **18** 72

Printaniers **14** 97

Priory cookies **13** 15

Provençal
- definition **14** 26
- dip **5** 47
- sauce **12** 42

Prunes
- with ballotines of chicken **16** 106
- with beef and red wine **13** 38
- and farfel tzimmes **9** 25
- flan (tarte aux pruneaux) **10** 54
- with pork tenderloin **13** 51
- to soak **13** 38
- spiced **1** 39
  - with cranberry relish **7** 84
- stuffing, with apple and pecan **8** 49

Puchero **12** 105
- mock **5** 38

Pudding(s)
- cherry **3** 12
- chocolate **1** 67
- christmas **8** 84–88
- Cumberland **11** 49
- custard **2** 92
- date **1** 66
- Eve's **5** 106
- leftover **8** 86
- rich **8** 86

Pudding(s) *continued)*

  sponge **1** 66
    lemon **6** 105
  summer **3** 57
  Valencia **1** 66
  Yorkshire **1** 30
Puerto Rican cake with coconut
  custard (Bien me sabe) **11** 84
Puff pastry **12** 73, **15** 15, **18** 90
Puffs
  cheese **8** 45, **13** 48
  choux **8** 45
  fried **8** 112
  zeppoté alla napolitana **8** 112
Pumpkin
  to cook **8** 52
  fritters **5** 124
  pie **8** 53
  soup **4** 111

Punch **6** 99
  brandy milk **8** 55
  cardinal's **8** 57
  claret **8** 57
  hard cider **8** 55
  rum **8** 55
    milk **8** 55
  simple milk **8** 56
  spiced milk **8** 56
  whiskey **8** 57
    milk **8** 55
Purée (fruit) to freeze **16** 39
Puris (Indian bread) **13** 97

Quail **17** 111
  stuffed, en cocotte alsacienne **17** 113
Quenelles **16** 91
  de brochet **18** 22
  without molds **16** 91
  Nantua **18** 20
  to poach **16** 91
Quesadillas **15** 33
  dough for **15** 33
    cheese **15** 33
    chili **15** 33
Queso y chile (cheese and chile) **15** 31
Quiche
  clam **3** 104
  leek **3** 32
    and cheese **10** 118
  Lorraine **3** 32
  onion **11** 14
  salmon, smoked **3** 32
  tuna **1** 101
Quick consommé (hot and cold) **11** 22
Quick aspic **16** 42

Rabbit
  fricassée **3** 24
  lapin dijonnaise
    (rabbit in mustard sauce) **6** 120
  mousseline of **16** 91
  quenelles **16** 91
  wild, with lentils **17** 119
    in red wine **17** 119
Radish(es)
  pickled **16** 54
  roses **8** 104
  white (daikon) **16** 57

Ragoût
  definition **3** 16
  of beef bourguignonne **10** 83
Raised pies (definition) **14** 44
  of lamb **16** 31
Raised pie molds **9** 48
Raisin(s)
  cake
    spice **9** 60
    and walnut **1** 112
  coffeecake, Danish **12** 29
  drippings cake **14** 53
  oatmeal drops **9** 119
  pilaf **15** 22
    with pistachios **7** 115
  sauce **1** 45
    with maple baked ham **7** 25
Raita **13** 95
Ramekins **9** 38
  cheese **15** 99
  crab **15** 119
  definition **5** 22
Rarebit
  ham **10** 124
  Welsh **15** 99
Rasgulla (cheese balls in syrup) **13** 98
Raspberry(ies) **3** 54–55
  compote
    Danish, with cream
    (rødgrød med fløde) **12** 25
    with yogurt cream and
      cranberries **6** 15
  crème suisse **3** 55
  feuilletées **8** 83
  frappé **11** 113
  ice cream **11** 106
  jam **7** 79
  linzer torte **3** 55
  in Melba sauce **3** 54
  parfait **2** 41
  purée **11** 106
  shake **4** 63
  sherbet **11** 109
  shortcake, Danish **1** 73
  soufflé, cold **17** 17
  syllabub **10** 89
  vinegar **16** 100

Rassolnik soup	**6** 102
Ratatouille	**6** 122
omelet provençale	**10** 121
Rava	**13** 98
Ravigote sauce	**2** 53
Ravioli	**5** 90
cheese filling	**5** 90
in consommé	**5** 90
dough	**5** 90
savory meat filling	**5** 90
spinach and ricotta filling	**5** 90

Rebhuhner im sahne mit	
weintrauben (Partridge in	
cream with grapes)	**11** 131
Red cabbage, braised	**17** 105
Red bean	
paste (definition)	**17** 64
soup	**6** 56
Red currant	
cake	**14** 90
compote, with cream	
(rødgrød med fløde)	**12** 25
frosted	**14** 90
jelly	**7** 81
glaze	**1** 55
with pears	**7** 127
sauce, with orange	**6** 73
Red jam sauce	**9** 124
wine sauce	**9** 125
Red snapper	**11** 60
Basquaise	**14** 79
boulangère	**18** 79
Fijian steamed, with sweet	
potatoes	**11** 89
fish couscous	**12** 94
Mentonnaise	**18** 79
Niçoise	**11** 60
poached	**11** 60
Redfish, see Perch	
Refresh vegetables, to	**1** 94
Refrigerator rolls	**16** 39
Refrigerators	**2** 124–129
Relish(es) see also Pickles	**7** 82–85
bean, green	**7** 85

beet	**7** 85, **11** 15
and cabbage	**9** 25
and horseradish	**8** 65
cabbage	**7** 85
celery and cheese	**11** 15
corn	**7** 85
cranberry, with spiced prunes	**7** 84
cucumber, spiced	**11** 15
Italian	**11** 15
mustard	**11** 41
onion	**11** 15
pear	**11** 41
sweet pepper	**11** 41
tomato and anchovy	**11** 15
Relleno	
de carne (meat filling for	
tamales)	**15** 34
de jamón y chile (ham and	
chili filling for tamales)	**15** 34
de papas (potato filling for	
quesadillas)	**15** 33
stuffed chilies	**15** 36
Rêve de Bébé	**18** 120
Revel buns	**14** 46
Rheinischer sauerbraten	
(Rhineland marinated beef)	**11** 129
Rhubarb	
charlotte	**4** 21
fool	**4** 21
jam	
with ginger	**16** 96
with orange	**7** 80
poaching	**4** 17
Rice	
with beef casserole	**17** 69
Brazilian (Arroz brasileiro)	**11** 86
to boil	**2** 64, **15** 73
boiled	**13** 84
brown	**4** 98
chicken with	**16** 122
cooking with	**2** 63
cream	**4** 60–67
with pineapple	**14** 14
with pistachios	**13** 98
with tangerines	**9** 57
Tyrolhof	**4** 60

croquettes de riz	**6** 126
to dry	**5** 30
fried	**13** 84, **16** 44
Chinese	**17** 66
Indian	**13** 84
in Indian and Pakistani	
cooking	**13** 84, 89, 98
à l'impératrice	**18** 40
jambalaya	**2** 64
kedgeree	**2** 65
with mussels	**10** 26
paella	**2** 67
pilaf	
chicken	**9** 96
currant and pistachio	**12** 91
ham	**13** 39
okra	**4** 111
seafood	**9** 95
tuna	**3** 124
pilau, vegetable	**13** 89
plum Condé	**4** 22
pudding	**4** 61
Spanish	**16** 127
rijstafel, Indonesian	**11** 93
risi-bisi	**11** 29
risotto	**2** 64
bolognese	**2** 65
alla certosina	**2** 65
milanese	**8** 104
round grain (note)	**2** 64
salad	**17** 29, **18** 44
with crab	**15** 67
with lima bean	**17** 84
with pistachios	**1** 95
with tomato and ripe olive	**13** 58
simla	**3** 95
saffron	**11** 119, **13** 84
savory	**10** 80
sweet	**13** 98
soup	
Japanese cake	**16** 58
with leeks	**16** 104
with shrimp	**6** 56
with tomato	**6** 55

Rice continued
steamed (Chinese) **17** 66
stuffing **2** 85
with pistachios **12** 62
and vegetable pilau
(sbzika chaval) **13** 89
vinegared **16** 51
and fish in seaweed
(Norimaki sushi) **16** 50
wild **17** 101
stuffing **8** 49
Rich pie pastry **11** 12
Ricotta
pie **4** 40
tartlets **18** 46
Rigatoni con quattro formaggi **5** 89
Rijstafel, Indonesian **11** 93
Rillettes **9** 38
Rinderrouladen (beef rolls) **11** 131
Ris de veau braisé au vin blanc **5** 59
Risi-bisi **11** 29
Risotto **2** 64
bolognese **2** 65
alla certosina **2** 65
milanese **8** 104
Rissoles **13** 43, 45
Riz à l'impératrice **18** 40
Roasting **1** 26–27
see also names of various meats
rotisserie **9** 130–133
slow oven **9** 130–133
for special occasions **2** 86–89
times, regular **1** 26
Robert sauce **2** 49
Rochers aux amandes
(almond rocks) **16** 132
Rock cakes **4** 123
Rock Cornish game hens,
casserole **4** 87
Rødgrød med fløde (Danish
berry compote with cream) **12** 25
Rognons sauté au vin blanc **10** 81
Roll(s)
to bake and shape **7** 64
potato refrigerator **16** 39
small, to heat **16** 77

Roman salad with noodles **15** 64
Romanoff (definition) **3** 46
Romesco sauce **5** 122
Root celery (definition) **6** 32
Roquefort cheese **7** 11
balls **17** 135
cream with stuffed tomatoes **15** 95
mousse **15** 92
salad **15** 96
walnut **15** 96
spread **17** 135
tartlets **7** 11
topping **13** 10

Rose, marzipan **15** 81
Rose geranium jelly **7** 82
Rose geranium punch **18** 133
Rose petal vinegar **16** 101
Rose water (definition) **13** 83
Rosebud and carnation salad **18** 132
Rosinbrød (Danish raisin
coffeecake) **12** 29
Rothschild soufflé **10** 44
Roti de veau en croûte **18** 33
Roulade(s) **10** 44–47
beef **16** 66
case **10** 45
cheese pastry, savory **7** 49
chocolate **7** 102
fish **10** 46–47
of ham **8** 21
salmon **10** 46
smoked **7** 46
spinach **10** 44
steak, with celery stuffing **16** 31
Royal icing **9** 71, **14** 87, **18** 53
Royal salad **4** 30
Rudjak (Indonesian spiced fruit
salad) **11** 95
Rum
cake, Austrian **16** 39
milk **8** 55
punch **8** 55
omelet **10** 43
pie **8** 52
punch **8** 55

sauce **9** 128
with apricots **11** 47
hard **8** 89, **9** 126
Rundstykke (Danish light rolls) **12** 30
Russe **17** 125
Russian tipsy cake **13** 79
Rye
bread
dark **7** 69
Swedish (limpa) **12** 29
flour (definition) **7** 69

S

Sabayon sauce, hot and cold **9** 127, **6** 67
Sablés, cheese **6** 42
Sachertorte **18** 67
Sacristans **8** 83
Saddle of lamb, jardinière **18** 12
Saffransbröd (Christmas saffron
buns) **12** 30
Saffron
buns **14** 46
Christmas (saffransbröd) **12** 30
definition **13** 83
loaves **12** 30
rice **6** 44, **11** 119, **13** 84, 98
savory **10** 80, **14** 130
Sage and onion stuffing **1** 39
Sah bok jing don (steamed eggs
with clams) **17** 78
Sai yong choy yuke gung
(watercress beef soup) **17** 65
Salad(s)
Alice **15** 63
antipasto **13** 65–61
apple, stuffed **6** 42

Salad(s) *continued*
artichoke
  and mushroom   **6** 32
  and tomato   **6** 30
avocado   **2** 11, **11** 29, **15** 37
  with orange and grapefruit   **6** 37
  with tomato   **12** 46
basque   **17** 85
bean   **6** 30
  with tomato and cucumber   **6** 36
beef   **4** 28
beet
  celeriac and walnut   **6** 32
  gelatin   **8** 27
  and green pea   **6** 98
  Ukrainian   **7** 116
Breton   **15** 63

carrot and raisin   **6** 99
cauliflower with mustard
  mayonnaise   **6** 32
celeriac rémoulade   **6** 32
celery
  apple and walnut   **6** 35
  and green bean   **8** 64
  potato and olive   **17** 87
cervelat   **4** 27, **12** 131
cherry tomato   **14** 122
chicken   **18** 44
  and avocado   **4** 29
  and cherry   **4** 29
  coriander (so see gai)   **17** 73
  Milanaise   **13** 104
chick-pea   **12** 110
chicory   **6** 35
chorizo   **12** 131
Clementine   **4** 102
cole slaw   **6** 37, 98
  cheese   **6** 37
  with cream   **6** 37
  pineapple   **6** 37
  savory   **6** 37
  shrimp   **6** 37
composée (combination)   **17** 86
corn and pickled onion   **8** 64

corned beef   **4** 28
crab   **18** 86
  printanier   **18** 86
  and rice   **15** 67
  with cream cheese dressing   **15** 67
cucumber   **1** 71, **17** 13
  and bean   **17** 84
  gelatin   **8** 27
  and tomato   **17** 84
egg
  aurore   **4** 27
  and beet   **4** 27
  stuffed   **3** 38
endive and orange   **8** 64
escarole   **6** 35
florentine   **17** 87
fruit
  fresh   **14** 111
  Indonesian spiced   **11** 95
  platter   **4** 30
grape   **8** 28
  and grapefruit   **8** 44
  melon and mint   **17** 87
green   **1** 22
  with fresh pineapple   **2** 100
  Goddess   **4** 30
Harlequin   **15** 64
herring   **10** 108
  and apple   **10** 70
Italian   **13** 59
for lunches   **15** 61–67
insalati di legumi   **8** 104
Japonais   **15** 67
leek and egg   **6** 30
lettuce and cucumber   **12** 80
light lunches   **15** 61–67
lima bean   **13** 106, **17** 84
liver sausage   **12** 131
lobster, Valencia   **5** 122
Louis   **4** 29
Lyonnaise   **17** 86
melon   **4** 10, **15** 67
mixed, with taratoor dressing
  (salata)   **12** 88
molded   **8** 27–29
mushroom in Gruyere   **15** 64
niçoise   **15** 16
orange   **17** 102
  celery and chestnut   **17** 87
  and onion   **7** 31
  and pineapple   **6** 36
parisienne   **8** 60
peach and ginger   **17** 21
pear and walnut   **9** 52
peas and carrot   **8** 21
pinwheel   **9** 120
pistachio rice   **1** 95
poetic   **18** 132

pork   **4** 28
potato   **6** 35, **14** 122
  celery and apple   **6** 35
  German   **6** 103
  with hot garlic sausage   **12** 130
  spicy   **3** 96
provençal   **4** 117
red cabbage   **9** 14
rice   **17** 29, **18** 44
Roman, with noodles   **15** 64
roquefort   **15** 96
royal   **4** 30
salmon, en gelée   **4** 26
sardine   **4** 27
sauerkraut   **17** 102
scallop   **15** 123
seafood   **3** 106
shrimp   **4** 26
  and orange   **10** 124
side   **17** 83–87
Spanish   **17** 86
spinach   **18** 47
  and bacon   **16** 68
Swedish pickled herring   **5** 123
Swiss   **15** 63
three bean   **4** 40
tomato   **9** 93
  anchovy and bean   **12** 110
  and artichoke   **16** 12
  and avocado   **17** 93
  and orange   **9** 89, **17** 87
tongue, jellied   **4** 30
tourangelle   **17** 87
tuna, deviled   **4** 26
turkey, Italian   **14** 122
Vancouver   **17** 87
various   **10** 53
veal   **13** 41
veal and peppers   **15** 64
vichy   **17** 84
vegetable   **8** 104, **13** 60
  mixed   **3** 96
  raw (Les crudités)   **11** 12
vinaigrette   **6** 30, **14** 122
winter   **6** 29–30
zucchini   **16** 109
Salad dressing(s)
boiled   **6** 38
with cream cheese   **15** 67
green   **11** 60
lemon cream   **6** 38
mayonnaise   **6** 38, **11** 45
sour cream   **13** 102
taratoor   **12** 88
tarragon cream   **15** 18, 67
thousand island   **4** 33
tomato   **11** 60
vinaigrette   **6** 38, **15** 63

Salambos	**6** 81
Salami	
canapé	**17** 128
definition	**12** 124
sandwich	
fillings for	**13** 11
open-face	**12** 10
with pickle	**14** 114
sausage (definition)	**12** 124
Salamis (definition)	**3** 16
Salata (mixed salad with taratoor	
dressing)	**12** 88
Salé (Swiss cheese pie)	**3** 34
Sally Lunn	**7** 70
Salmis of duck with olives	**14** 32
Salmon	**2** 107
in aspic	**17** 13
baked stuffed	**2** 107
boats	**17** 125
braised	**5** 57
canapés	**17** 128
and caviar checkerboard	**17** 127
with fennel or dill	**18** 76
marinated (gravlax)	**12** 18–19
mousse Nantua	**18** 22
Muscovite	**13** 60
with piquant sauce	**14** 38
potted	**10** 123
quiche, smoked	**3** 32
rolls, with shrimps,	
smoked	**9** 86, **18** 44
roulades	**10** 46
smoked	**7** 46
rounds, with cream cheese,	
smoked	**7** 52
salad en gelée	**4** 26
sandwich, open-face, smoked	**12** 13
smoked, with eggs en cocotte	**10** 118
smothered	**12** 55
steaks	
broiled	**3** 80
en chaudfroid	**15** 16
aux gourmets	**14** 79
with Madeira sauce	**2** 107
with white piquant sauce	**14** 38
tourtière	**18** 48
Salpicon (definition)	**9** 80
Salsa, in Mexican cooking	**15** 39–40
Salsa verde	**8** 104
Salt, pickling	**11** 36
Saltenas	**5** 124
Saltimbocca	**8** 102
Saltpeter (definition)	**7** 122
Sambals	**13** 92–93
Sambar (definition)	**13** 92
Sandwich(es)	
coffee party	**13** 10
coffee cheese and pineapple	**14** 114

crab meat	**14** 114
Danish open-face	**12** 10–13
ham and cream cheese	**14** 114
liver sausage and chutney	**14** 114
loaves	**17** 135
ribbon	**15** 23
roast beef	**14** 114
salami and pickle	**14** 114
shrimp	**14** 114
stacked	**7** 49
tongue and curry	**14** 116
wedding reception	**15** 23
Sang geong (definition)	**17** 64
Sangria	**16** 68
Saos saté katjang (Indonesian	
peanut saté sauce)	**11** 95
Sardine	**5** 38
deviled	**12** 54
omelet	**16** 116
salad	**4** 27
topping for sandwiches	**13** 11
Sashimi	**16** 51
definition	**16** 48
Saté(s)	
babi manis (Indonesian	
barbecued pork kebabs)	**11** 95
definition	**11** 95
sauce, Indonesian peanut	
(Saos saté katjang)	**11** 95

Sauce(s)	**2** 42–53
Alabama	**3** 108
apple	**8** 50
apricot jam	**9** 124
hot or cold	**4** 60
with rum	**9** 124
avgolemono	**5** 120
avocado	**15** 37
banana	**9** 124
barbecue	
blender	**3** 81
hot	**3** 81
bâtarde	**2** 53
béarnaise	**15** 59
béchamel	**7** 43
beurre blanc	**2** 52

bigarde	**2** 48
blanche au beurre	**2** 53
boiled dressing	**6** 38
bolognese	**5** 93
bordelaise	**2** 49
brandy, hard	**8** 89, **9** 126
bread	**17** 101
for broiled dishes	**3** 80–82
brown	**2** 47–49, **12** 65
basic (espagnole)	**2** 48, **13** 37
butter	**2** 50–53
butterscotch	**9** 128
caper	**2** 46, 53
caramel	**9** 128
chasseur	**2** 49
cherry, plain	**9** 125
chili, spiced	**11** 41, **15** 40
chocolate	**1** 67, **9** 126
orange	**7** 97
rich	**7** 100, **9** 126
Choron	**2** 52
clam, red and white	**5** 96
to coat with	**15** 56
conti	**5** 96
crab	**10** 39
cranberry	**8** 50, **11** 132
ketchup	**11** 40
cream	**5** 63
cream, caramel	**9** 128
cream cheese	**10** 67
crème à la vanille	**7** 98, **9** 128
Cumberland	**7** 122, **9** 125
curry hollandaise	**10** 39
demi-glace	**15** 19
dessert sour cream	**11** 47
devil sauce dip	**7** 53
duxelles	**16** 84
egg	**2** 46
eggplant salpicon	**5** 95
espagnole	**2** 48, **9** 87
fruit	**6** 78
spiced	**11** 40–41
fudge	**9** 126
genevoise	**2** 53
green	**11** 60, **15** 39
gribiche	**13** 39

Sauce(s) *continued*

harissa	**12** 93
herb tomato	**17** 127
hollandaise	**2** 51
blender	**2** 52
honey	**10** 128
horseradish	**5** 49
Danish (peberrodssvors)	**12** 21
jam	
hot	**6** 87
red	**9** 124
lemon	
Danish (citronsovs)	**12** 24
hard	**8** 96, **9** 127
liaisons	**2** 44
lobster	**10** 39
Madeira	**7** 31
madère	**15** 19

maltaise	**2** 52
marmalade	**9** 124
mayonnaise	**2** 36, **11** 45
green	**6** 38, **11** 60
tomato	**6** 38, **11** 60
Melba	**9** 124
Mexican cooking	**15** 37–40
milanese	**5** 95
mint	**1** 35
mornay (cheese)	**7** 39
mousseline	**2** 52
mushroom	**2** 45
cream	**16** 91
mustard	**2** 46, 53
cream	**16** 30
simple	**16** 20
Swedish (sennepssors)	**12** 18
napolitana	**5** 95
orange	
chocolate	**9** 126
cream	**9** 124
and red currant	**6** 73, **9** 125
oyster, with steak	**14** 38
parsley	**2** 46, **15** 40
for pasta	**5** 93–97
peanut saté (saos saté katjang)	**11** 95
périgueux	**2** 49, **16** 90

pesto	**5** 96
pimiento	**6** 11, **15** 40
pineapple	**9** 124, **11** 49
piquant(e)	**1** 65, **3** 108
white, with salmon	**14** 38
plum	**11** 40, **14** 63
provençal dip	**5** 47
Provençale	**12** 42
raisin	**7** 25
ravigote	**2** 53
Robert	**2** 49
rum	**9** 128
and apricot	**11** 47
hard	**9** 126
sabayon, hot and cold	**6** 67, **9** 127
salsa verde	**8** 104
shrimp, with halibut	**11** 22
soubise (onion)	**2** 46
sour cream	**14** 127
sour cream horseradish	**7** 112
spicy hard	**5** 49, **9** 127
strawberry custard	**9** 128
Suchard	**9** 126, **15** 51
suprême	**16** 90
sweet and sour	**3** 81
mustard	**7** 30
tartare	**10** 25, **13** 67
tomato	**7** 41, **11** 72, **15** 40
deviled	**5** 47
for pasta	**8** 119
simple	**5** 126
soy	**3** 82
tuna	**16** 104
vanilla custard	**6** 125, **7** 98
velouté	**16** 88
Venetian	**2** 53
walnut and apple	**9** 125
white	**2** 45–46
wine, red	**9** 125
yogurt	**10** 67
yoli	**15** 40

Saucer pancakes	**10** 67
Sauerbraten	**5** 68
definition	**11** 129
Sauerkraut	
braised	**5** 64
cooked (Gekochtes sauerkraut)	**11** 128

definition	**10** 60
filling for knishes	**9** 22
and frankfurters with bacon	**10** 60
salad	**17** 102
soup	**10** 108
stuffing	**1** 91
with sausages and pork (choucroûte alsacienne)	**12** 128

Sausages	**12** 120–131
blutwurst with apples	**12** 128
bockwurst	**12** 127
boudin blanc	**12** 127
bratwurst in beer	**11** 128
casserole, with tomato	**6** 100
cervelat salad	**4** 27
Chinese dried	
definition	**17** 64
steamed pork patty with	**17** 77
chorizo	**16** 114, 116
dishes	**12** 127–131
flan, with tomato	**3** 32
Italian with chicory	**12** 128
kebabs	**12** 130
kielbasa with cabbage	**12** 130
kinds of	**12** 123, 124
knackwurst	**12** 127
with lasagne	**11** 73
linguica	**16** 116
making	**12** 124–126
with navy beans	**12** 106
pie	**12** 130
pigs in a blanket	**5** 38
pizza	**8** 130
pork	**12** 124
with sauerkraut (choucroûte alsacienne)	**12** 128
to prepare and fill casings	**12** 124
rolls	**2** 32, **17** 122
soup	**12** 127
tostadas	**15** 31
weisswurst	**12** 127
in wine, red	**12** 128
Sauté	**4** 42–51

51

Savarin Chantilly · **4** 14
Savories · **14** 45
Savoy butter · **6** 57
Savoy cole slaw · **6** 37
Savoyarde
  escalopes · **17** 48
  potatoes · **12** 48
Scallion(s)
  brushes · **17** 67
  garnish · **15** 126
  preparation of · **16** 57
Scallops · **3** 100–103
  baked · **3** 103
  chowder · **10** 12
  à la crème · **3** 103
  curried · **2** 37
  Dugléré (coquilles St. Jacques) · **12** 114
  mornay · **3** 103
  paimpolaise · **16** 23
  parisienne · **3** 100
  provençale · **3** 100
  salad · **15** 123
  with wine (red) and
    mushrooms · **3** 103

Scampi · **3** 106
  in batter · **3** 108
  à la crème · **3** 109
Scandinavian cooking · **12** 16–31
Schav bortsch · **9** 21
Schrecklösschen (snow
  dumplings) · **11** 125
Schwäbisches reh (Swabian roast
  venison) · **11** 132
Schwarzwalder kirschtorte · **18** 68
Scones · **4** 127
  drop · **4** 127
  griddle · **4** 127
  potato · **4** 127
Scotch broth · **14** 36
Scotch eggs · **11** 10
Scotch woodcock · **5** 29
Scottish oatcakes · **14** 53

Scup · **11** 59
Sea bass · **3** 80
Sea soup · **3** 100
Seafood
  cocktail, with watercress · **17** 10
  crêpes · **13** 127
  filling for pastry fingers · **17** 131
  gratin of · **14** 11
  pie · **16** 21
  pilaf · **9** 95
  salad · **3** 106
  vinaigrette · **18** 82
  vol-au-vent · **8** 78
Seasonal luncheon menus · **17** 8–17
Seasoning · **1** 23
Seaweed, vinegared rice and fish in
  (Norimaki sushi) · **16** 50
See jup pai gwut (spareribs
  with black bean sauce) · **17** 77
See yow (definition) · **17** 64
Seed cake · **14** 46
Seekh kebabs · **13** 90
Seen mouie jeong (definition) · **17** 64
Selkirk bannock · **14** 50
Semolina · **8** 119
  definition · **5** 84
Sengalese fish balls
  (boulettes de poisson) · **11** 91
Sennepssovs (Swedish mustard
  sauce) · **12** 18
Serrano chili · **4** 93
  definition · **15** 28
Serraño ham · **16** 115
Sesame
  with chicken · **17** 71
  oil (definition) · **12** 84
  paste (tahina) definition · **12** 84
  seed cookies (koulouria) · **12** 95
  with spinach · **16** 52
Seviche, Mexican · **15** 35
Shad · **2** 109
  with bacon · **2** 109
  baked, with lemon stuffing · **2** 109
  broiled · **3** 80
Shallot vinegar · **16** 101
Shami kebabs (curried meatballs) · **13** 90
Shannon soup, iced · **17** 12

Shark's fin
  definition · **17** 66
  soup (yee chee tong) · **17** 66
Shashlik · **7** 116
Shellfish · **3** 99–111, **10** 16–31
  16 18–23
  (see also individual names) ·
  cioppino · **4** 85
  court bouillon for · **10** 18
  Louis · **15** 21
  sushi · **16** 58
Shepherd's pie · **14** 41
Sherbet(s) · **11** 108–112
  cranberry · **4** 22
  to freeze
    in a churn freezer · **11** 108
    in ice trays · **11** 108
  grapefruit with mint · **11** 112
  lemon · **11** 108
  orange · **11** 109
  pineapple · **11** 109
  raspberry · **11** 109
  sherry · **11** 109
  strawberry · **11** 109
    and orange · **18** 127
  tangerine · **16** 35
Sherry sherbet · **11** 109
Sherry trifle · **10** 105
Shortbread · **14** 50
Shortcake
  Danish raspberry · **1** 73
  strawberry · **3** 47
Shoyu (definition) · **16** 48
Shrimp(s) · **3** 106
  with Alabama dip · **10** 31
  in aspic · **8** 10
    couronne of · **14** 30
  and bacon kebabs · **14** 129
  in batter · **3** 108
  bisque · **18** 10
  boats · **17** 125
  en brochette · **10** 29
  broiled in soy sauce · **16** 57
  casserole Florentine · **10** 123
  chartreuse · **15** 63
  chowder, Chilean · **5** 124

Shrimp(s) *continued*

cioppino	**4** 85
cole slaw	**6** 37
creamed	**12** 55
Creole	**16** 22
crowned, open-face sandwich	**12** 13
curry	**13** 86
and egg	
bouchées	**8** 76
mousse	**8** 67
filling, with cheese	**15** 125
curried	**3** 123
flan	**3** 34
fried (dry) in shell	**17** 67
fritters, with corn	**11** 93
Frederick	**3** 108
garnish	**16** 48
gougère	**6** 83
gourmet	**16** 22
au gratin	**12** 76
kebabs	**17** 134
Mariette	**7** 54
in mayonnaise nantua	**17** 13
and oyster gumbo	**10** 66
Parsee khichri	**13** 90
pâté	**15** 123
pickle, Parsee	**13** 96
pie, curried	**18** 76
provençale	**10** 31
Ritz ✳	**5** 112
salad	
Green Goddess	**4** 30
with orange	**10** 124
with tomato	**15** 63
with tuna	**13** 57
sandwiches	**14** 114
open-face	**12** 13
topping for	**13** 11
sauce, with halibut	**11** 22
Sicilienne	**10** 31
soup	
chilled	**3** 118
with rice	**6** 56
spiced	**14** 45
with tomatoes	**15** 63
wiggle	**10** 131

with zucchini	**1** 94
Side salad	**6** 32, **17** 83–87
Sill pudding (Swedish herring and potato pie)	**12** 22
Sillgratin (Swedish herring pudding)	**12** 22
Sippets	**6** 57
Sieves	**6** 48
Simla belati (stuffed tomatoes)	**13** 93
Simnel cake	**14** 54
Simple mustard sauce	**16** 21
Singin' hinnie	**14** 49
Skillet corn bread	**4** 123
Sliced raw fish	**16** 51
Slices, coffee nut	**17** 16
Slow oven roasting	**9** 130–133
Smoked trout or Finnan haddie mousse	**14** 58
Smørrebrød table, Danish	**12** 8–15
Smothered beef casserole	**5** 41
Snails	
with mushrooms	**17** 130
with parsley butter	**10** 29
Snipe	**17** 113
Snowball, chocolate	**7** 96
Snow dumplings (Schrecklosschen)	**11** 125
Snow peas	
definition	**17** 64
with water chestnuts and bamboo shoots	**17** 80
So see gai (coriander chicken salad)	**17** 73
Sockerstruvor	**5** 132
Soda biscuits	**4** 126
Soda bread	**4** 120
Sole	**11** 60
andalouse	**4** 68
aux ananas	**18** 79
bonne femme	**12** 48
caprice	**14** 76
Catalan	**14** 76
délices de au parmésan	**15** 46
en eventail	**14** 77
fillets of	
in aspic	**8** 23

dorothea	**17** 38
mornay	**5** 10
Georgette	**11** 116
à l'indienne	**11** 63
Lasserre	**18** 77
meunière	**14** 108
aux moules	**11** 60
mousseline	**18** 104
Nantua	**14** 77
Orly, with pimiento sauce	**6** 11
suchet	**18** 77
Solianka	**7** 112
Sopa de ajo (Spanish garlic soup)	**16** 115
Sothi (Malaysian coconut soup)	**11** 96
Soubise (onion) sauce	**2** 46
Soufflé	**14** 56–65
apple dish	**8** 96
cauliflower, with mornay sauce	**11** 118
cheese	**10** 35
cold	**15** 91
rich	**10** 36
chicken	**14** 62
chocolate, cold	**6** 44
corn and cheese	**10** 36
crab	**10** 39
crêpes	**18** 36
dish	**10** 35
preparation of	**10** 34, **14** 58
eggplant	**7** 35
fish	**10** 39
ginger	**15** 21
Grand Marnier	**10** 43, **18** 41
grapefruit	**10** 128
ham	**13** 39
hot	**10** 33–43
Italian	**10** 38
lemon	**10** 41
cold	**7** 12
moka praline	**14** 64
Monte Cristo	**10** 75
mushroom	**10** 36
omelet	**10** 43–44
orange	**10** 41
Nantaise	**15** 51
peach	**14** 64
preparation of	**10** 33–34
raspberry, cold	**17** 17
Rothschild	**10** 44
roulades	**10** 44–48
savory	**10** 35–39
sweet	**10** 40–44
Soup(s)	**3** 113–119, **6** 47–57
almond and grape	**3** 117
avocado	**2** 98, **3** 117
bean	
Galician white	**16** 115
with leek	**12** 105
and tomato	**9** 120

Soup(s) *continued*
beer
    cold (bierkaitschale) **11** 125
    hot (biersuppe) **11** 125
berry (bärsoppa) **12** 25
bisques **3** 118
blueberry **3** 52
black bean **12** 100
bouillabaisse (Mediterranean
    fish stew) **6** 113
buttermilk **4** 57
caraway seeds **10** 108
chicken **9** 20
    broth **7** 107
        mushroom **6** 53
    cockie-leekie **6** 51
    with matzo balls **9** 12
Chinese **17** 65–66
chowder
    clam
        Manhattan **6** 53
        New England **3** 106
    corn **6** 51
    fish **6** 51
    mussel **1** 42
    shrimp, Chilean **5** 124
clam **8** 101
    chowder **6** 53
coconut, Malaysian (sothi) **11** 96
consommé
    with caviar **13** 17
    with mushrooms **9** 93
    quick (hot and cold) **11** 22
crab, she **3** 109
cream
    apple and apricot, iced **5** 123
    asparagus **17** 54
    beet **8** 92
    carrot **6** 55
    cheese **13** 48
    chestnut **8** 35
    corn **8** 44
    fish **14** 117
    leek and rice **16** 104

    lettuce **3** 63
    onion **13** 75
    pimiento and zucchini, iced **14** 120
    potato **6** 55
    spinach **14** 10
    turnip **14** 68
crème St. Germain **3** 114
crème normande **3** 117
cucumber, iced **3** 114
curry, iced **12** 115
of the day **1** 103
duck **6** 51
egg flower **17** 66
fava bean **12** 105
fish
    cream of **2** 10
    Norwegian (fisksoppa) **12** 18
    solianka **7** 112
fruit, swedish (fruktsoppa) **12** 25
garbure paysanne **6** 109
garlic **16** 115
garnishes **6** 56–57, **16** 48
gazpacho
    alicantina **16** 115
    cold **15** 110
Georgette **4** 103
giblet **11** 124
green (vert) **16** 77
    pea **12** 103
herb tomato **4** 37
hollandaise **3** 117
iced **3** 114–117
    Shannon **17** 12
kale **16** 116
kidney **10** 81
lemon (avgolemono) **6** 10
lentil **12** 101
    Moroccan (harira) **12** 84
lettuce, cream of **3** 63
lobster **3** 118
Madrilène, simple **12** 80
meatball, Turkish **5** 120

minestra **6** 53
minestrone **6** 53
mulligatawny **6** 56
mushroom **3** 10, **3** 117
    and watercress **17** 15
mussel chowder **1** 42
New England clam chowder **3** 106
à l'oignon (French onion) **6** 109
onion
    cream of **13** 75
    simple, French **6** 48

oyster **16** 49
and mushroom **10** 23
petit marmite **6** 114
pondicherry **16** 104
potage
    bonne femme **4** 111
    crème d'or **15** 71, **18** 104
    cultivateur **4** 111
    freneuse **14** 69
    palestrine **6** 55
    parabère **11** 76
pumpkin **4** 11
rassolnik **6** 102
red bean **6** 56
red pepper, sweet **11** 82
rice cake **16** 58
Russian bortsch **7** 113
sauerkraut **10** 108
sausage **12** 127
scallop chowder **10** 12
Scotch broth **14** 36
sea **3** 100
Shannon, iced **17** 12
Shark's fin **17** 66
shrimp
    chilled **3** 118
    and oyster gumbo **10** 66
    and rice **6** 56
soy bean paste (misoshivu) **16** 49
squash and pigeon **17** 65
stracciatella **8** 101
stocks **6** 48
    Chinese **17** 65

Soup(s) *continued*
tomato
  and orange **5** 11
  and rice **6** 55
  special **3** 124
  spicy **10** 50
 tripe **15** 35
 Turkish meatball **5** 120
 vegetable **14** 114
 velouté **3** 114
 vichysoisse **3** 114
 vongole, zuppa di **8** 101
 walnut **3** 114
 watercress, chilled **16** 70
 Welsh granny's broth **14** 36
 yoghurt (cacik) **12** 84, **16** 106
Soupe au poisson **14** 117
Sour cream
 cake **4** 59
 and dill with summer squash **10** 110
 dressing **13** 102
 horseradish sauce **7** 112
 mold, with cranberry and
  apple compote **6** 100
 omelet, with chives **10** 118
 pastry **7** 113
 sauce **14** 127
  dessert **11** 47
 with wild duck **17** 110
Sourdough bread **7** 72
 starter **7** 72
South American cooking **11** 86–87
Southeast Asian cooking **11** 93–97
Soybeans **12** 100
 paste soup **16** 49
Soy sauce
 with broiled shrimps
  (Onigari-yaki) **16** 57
 definition **16** 48, **17** 64
Spaghetti
 alla carbonara **5** 88
 Grimaldi **14** 118
 and ham au gratin **6** 102
 with mushrooms **3** 124
Spanakopita (Greek spinach pie) **12** 89
Spanish dishes **16** 111–129
 chicken casserole **4** 88

salad **17** 86
Spareribs
 with black bean sauce **17** 77
 spiced **16** 61
 sweet sour **4** 38
Spätzle **10** 63, **11** 129
Speculas (Dutch spice cookies) **12** 70
Spezzatino di pollo all trasteverina **8** 104
Spiced
 apricots **18** 105
 chicken **16** 29
 pork **16** 44
 shrimps **14** 45
 tangerines **16** 97
 vinegar **16** 101
Spice(s)
 cookies (speculas) **12** 70
 cooking with **3** 84–91
 in Indian and Pakistani
  cooking **13** 82–85, 88
 pickling **11** 36
Spinach
 with bean cake sauce **17** 80
 bortsch **9** 21
 canapés **17** 128
 creamed **7** 31
 crêpes **9** 103
 galette **14** 20
 leaf **2** 84
 mold **7** 39, **11** 46
 pie (spanakopita) **12** 89
 purée, with fricandeau **5** 63
 roulade **10** 44
 salad **18** 47
  with bacon **16** 68
 with sesame **16** 52
 soufflé **10** 38
 soup, cream of **14** 10
Split peas **12** 100
Sponge
 cakes **4** 78, **6** 59–69
  crusty top **18** 45
 puddings **1** 66
Spreads for hors d'oeuvres **17** 135
Springerle (molded Christmas
 cookies) **11** 137
Spun sugar **18** 16
Squab
 bonne femme **15** 49
 en cocotte normande **17** 108
 in cranberry cream sauce **5** 123
 in lettuce cups **17** 73
 pie, Moroccan (bistaela) **12** 94
 with raisins **4** 90
 roast, St. Hubert **17** 106
 and steak tourtière **7** 123
 stuffed en cocotte with olives **16** 70

Squash **1** 64
 acorn, baked **8** 51
 baked **4** 113
 blossoms, stuffed **18** 132
 buttered **1** 30
 buttered **1** 30
 definition **4** 113
 fuzzy (definition) **17** 64
 à la greque **4** 115
 soup, with pigeon **17** 65
 steamed stuffed **1** 65
 summer, in dill and sour cream **10** 110
Squid
 with anchovy **11** 63
 calamari **11** 63
 to clean **16** 119
 with tomatoes **8** 101, **11** 63
Star anise **17** 75
Steak, see Beef
Steak and kidney pudding **14** 41
Steam, how to **3** 15–25
Steamer, Chinese **17** 62
Stencil, cardboard, to make **7** 100
Stew **3** 15–25
 (see also names of various meats)
 Portuguese and Spanish
  cooking **16** 119, 120, 122
Sticky ginger cake **4** 41
Stilton cheese **15** 88
Stir-frying **17** 63
Stirrup cup **8** 55
Stock
 beef, for consommé **8** 20
 broth, clear (note) **2** 19
 brown
  for aspic **8** 19
  bone **2** 18
 chicken **11** 118
  for consommé **8** 20
 Chinese **17** 65
 consommé (note) **2** 19
 court bouillon **5** 122
  for shellfish **10** 18
 duck **2** 19
 fish **11** 56, **16** 22

Stock *continued*

for aspic	**8**	19
jellied	**5**	56
mixed	**2**	18
vegetable	**2**	19
white		
for aspic	**8**	19
bone	**2**	19
Stocking the kitchen		
cupboard	**3**	121–124

Stollen	**13**	20
Stracciatella	**8**	101
Strasbourg sausage		
definition	**12**	124
omelet alsacienne	**10**	121
Strasbourgeoise	**17**	124
Strawberry(ies)	**3**	46–49
with angel cake	**1**	97
bombe	**18**	115
butterscotch	**10**	131
cake		
fresh	**9**	63
gateaux aux fraises	**14**	95
walnut cream	**3**	49
cardinal	**16**	109
charlotte	**16**	36
coeur à la crème	**10**	130
compote with cream		
(rødgrød med fløde)	**12**	25
coupe française	**10**	105
cream in fruit	**16**	39
cream roll	**6**	69
cremè Margot	**3**	66
cup, with melon	**10**	130
custard	**11**	20
sauce	**9**	128, **18** 115
flan	**3**	47
frappé	**11**	113
galette	**3**	47
gâteau	**15**	17
chocolate	**7**	98
Margot	**13**	109
ice cream	**11**	106
jam	**7**	77
japonais	**8**	38
Jeanne Granier	**18**	120

marquise	**18**	39
meringue basket	**4**	77
mille feuilles	**18**	90
mousse	**14**	62
iced	**11**	121
purée	**11**	106
in raspberry cream	**3**	46
Romanoff	**3**	46
sherbet	**11**	109
orange	**18**	127
shortcake	**3**	47
sundae, with orange	**5**	53
swans	**6**	79
syllabub	**10**	87
tabatières	**3**	49
tartlettes coeur à la crème	**3**	49
tartlets	**1**	55
Streusel kuchen	**13**	18
apple	**13**	20
Striped bass à la kan	**17**	69
Strudel		
almond	**9**	33
apricot and almond	**15**	115
basic dough	**10**	114
cherry	**9**	33
cream cheese	**4**	55
definition	**4**	55
fillings	**10**	114
rolled	**9**	32
Stufato di manzo alla romana	**8**	103
Stuffed artichokes vinaigrette	**16**	10
Stuffed lobster tails	**17**	67
Stuffed squabs, en cocotte		
with olives	**16**	70
with peas and carrots	**18**	29
Stuffing		
apple, pecan and prune	**8**	49
balls	**17**	110
beef (for peppers)	**4**	112
Brazilián	**8**	49
celery	**16**	31
apricot and pecan	**8**	48
chestnut	**8**	48
corn (for peppers)	**4**	112
herb and onion	**2**	85
lemon stuffing balls	**4**	99
mousseline	**14**	77

mushroom and rice (for peppers)	**4**	112
onion	**12**	62
Passover	**9**	14
pecan	**2**	85
pork	**8**	48
potato and apple	**8**	49
quantity guide	**8**	48
rice	**2**	85
and pistachios	**12**	62
wild	**8**	49
sage and onion	**1**	39
sauerkraut	**1**	91
summer pudding	**3**	57
sweet potato and celery	**1**	91
veal	**8**	48

Stummer sausage (definition)	**12**	124
Succotash	**4** 114, **12** 63
Suchard sauce	**9** 126, **15** 51
Sucking pig, roast	**12**	62
Suédoise	**18**	15
apricot	**5**	14
definition	**5**	14
plum	**4**	21
Sugar		
cane crystals (definition)	**13**	82
scraper	**13**	120
syrup	**13** 120, **14** 111
stages and tests for boiling	**13**	112
thermometer	**13**	112
types of	**6**	130–131
vanilla	**4**	77
Sugar cookies, American	**12**	71
Sugar scraper	**13**	120
Suisse, tartlets	**17**	124
Sukiyaki	**16**	54
Sultane	**17**	125
Summer pudding	**3**	57
Summer squash in dill and		
sour cream	**10**	110
Summer vinegar	**16**	100
Sundaes, ice cream	**5**	53
Suprême		
of chicken with cream	**15**	107
de chocolat	**7**	98
definition	**10**	72
de poisson parisienne	**18**	23

Suprême continued
de poulet Villeroi | **14** 109
sauce | **16** 90
Sushi
Norimaki (vinegared rice and fish in seaweed) | **16** 50
shellfish | **16** 58

Swabian roast venison (Schwabisches reh) | **11** 132
Swedish dishes
apple charlotte | **5** 104
meatballs (köttbullar) | **17** 135
Sweet Bread (Spanish) | **16** 125
Sweet potato(es)
candied | **1** 39
casserole | **4** 99
glazed | **8** 50
with orange | **10** 101
with steamed fish | **11** 89
stuffing with celery | **1** 91
Sweet sour
ham | **10** 131
sauce | **3** 81
spareribs | **4** 38
Sweetbreads | **13** 65–69
bonne maman | **13** 68
braised, with white wine | **5** 59
with chestnuts | **13** 67
Dauphine | **13** 69
fricandeau of | **13** 66
fritot of | **13** 67
to prepare | **8** 107, **16** 12
provençale | **13** 68
soubise | **13** 68
tante Marie | **10** 12, **16** 12
vol-au-vent | **8** 78
Swiss cake | **18** 72
Swiss cheese fondue | **15** 95
Swiss dishes
omelet | **10** 118
salad | **15** 63
Syllabub | **4** 59
definition | **7** 128
orange macaroon | **13** 52

Syltede
agurker (Danish pickled cucumber) | **12** 25
rødbeder (Danish pickled beets) | **12** 25
Syrup
golden (definition) | **10** 94
for savarin | **4** 14

Tabatière (definition) | **3** 49
Tabasco (definition) | **15** 28
Tacos | **15** 32
en cazuela (casserole with beef) | **15** 32
de gueso (cheese) | **15** 32
Taffy | **13** 115
Tagliatelle
con pepperoni | **5** 88
al prosciutto | **8** 116
basic dough | **8** 116
verde al pomodoro | **8** 116
Tahina (sesame paste)
definition | **12** 84
Tamale(s) | **15** 34–35
basic dough | **15** 34
fillings for | **15** 34
pie, American | **11** 73
Tamarind (definition) | **13** 83
Tammy cloth/strainer | **7** 31
Tandoori murgh (barbecued chicken) | **13** 88
Tangerine(s)
cream | **2** 95
marmalade | **16** 95
mousse | **16** 104
with rice cream | **9** 57
sherbet | **16** 35
spiced | **16** 97
Tante Marie sweetbreads | **16** 12
Tapas | **16** 112
Taramasalata | **12** 88
Taratoor dressing | **12** 88

Tarragon
with chicken (poulet à l'estragon) | **17** 22
cream dressing | **15** 18, 67
avocado in | **8** 44
vinegar | **16** 100
Tartare sauce | **13** 67

Tarte
almond | **14** 97
apple, tatin | **5** 106
asparagus | **7** 50
beauceronne | **3** 31
cannelle (cinnamon flan) | **3** 54
aux citrons (lemon flan) | **3** 29
française | **2** 29
aus pommes à l'orange | **10** 14
aux pommes grillée | **14** 32
aux pruneaux | **10** 54
coeur à la crème | **3** 49
Danish | **15** 121
fruit | **1** 54
hors d'oeuvres | **17** 124–125
lobster boats | **7** 50
maids of honor | **4** 57
niçoise | **7** 52
fillings | **7** 52
perlées | **18** 62
Roquefort | **7** 11
savory | **15** 23
shells | **7** 50
strawberry | **1** 55
Welsh cheese, or cakes | **1** 111
Tartelettes amandines | **14** 99
Tayglach | **9** 31
Telor genbung (Indonesian spiced shredded 'omelet') | **11** 93
Tempura | **16** 52
definition | **16** 48
Tequila (definition) | **15** 43
Terrine(s) | **9** 37–49
chicken | **16** 29
duck | **16** 29
game | **9** 46
maison | **9** 45

Terrine(s) *continued*

molds	**9** 42	
pork	**9** 46	
simple	**9** 42	
Thai meat curry		
(Kaeng phet nua)	**11** 96	
Thanksgiving Day ideas	**8** 40–57	
Thaw frozen foods	**16** 27	
Thermometer, sugar	**13** 112	
Thickening agents	**5** 57	
Thourin, le (cream of onion soup)	**13** 74	
Thousand island dressing	**4** 33	
Three bean salad	**4** 40	
Thüringer sausage (definition)	**12** 123	
Ti leaves (definition)	**11** 82	
Timbale à l'Indienne	**18** 76	
Timbale Orta	**6** 67	
Tipsy cake	**7** 92	
porcupine	**7** 128	
Russian	**13** 79	
Tiropetes (Greek cheese pastries)	**15** 92	
Tiropita (Greek cheese pie)	**12** 89	
Toast	**12** 110	
melba	**17** 54	
toffee French	**5** 42	
tomato and gruyère	**15** 47	
Toffee French toast	**5** 42	
Tom Pouce	**18** 63	
Tomato(es)		
and anchovy relish	**11** 15	
and apple chutney	**11** 34	
avocado ice	**5** 125	
baked	**11** 52	
with beef and zucchini	**13** 37	
bhartha	**13** 93	
bruxelloise	**15** 123	
butter	**14** 38	
calamari al pomodoro	**8** 101	
canapé		
with egg	**17** 128	
with onion	**17** 128	
caramelized	**14** 19	
chartreuse	**8** 28	
with shrimps	**15** 63	
cherry		
pickled	**7** 84	
salad	**14** 122	
stuffed	**7** 47	
chutney		
with apple	**11** 34	
ripe	**11** 34	
coulis	**4** 42	
eggs baked in	**12** 76	
flan	**11** 14	
fondue	**13** 61	
au fromage	**13** 76	
garnish	**15** 127	
for egg mousse	**10** 51	

Gervais	**1** 15	
and gruyère toast	**15** 47	
and lemon purée	**4** 68	
mayonnaise	**6** 38, **11** 60	
mold, with fish	**16** 87	
omelet	**1** 76	
for pasta	**5** 88	
paste	**16** 84	
to peel	**4** 102	
pickle	**11** 40	
ripe	**11** 40	
sweet green	**11** 40	
provençale	**16** 62	
purée, fresh	**17** 38	
relish, with anchovy	**11** 15	
salad	**9** 93	
and artichoke	**16** 72	
with avocado	**12** 46, **17** 93	
bean and anchovy	**12** 110	
bean and cucumber	**6** 36	
orange	**9** 89	
Clementine	**4** 102	
with cucumber	**17** 84	
with lemon dressing	**13** 57	
and orange	**9** 89, **17** 87	
for pasta	**8** 101	
with rice and ripe olive	**13** 58	
sauce	**7** 41, **11** 72, **15** 40	
chaudfroid	**18** 95	
deviled	**5** 47	
with herbs	**17** 127	
for pasta	**8** 101	
simple	**16** 87	
to seed	**4** 102	
soup		
with beans	**9** 120	
Georgette	**4** 103	
herb	**4** 37	
with orange	**5** 11	
with rice	**6** 55	
special	**3** 124	
spicy	**10** 50	
soy sauce	**3** 82	
with squid	**8** 101	
stuffed	**7** 36, **13** 41	
with roquefort cream	**15** 95	
simla belati	**13** 93	

Valaisanne	**14** 20	
vinegar	**16** 101	
Tongue(s)	**13** 69–71	
baked, with chutney	**3** 124	
braised		
Bigarade	**13** 71	
Florentine	**11** 46	
to carve	**11** 46	
and chicken filling	**15** 125	
dijonnaise	**10** 131	
filling for sandwiches	**13** 11	
Montmorency (calves')	**13** 70	
mousse	**14** 61	
pâté, smoked	**16** 66	
rolls, with chicken	**16** 30	
salad, jellied	**4** 30	
sandwich, and curry	**14** 116	
spread	**17** 135	
Tongue press (definition)	**13** 69	
Toppings		
for coffeecake	**13** 14	
for sandwiches	**13** 10	
Torisashi (chicken sashi)	**16** 52	
Torta d'Amatio	**18** 73	
Torta di formaggio	**8** 112	
Torte, Czech	**10** 112	
Torte de elode (corn casserole)	**15** 36	
Tortellini	**5** 93	
Tortilla	**15** 30, **16** 116	
Balear	**16** 116	
basic	**16** 116	
Granadina	**16** 116	
à la jardinera	**16** 116	
Tortilla press	**15** 30	
Tortelli	**8** 116	
Tostadas	**15** 31	
Toucinho do céu (Portuguese 'bacon and heaven' cake)	**16** 128	
Tourangelle	**17** 86	
Tournedos		
chasseur	**15** 56	
clamart	**15** 54	
definition	**15** 54	
mâconnaise	**17** 47	
parisienne	**15** 54	
à la Russe	**10** 72	
Seville	**17** 48	

Tourtière (definition) **7** 123
Trifle
  fruit **1** 103
  sherry **10** 105
Tripe
  Italian style **9** 83
  à la mode de Caen **6** 114
  soup (menudo) **15** 35
Trois frères, chicken **17** 21
Tropical cooking **11** 81–97
  ingredients **11** 82
Trout
  in aspic **18** 23
  belin **14** 80
  blue (forelle-blau) **11** 125
  broiled **3** 80
  à la Genevoise **11** 65
  how to bone **14** 80
  mousse **14** 58
  smoked
    meunière **15** 70
    in parsley aspic **15** 103
    pâté **11** 65
  stuffed **14** 79
  stuffed nantua **18** 82
Truffle(s) **1** 79
  chocolate **18** 128
  definition **17** 56
  omelet **1** 79
  with pheasant **17** 102
Truite en gelée **18** 23
Tub of mushroom cake **15** 84
Tuiles aux amandes **5** 80
Tumeric (definition) **13** 83
Tuna
  with chicken **16** 79
  cream, with egg **5** 37
  with eggs **5** 34
  fresh **11** 67
  pilaf **3** 124
  quiche **1** 101
  sauce **16** 104
  salad
    deviled **4** 26
    and shrimp **13** 57

spread, with walnuts **17** 135
  with tomatoes **5** 38
Turinois **10** 92
Turkey **17** 110
  braised **5** 57
    alsacienne **5** 57
    with champagne **10** 84
  broth **7** 107
  to carve **8** 46
  cooking times **8** 45
  croquettes **8** 60
  curry **8** 60
  devilled **8** 60
  dinde braisé au champagne **10** 84
  divan **8** 60
  French roast **8** 46
  galantine **8** 65
  en gelée **15** 10
  mole **15** 39
  mousse **8** 61
  and mushroom loaf **8** 61
  with Passover stuffing **9** 14
  kebabs, deviled **4** 38
  pâté with ham **9** 46
  ragoût de dinde à la bourgeoise
    (ragoût with vegetables) **6** 117
  roast, with oyster stuffing **10** 101
  salad
    Italian **14** 122
    Louis **4** 29
    parisienne **8** 60
  to slow roast **8** 45
  to stuff **8** 49
  stuffings for **8** 48–49

Turkish meatball soup **5** 120
Turnips
  braised **6** 122
  buttered **8** 51, **17** 102
  chrysanthemum **16** 57
  creamed **1** 30
  with duck, roast **17** 30
  with onions **14** 19
  soup, cream of **14** 68
Turnovers
  fruit **8** 79

ham and cheese **8** 131
  miniature (empanadillas) **16** 112
Turtle beans **12** 100
Tutti frutti **11** 106
Twelfth Night cake **11** 17
Twists (Danish pastry) **13** 29
Tzimmes (definition) **9** 14
  beef and prunes **9** 14
  prune and farfel **9** 25

UV

Upside down gingerbread **10** 67

Vacherin aux marrons **10** 56
Valencia pudding **1** 66
Vallée d'Auge (braised pheasant) **17** 103
Vancouver salad **17** 87
Vanilla **2** 92
  cream **13** 27
  crescents **18** 68
  custard sauce **6** 125, **9** 128
  ice cream **11** 103
    egg mousse base **11** 104
  soufflé **10** 41
  sugar **4** 77, **14** 84
Vanillekipfeln **18** 68
Variety meats **9** 77–83
Vatrushka **7** 118
Veal
  blanquette **3** 22
  braised
    breast
      poitrine de veau
      braisé farci (braised stuffed
      breast) **6** 118
      with tomatoes **11** 77
  Orloff **15** 73
  sweetbreads with white wine **5** 159
  for broiling **3** 77
  carving **6** 24
  casserole bolognese **4** 95

Veal *continued*

with cheese and ham **17** 93
chops
  bonne femme **4** 104
  broiled **3** 77
  Judic **15** 58
  monarque **17** 48
  Hongroise **12** 37
  with mustard **4** 95
  portugaise sauté **4** 46
cordon bleu **17** 93
costolette bolognese **8** 102
cuts and how to cook them **6** 24–27
cutlets sauté normande **4** 47
escalopes **15** 56–57
  coupole **10** 84
  to flatten **12** 34
  Italienne **12** 34
  with olives **12** 37
  with orange **12** 37
  provençale **17** 39
  savoyarde **17** 48
  tapenade **15** 105
fricadelles in tomato sauce **3** 40
fricandeau with spinach purée **5** 63
galantine **7** 125
goulash **11** 25
grenadins
  de veau à l'Hongroise
    (Hungarian grenadins of) **17** 51
  definition **17** 51
and ham pie **2** 28
Hongroise **15** 105
kidneys
  broiled **3** 77
  Robert **12** 80
kromeskis **13** 45
mold **16** 89
mousseline **16** 91
osso buco **8** 105
paprika **10** 112
parisienne **9** 93
in pastry **18** 33
paupiettes de veau
  citronnées **9** 89

pie, with ham **2** 28
poitrine de veau braisé farci
  (braised stuffed breasts) **6** 118
Pojarski cotleti **7** 115
quenelles **16** 91
roasting **2** 82–84
  times **6** 18
salad **13** 41
  with pepper **15** 64
saltimbocca **8** 102
sauté **16** 91
  chasseur **16** 31
  with cheese **16** 30
  Marengo **4** 48
scaloppine à la crème **4** 47
serving, suggestions
  for **2** 84–85, **6** 26–27
shoulder of hongroise **8** 12
stuffed rolls Bayonne **15** 58
stuffing **8** 48
with tuna sauce **16** 104
wiener schnitzel **12** 34

Venison **17** 114
  braised **5** 73
  fillets of (poivrade) **17** 116
  grenadins **17** 116
  roast, Swabian
    (Schwabisches reh) **11** 132
Vénitienne (Venetian) sauce **2** 53
Venitiennes **14** 103
Véronique chicken **17** 11
Vert-pré (definition) **2** 117
Vet's midnight snack, open-face
  sandwich **12** 10
Vichy salad **17** 84
Vichysoisse **3** 114
Viennese curd cake **4** 56
Viennese wafers **14** 104
Viking galley open-face
  sandwich **12** 13
Vinaigrette dressing **6** 38, **15** 63, **17** 84
Vinaigrette leeks **10** 70
Vinaigrette salad **6** 30, **14** 122
Vine leaves, stuffed (dolmas) **12** 86
Vinegar
  definition **13** 83
  homemade **16** 99–101
  spiced **11** 36
Vitello tonnato (veal with tuna
  sauce) **16** 104
Vol-au-vent **8** 74
  cases **8** 74
  aux fruits de mer **8** 78
  seafood **8** 78
  sweetbread **8** 78

Vegetable(s), see also individual
  names **14** 16–23
  baby, chartreuse of **8** 23
  in béchamel sauce **7** 43
  braising **5** 56
  cooking with **4** 108–117
  entrées **7** 33–43
  à la greque **4** 115
  ratatouille **6** 122
  to refresh **1** 94, **14** 19
  salad **8** 104
    fresh (Les crudités) **11** 12
    mixed **3** 96
  to sauté **4** 44
  to serve with broiled dishes **3** 82–83
  soup **14** 114
  stew **16** 119
  stock **2** 19
Velouté sauce **16** 88
Venetian cookies **14** 103

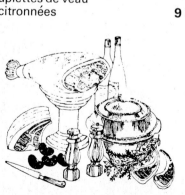

Waffles **5** 129–133
Wah yeem (definition) **17** 64
Wafers **14** 102
  almond **14** 130
  Viennese **14** 104

Waldmeister-bowle (Woodruff or May Wine) **11** 137, **18** 113
Walnut(s) **10** 97
  and apple sauce **9** 125
  bread **10** 94
    wholewheat **4** 123
    rolls **1** 16
  brittle **13** 117
  cake
    layer **1** 115
    nusstorte **18** 67
    raisin **1** 112
    sponge (chocolate) **10** 94
  candy, Caucasian **7** 118
  caramelized **18** 67
  with chicken **17** 71
  cookies **13** 12
  galette **1** 102
  kisses **10** 94
  marzipan **13** 117
  muffins, with honey **4** 124
  pickled **11** 39
  salad, with beet and celeriac **6** 32
  soup **3** 114
  spread, with tuna **17** 135
Wassail (definition) **11** 17
  bowl **11** 17
Water bath, cooking in **2** 92
Water chestnuts
  definition **17** 64
  with snow peas and bamboo shoots **17** 80
Watercress
  cocktail, with seafood **17** 10
  garnish for egg mousse **10** 51
  soup **16** 70
    with beef **17** 65
    with mushrooms **17** 15
Watermelon
  rafraîchis **16** 64
  rind pickles **11** 37
Wedding
  lunch **15** 9–13
  reception **15** 14–25
Weekend cooking **1** 98–103
  menus for one **12** 74–81
Weisswurst sausage
  definition) **12** 124
  to make **12** 127
Welsh cooking
  cakes **14** 46
  cheese cakes or tartlets **1** 111
  granny's broth **14** 36
  pancakes **14** 50
Welsh rarebit **15** 99
Wheat
  bread
    cracked **7** 70

  definition **12** 84
  fine wholewheat **7** 67
  wholewheat **7** 67
  kasha **7** 116
Whiskey
  apples **10** 131
  milk punch **8** 55
  punch **8** 57
White beans **12** 100
White sauce **2** 45, **18** 94
Whitefish **11** 67
  broiled **3** 80
  Florentine **11** 67
White fruit cake **9** 68
White wine with mushrooms **16** 76
Whiting **11** 67
  Alsacienne **11** 67
Whole peas **12** 100
Wholewheat biscuits **4** 126
Wholewheat bread **7** 67
  Grahamsbröd **12** 30
  ice cream **11** 106
Wiener schnitzel **12** 34
Wieners (frankfurters)
  definition **12** 123
Wild goose **17** 110
  roast with mushroom cream sauce **17** 108
Wild duck **17** 108
  roast with orange gravy **17** 110
  roast with sour cream **17** 101
Wild rice **17** 110
Wild turkey **17** 110
  braised **17** 110
Wine
  cooking with **10** 76–87
  cup, Rhine **8** 55
  sauce **9** 125
    white **13** 65
  White, with mushrooms **16** 76
Winter buffet **11** 9–17
Winter melon (definition) **17** 64
  soup **17** 65
Winter salads **6** 29–39
Wok **17** 62
Woodcock **17** 113
  Scotch **5** 29
Wrap cooked dishes **16** 27

Yams (definition) **11** 82
Yeast **13** 18
Yee chee tong (shark's fin soup) **17** 66

Yeong jow chow fon (yeong jow fried rice) **17** 66
Yeong loong hah mei (stuffed lobster tails) **17** 67
Yogurt
  definition **12** 84
  with lamb **10** 112
  sauce **10** 67
  soup (cacik) **12** 84, **16** 106
Yoli sauce **15** 40
Yorkshire dishes
  applecake **1** 53
  oatcakes **14** 53
  parkin **14** 49
  pie **12** 66
  pudding **1** 30
Yow
  Chinese chard with oil and salt **17** 78
  definition **17** 64
Yuen sai (definition) **17** 64

Zabaione **10** 87
Zakouski (definition) **7** 112
Zarzuela (Basque fish stew) **16** 120
Zeppole alla napoletana **8** 112
Zoni (rice cake soup) **16** 58
Zucchini
  with beef and tomatoes **13** 37
  buttered **3** 83, **15** 49
  casserole, with corn **4** 95
  and eggplant au gratin **14** 20
  aux fines herbes **4** 70
  flower fritters **18** 132
  au gratin **4** 104
  à la greque **16** 85
  mold **4** 115
  omelet **1** 79
  and pimiento soup, iced **14** 120
  salad **16** 109
  with shrimps **1** 94
  with tomatoes **15** 36
Zuger kirschtorte **18** 72
Zuppa inglese **8** 110
  definition **8** 110
Zuppa di vongole **8** 101
Zwetschgenknödel (plum puddings) **11** 127

A GLOSSARY OF COOKING TERMS AND TECHNIQUES

BY   SHERYL JULIAN

Acidulate means to add an acid such as lemon juice or vinegar to a liquid.

Agar agar is a setting agent made from seaweeds and is used in jellies, ice cream and for clarifying the Japanese rice wine, sake.

Aiguillettes are long, thin strips of duck breast. To make them remove the breast from the duck in one piece and then cut lengthwise into strips.

Aioli is a sauce from Provence, similar to mayonnaise but heavily flavored with garlic. The Spanish version is called ali-oli (garlic-oil) and both are popular with fish.

Al dente ('to the tooth' in Italian) is the term used to describe pasta that is cooked until almost tender, but still has perceptible resistance to the teeth.

Allspice is the berry from the allspice tree. Pungent and aromatic, it is primarily used in pickling liquids, marinades, and spice and fruit cakes.

Allumettes ('matchsticks' in French) refer to pastry and potatoes cut into very thin sticks.

Almonds, to brown and grind: blanch and remove skins of almonds before browning. Bake in a moderately hot oven (375°F) for 8–10 minutes or until browned. Grind in a rotary cheese grater or a few at a time in the blender.

Alsacienne (à l') refers to a dish characterized by pâté de foie gras – liver pâté made from specially fattened geese. The pâté is a specialty of Alsace in France. It can also refer to a sauerkraut garnish.

Américaine (à l') usually refers to a garnish of tomatoes and garlic, originally created for a lobster dish by a Parisian chef named Pierre Fraisse, who was born in Provence (which may account for the typically Provencal ingredients). The same dish is sometimes called lobster Amoricaine and experts disagree about which title is correct.

Amoricaine (à l') refers to dishes that originated in Amorica, the Roman name for Brittany. In the 17th century the main port of the region, Nantes, was a center for the spice trade; therefore, many local recipes are spiced. See Américaine.

Ancienne (à l') usually refers to dishes with a long history; often two or more garnishes are combined.

Andalouse (à l') usually refers to a dish characterized by tomato paste, sweet peppers or pimientos, and often chipolata sausages. The name comes from the province of Spain, Andalusia.

Andouilles are large salted or smoked tripe or chitterling sausages, usually eaten cold in slices. Andouillettes are the same, only smaller, and usually cooked in fat to be served hot. The best of these sausages come from Normandy, northern France.

Angelica is a herb valued for its leaves and its root, used in cordials and liqueurs such as Chartreuse. Candied angelica is made from the stalks. It comes in wide, flat strips and is usually cut into diamond shaped pieces to use with other candied fruits for decoration.

Anglaise (à l') usually refers to food cooked plainly in boiling water or by roasting.

Anise is a sweet-smelling herb with feathery leaves producing aniseed. Its principle use is in the making of liqueurs, but it can also flavor cookies, cakes, breads, sauces for fish and meat. It is a favorite herb in Chinese cooking.

Argenteuil always refers to a dish characterized by asparagus. The Argenteuil region (a suburb of Paris) has sandy soil in which the best asparagus used to grow.

Aromatics are herbs, spices, garlic and flavorings that are added to a dish during cooking or when the dish is finished.

Arrowroot is a starch made from the roots of tropical plants, and is used to thicken sauces and sometimes in baking. It is mixed with a little cold liquid to a smooth paste, then gradually whisked into the hot liquid to be thickened. Arrowroot leaves a sauce clear after it has thickened.

Jerusalem artichokes are the roots of a type of sunflower. They have nothing to do with the city of Jerusalem, but instead are native to the U.S. and were a common vegetable in colonial days. The name is a corruption of 'girasole', the Italian word for sunflower.

Asparagus cookers are tall narrow pans with an inner basket, designed so the asparagus stems can cook in boiling water in the bottom of the pan while the more delicate heads steam at the top.

Aspic is clear jelly used to coat cold foods. It is made by clarifying stock with egg whites and sometimes egg shells. Wine or liqueur may be added to the stock and, if necessary, gelatin may be used to set it but, if possible, the stock used for aspic should be so well-flavored that it sets naturally. Chicken, meat or fish stock may be used, depending on the food it will coat.

Attelets are small skewers with ornamental heads used to decorate very elaborate dishes.

Aurore ('sunrise') usually refers to a sauce or dish flavored with tomato paste or tomatoes.

B

Babas are small raisin-filled yeast cakes that are soaked in rum-flavored sugar syrup after baking.

Bain Marie See water bath.

To bake is to cook by dry heat in an oven.

To bake blind is the term used for baking unfilled pastry without the sides falling in or the bottom rising. The pastry is lined with foil or a triple thickness of tissue paper, then filled with rice or dried beans. The paper and beans are removed when the pastry is set, so that it can become crisp and brown.

Baking powder is a leavening agent used in baking. Baking powder is usually a compound of acid salt, bicarbonate of sodium (baking soda) and a stabilizer such as cornstarch. There are three kinds of baking powder: tartrate, phosphate and double acting. Double acting baking powder is most commonly used today.

Baking soda (or bicarbonate of soda) is made from soda and is sometimes used in place of baking powder. In baking it reacts with acid ingredients such as sour milk to make breads and biscuits to rise.

Ballotine refers to a piece of meat, poultry, game or fish that is boned, stuffed and rolled into the shape of a bundle – a 'ballot'. It is tied with string to keep its shape, or secured with skewers or poultry pins. A ballotine is usually roasted and served hot or cold.

Balm is a herb that is seldom used in cooking, but a large handful of fresh or dried balm can be infused in boiling water to make a herb tea.

To barbecue is to broil or roast on a rack, normally over charcoals. The term is said to have come from Florida, where French settlers spit-roasted goats 'de barbe en queue' (from head to tail). Alternatively the word barbecue may be derived from the Spanish 'barbacoa' meaning a frame of wooden sticks used to support meat for roasting.

To bard is to cover lean meat or game with thinly sliced fat before cooking to prevent the flesh from drying out. The fat is usually tied on with string and barding can be done with strips of bacon or with thin even slices of pork fat.

Basil (also known as sweet basil) is a sweet aromatic herb with a natural affinity for tomatoes. Basil used to be a royal herb (*Basileus* means 'king' in Greek) and it was once said 'the smell thereof is so excellent that it is fit for a king's house'.

Basque country lies both in France and Spain, divided by the Pyrenees, and the cooking of the region reflects both influences. Basque dishes are characterized by pimiento, red and green peppers, and garlic – showing the Spanish influence – but recipes also have a French finesse. Often ham, a specialty of Bayonne, the Basque capital, is included.

Basting is the process of spooning hot fat or liquid over food as it roasts to keep it moist and juicy.

Batterie de cuisine is the French term for cooking equipment.

Bavarian cream (Bavarois) is a rich egg custard stiffened or set with gelatin and with whipped cream added.

Bay leaf is an evergreen member of the laurel family, used as a flavoring for soups, stews, meats, fish, poultry and marinades. It is included in a bouquet garni and at one time the withering of a bay tree predicted an evil event.

Beet gelatin salad

Barbecue

B *continued*

Béarn, a French province in the Pyrenees, is well known for its good food and wines. Its most famous namesake, sauce Béarnaise, did not originate in Béarn, but was the creation of a chef of the restaurant Pavillon Henri IV at St. Germain near Paris. Henri IV – the 'grand Béarnais' – was from Béarn and the sauce was named after him. See sauces.

To beat is to stir vigorously with a circular motion using a spoon or whisk to give lightness to a mixture.

Béchamel is the French name for a white sauce made from milk infused with flavorings and thickened with butter and flour. The name is said to come from Marquis Louis de Béchamel, a 17th century French financier. See Sauces.

Beeton, Isabella (1836–1865) is the author of an English book called 'The Book of Household Management', a guide for the mid-Victorian housewives that includes over 2,000 recipes and 3,500 articles. Mrs. Beeton published her book when she was only 21 years old. It remains a classic.

Beignets are light French fritters that are made of choux pastry, or dipped in batter and deep fat fried. They can be sweet or savory; the sweet ones are usually sprinkled with sugar and the savory ones with grated cheese.

Bel paese is a mild Italian cheese that is ivory-colored and semi-soft.

Bigarade is the French name for the bitter Seville orange that is used in a classic savory sauce and to make marmalade. Sauce bigarade can be made with a sweet orange and a squeeze of lemon juice for sharpness. See Sauces.

Bigarreau is a type of cherry (often called 'white-hearts') with a very hard flesh.

To bind is to moisten with liquid such as egg to keep a mixture together.

Bisque is a smooth creamy soup made from either lobster, shrimp, crayfish, clams or oysters. Originally, a bisque was made from a purée of game such as quail or pigeon.

Bitkis are small balls or flat rounds of ground meat bound with breadcrumbs and cooked in fat; they are of Russian origin.

To blanch means to whiten meats or to remove strong flavors from vegetables by immersing in cold water, bringing to a boil, and draining before further cooking. Green vegetables should be put directly into boiling water and cooked for up to 1 minute.

Blanquette is a stew of lamb, veal, chicken or rabbit with a rich sauce made from the cooking liquid, milk or cream, and egg yolks; it is often garnished with small onions and mushrooms.

To blend is to stir a mixture until it is completely combined and smooth.

Bleu is a method of cooking trout by killing it, tying tail to head, then immediately plunging it into vinegar-flavored court bouillon at which point the fish takes on a bluish tinge. The fish must be killed not more than 10 minutes before cooking.

Blini are tiny Russian pancakes made from buckwheat flour. They are most often associated with caviar but can be served with smoked salmon, smoked sturgeon or salted herring.

Blue-veined cheeses are marbled with mold. They include English Stilton, French Roquefort and Italian Gorgonzola. See individual names.

To boil is to immerse food in water or stock when the liquid has reached 212°F and is bubbling vigorously.

Bombe is a molded ice cream that is made in a traditional bomb-shaped mold, almost spherical with a flat bottom. The mold can be filled with one kind or a combination of ice cream, sherbet or parfait and different flavors can be layered on the bottom and sides of the mold so the bombe is striped when cut in wedges like a cake for serving.

Bonne femme (à la) (literally 'good woman') usually refers to homey traditional food and often to a garnish of onion, bacon and potato. The term can be applied to dishes as varied as beef broth garnished with vegetables, or a rich wine sauce flavored with mushrooms and enriched with egg yolks and cream.

Bordelaise (à la) refers to a dish containing red or white Bordeaux wine and beef marrow.

Bortsch is the national soup of the Ukraine and the name is an old Slav word for beet. There are many ways of making bortsch and it always contains root vegetables, usually with a large proportion of beet. Sometimes as many as three different kinds of meat may be added.

Bouillabaisse is a Mediterranean fish stew that originated in Marseilles, France. It is traditionally made with red mullet, sea perch, rascasse, whiting, spiny lobster, tomatoes, saffron, garlic and onions. It is served in 2 dishes, one for the pieces of fish and the other containing slices of French bread with the broth poured on top.

Bouillon is meat or vegetable stock.

Boulangère (à la) – French for 'baker' – usually refers to meat or poultry cooked on a bed of sliced potatoes. Years ago, in country districts of France, small houses had no ovens and the Sunday lunch of leg of lamb was set in a dish with sliced potatoes and onions. This was left with the local baker to cook while the family was at church, then collected piping hot for the midday meal.

Bouquet garni is a bunch of herbs traditionally made with 2–3 stalks of parsley, a sprig of thyme, and a bay leaf tied together with string and used to flavor stews and sauces. It is always removed before serving.

Bourgeoise (à la) always refers to a garnish of diced bacon, baby onions and carrots cut to a uniform size.

Bourguignonne (à la) refers to a dish cooked in the style of Burgundy, France, with mushrooms, onions and red Burgundy wine.

Boursault is a triple cream soft cheese from France.

To braise is the process of cooking meat, poultry, game, fish or vegetables in a small amount of liquid in a pot with a tight-fitting lid so the food cooks in the steam from the liquid. First the food is browned in fat, then the cooking is continued on a bed of diced vegetables (see Mirepoix), that are discarded before serving.

Braisière is the traditional pan for braising, designed for old-fashioned French kitchens that had no ovens. The pots have indented lids in which live coals were placed so that the pan was heated from the top as well as from the bottom. Often braising pans are still made in this shape, although the indented lid is no longer necessary.

Bran is the outer covering of grain that is often removed during processing. It can be combined with wheat and eaten as a breakfast cereal or used for bread-making.

Brandade is a mousse of salt cod (morue) made by beating in warm oil and milk drop by drop and flavoring with garlic. Brandade de morue originally comes from Nîmes in the Languedoc region of southern France.

Bratwurst is a mildly spicy German pork sausage, made from coarsely ground pork often with veal added.

Bretonne (à la) refers to dishes cooked in the style of Britanny, on the northwest coast of France; beans are usually included in the dish.

Brie is a French cheese with a soft creamy yellow inside when ripe. Connoisseurs regard it as the queen of table cheeses.

Brillat-Savarin, Jean Anthelme (1755–1826) was a French lawyer, gourmet and politician, who left France in 1793 during the Revolution and worked his way to New York, giving French lessons and playing the violin. On returning to France, he became well known for his grand dinners and knowledge of food and his book 'La physiologie au goût' is a famous collection of witty anecdotes about food and dining.

Brine is a salt and water solution used in preserving food.

Brioche is a rich yeast dough usually shaped into characteristic small balls with 'heads' and baked in fluted brioche molds. Brioche can also be baked as a large loaf, sometimes with a filling such as a sausage or truffle.

Broche (à la) means to cook on a spit.

Brochette (en) is the term used for small pieces of meat, fish, poultry or vegetables threaded on a skewer and broiled.

To broil is to cook meat, fish or poultry by direct heat, usually under an oven broiler or over a fire.

Bruxelloise (à la) means in the style of Brussels and usually refers to a garnish of Brussels sprouts.

Bulgur (cracked wheat) is made by boiling, drying, then crushing grains of wheat. It can then be made into pilaf or added to soups and stuffings.

Butter
  Beurre blanc is a sauce of butter, white wine, wine vinegar, fish stock and chopped shallots that is served with fish.
  Beurre manié (kneaded butter) is a liaison of twice as much butter as flour worked together into an uncooked paste. It is added in small pieces to thicken a liquid at the end of cooking.
  Beurre noir is clarified butter cooked to a deep brown, then sharpened with a squeeze of lemon juice or vinegar. Used mainly for fish and brains, it can also contain parsley or capers.
  Beurre noisette is clarified butter cooked to a nut-brown color.
  Clarified butter: See Clarify 2.

Kidney brochettes

Ragoût of Beef

Caen (à la mode de) means to cook with white wine and Calvados, an apple brandy; it is a favorite way to prepare tripe. The town of Caen lies at the edge of the Calvados region of Normandy in northern France.

Caerphilly is a hard white granular cheese of the Cheddar family; it is made in Wales.

Camembert is a soft-ripened French cheese with a creamy interior and a subtle flavor, though when overripe it becomes very pungent. It has been called the king of cheese.

Canapés are small open-faced, garnished pieces of bread or toast that can be triangular, round, square, rectangular, oval or crescent-shaped. They are always small and can be served as an appetizer or with cocktails.

Capers are unopened flower buds of the caper bush, that grows wild on mountain slopes. Capers are sold packed in salt or vinegar and used to add piquancy to hot and cold sauces.

Capsicum: See Chili and Peppers.

Caramelize: 1 To dissolve sugar slowly in water then boil steadily, without stirring, to a deep honey color. 2 To give a thin caramel topping by sprinkling surface of a dessert with granulated or brown sugar and broiling slowly.

Caraway seed is a flavoring for rye bread and is also widely used in cakes, cheeses, cookies and hearty root vegetable dishes. It is a favorite flavoring in German cooking.

Carbonade used to refer to any dish that was simmered for a long time over coals (charbon) but it has come to be associated mainly with a rich beef stew made with ale or beer.

Cardamom seeds are the dried ripe fruit of the reed-like cardamom plant; there are 8 kinds and the best known are whitish pods that contain black seeds that are used to give an aromatic touch to pastries, cookies, curry powders and Turkish delight.

Cardinal refers to a dish characterized by a sauce of red color; for savory dishes, the sauce usually contains lobster coral (roe), tomato paste or pimiento; and for sweet dishes, a strawberry or raspberry sauce.

Carême, Marie-Antoine (1784—1833) was a celebrated French chef. Renowned for his pièces montées — grand creations of raw or cooked food built with architectural precision — Carême said that ''Of the five fine arts, the fifth is architecture, whose main branch is confectionery.'' Carême became better known than any cook before him and worked as chef to the French statesman Talleyrand, to the Rothschild and to the Prince Regent of England. He wrote several books that became encyclopedias for future chefs, describing French classical cooking in more detail than ever before.

Carrageen (or Irish Moss) is a kind of edible seaweed named after a small town in Ireland. It is used to clarify malt drinks or to make a medicinal beverage with milk, sugar and lemon juice added.

Cassava is an edible root up to 3 feet long, that is used in tropical cooking.

Casserole is a stewpan or Dutch oven in which stews of meat, game, fish, poultry and vegetables are cooked very slowly in liquid or sauce. The pot and the food cooked in it are both referred to as casseroles.

Cassolettes or little casseroles, are little containers made from pastry or vegetables like cucumber.

Cassoulet is a popular French stew made with haricot beans and usually contains goose or duck with lamb or pork; it comes from Toulouse, France, known for its geese.

Cayenne is a very hot pungent pepper in dried form that must be used sparingly with meat, egg and cheese dishes. It is made from dried and ground red chilies. See Chilies.

Celeriac (or root celery) is a large nobbly root resembling a turnip or rutabaga with a taste of celery. It is peeled before adding to beef or lamb stews or cut into julienne strips and tossed with a remoulade dressing.

Celery seeds are a spice that comes from a variety of wild celery known as 'smallage'. They give a pleasant flavoring to soups, pickles, pastries and hearty salads.

Cèpes are a fungus similar to mushrooms with brown shiny caps, thick white stems and elastic gills. They are prepared like button mushrooms.

Challah is a rich braided bread served each week on the Jewish Sabbath.

Chapons are small crusts of French bread that are rubbed with garlic and tossed with a salad to add flavor; they may be removed before the salad is served.

Chantilly cream is heavy cream that is whipped and flavored with sugar and vanilla. It is used to decorate cold desserts, fresh fruits and many pastries and confections.

Charcuterie — literally 'food from the pork butcher' — is the term used to refer to all sausages and prepared pâtés and terrines. In France the name also refers to the shop where they are sold.

Chard (or Swiss chard) is a variety of the beet family; only the leaves and stalks are used in cooking. It is available during the summer months.

Charlotte refers to the bucket-shaped mold with two handles used for all kinds of mixtures varying from cakes to creams like the famous charlotte Russe. The name is said to come from the old English 'charlet', meaning custard.

Chartreuse is the name given to hot and cold molded dishes. Near Grenoble, France, there is a Carthusian monastery called La Grande Chartreuse where the monks are vegetarians. They invented a vegetable dish which they made and cooked in molds — some very elaborate. Many molded dishes are now called Chartreuse, although correctly the name should be given only to vegetarian dishes. Chartreuse is also the name of a liqueur.

Chasseur means 'hunter-style' and refers to a mushroom garnish that is flavored with shallots and white wine. It is also the name of a brown sauce. See Sauces.

Chaudfroid means hot-cold and is a cold dish of cooked fish, game or poultry that is first coated with a cold velouté or béchamel-based sauce (called a chaudfroid sauce), then coated with a layer of aspic. The term is thought to date from mid-18th century, when the Maréchal de Luxembourg, who was giving a banquet, was suddenly called away. When he returned late, he tasted only one dish — a fricassée of chicken that had become cold in its own sauce. It was so delicious that he began a fashion for chaudfroids.

Chayote is a greenish gourd-like fruit cultivated in California and the southern states. It is usually eaten as a vegetable and cooked like squash — either boiled or stuffed and baked.

Cherries, to pit: either use a special cherry pitter, a small, pea-sized vegetable scoop, the point of a potato peeler or the bend of a hairpin. Insert at the stem, give a twist and draw out the pit.

Chervil is a delicate fern-like herb that is a member of the parsley family. It is sweeter and more aromatic than parsley and one of the traditional 'fines herbes'. Chervil is often combined with tarragon and also to flavor sauces and vinegars.

Cheshire is a salty relative of Cheddar cheese made in England.

Chestnuts, how to peel: pierce each nut with the point of a knife, cover them with cold water in a pan, bring to a boil and take from the heat. Lift them out of the water one at a time with a slotted spoon and peel away the outer and inner skins.

Chili is a tropical plant of the Capsicum family with elongated pods and there are many kinds, including sweet bell peppers, pimientos and chili pepper, most of them fiery hot. Pungent red chilies include ancho, mulato, pasilla and hontaka; green include Senano, Poblano, and Jalapeño. To prepare *dried chilies*, wash them in cold water, remove veins, stems and seeds and cut chilies into small pieces. Pour on boiling water and about 2 teaspoons vinegar and soak for 30 minutes. **Fresh chilies** should be soaked in cold salted water for 1 hour to remove some of the hot taste. *To peel fresh chilies and bell peppers*, hold each one over a flame with a fork or roast them in a hot oven (400°F) until blistered. Wrap in a damp towel, then peel off the skin, split in half and trim away seeds and core. The oils in the flesh of hot chilies can burn your skin so wear rubber gloves. *Canned* chilies and pimientos should be rinsed in cold water and drained.

To chill means to cool food in the refrigerator or over ice without freezing.

Chinois is a cone-shaped strainer with very tiny holes used for straining sauces.

Chipolata is a highly seasoned fresh pork sausage of Italian origin. Chipolatas are very small, and come linked about 18 to the lb.

Chives are a delicate herb belonging to the onion family. They grow well in a pot on the windowsill and their bright green color and delicate onion flavor makes them an attractive garnish for soups, salads, eggs and vegetables.

Chocolate caraque are scrolls of chocolate used to decorate desserts.

Chorizo is a spicy Spanish pork sausage flavored with pimiento, red pepper and garlic.

Choux pastry or pâte à choux is made by adding flour to a boiling water and butter mixture to make a firm paste. Then eggs are beaten in so that, during baking, the pastry puffs rise to form a hollow inside. Choux pastry is used to make profiteroles, éclairs, cream puffs, and savory gougère.

Chowder usually refers to a soup based on fish, but there are also meat and vegetable chowders. Chowder was brought to the U.S. by early French settlers and the word originates either from 'Chaudrée de Fouras', a fish soup from the Fouras region of France, or from 'chaudière' (kettle).

Churros are Spanish crullers (similar to doughnuts) that are dropped into hot deep fat from a special tube and served sprinkled with sugar.

Chutney is an Indian relish usually made from mangoes, chilies and other seasonings.

CHICKEN
cutting up raw

1 Hold chicken firmly on board with one hand. With a sharp knife, sever skin between leg and breast. Then, pressing flat of knife against carcass, take leg in other hand and bend it sharply outwards until bone breaks away from carcass.

2 Slide knife around leg joint, cutting down towards pope's nose, keeping it between oyster and backbone. The leg is now separated from carcass and has oyster bone (from beneath carcass) attached. Remove remaining leg in the same way.

3 Make slantwise cut with knife halfway up breast across to top of wishbone from neck to end of wing joint. With scissors or poultry shears, cut down through wishbone and ribs to detach wing with a good portion of breast.

4 Twist wing pinion out and tuck it under this breast meat to hold the piece flat. This makes for even browning of meat. To obtain both wings of even size, make slantwise cuts at the same time, then detach other wing in the same way.

5 Cut away the breast meat in one piece with the scissors. All that is now left of the carcass are the ribs, the backbone and the pope's nose.

6 The chicken pieces are ready for cooking. The carcass may be cut in half and then sautéed with the other pieces to give the finished dish more flavor.

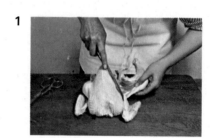

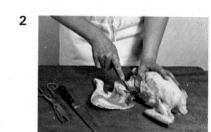

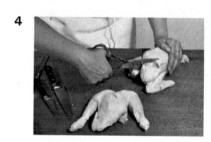

Chicken, splitting a raw broiler
1 Hold bird firmly on board with one hand; make a cut with a sharp knife through skin and flesh on top of breast.
2 Split in half with scissors, starting at wishbone, cutting through on one side of backbone. When divided, trim away backbone from other half of bird.
3 Trim the knuckle end of each drumstick and ends of wing pinions after cooking.

To split a cooked broiler
Lift bird carefully from pan onto a board. Cut and draw out trussing strings before splitting as above.

CHICKEN
how to bone

1 Remove the trussing string or skewer. With a sharp knife, slit the skin along the backbone. Work skin and flesh from this area of carcass with the small knife until leg joint is reached.

2 Hold the end of the ball joint firmly in one hand. Cut away flesh with knife and scrape the thigh bone completely clean, always working from the inside of the leg

3 Continue cleaning the drumstick until the whole leg bone is free of flesh. Now cut the leg bone from the flesh and repeat this cleaning process with the other leg, freeing the leg bone of all flesh.

4 Sever the wing joint from carcass, leaving bone attached to chicken meat. Still using knife, separate white meat from breastbone, leaving carcass intact; stop there. Now free the other wing and breast.

5 Carefully cut away skin from top of breastbone without splitting skin; keep both sides of bird attached so that it remains in one piece for stuffing.

6 Lay the chicken flat ready for the stuffing to be spread over the cut surfaces. Then sew up or secure with poultry pins and string; it is now ready to truss.

1

2

3

4

5

6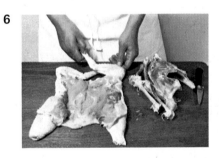

CHICKEN
how to truss

The best way to truss a chicken is to use string and a special long trussing needle. However, it is quite possible to hold the bird firmly together in the same position by using skewers and tying string around them.

Fold flap of skin over back of neck end, fold ends of wing pinions backwards and under to hold neck skin in position. Place bird on back, press legs down into sides to plump up breast.

To truss with a needle:
1 Thread trussing needle with a strong thread or thin string. Insert needle through wing nearest you, then through thigh and body to emerge in same position on far side.
2 Insert needle again into one end of other wing, then into far end of same joint (leaving a stitch showing 1–2 inches long, depending on size of wing) and pass back through body and out at corresponding part of the first wing.
3 Tie the two thread ends into a bow.
4 Re-thread needle, insert through fleshy skin at end of one drumstick, through the gristle on each side of the pope's nose, and out through skin of other drumstick end.
5 Re-insert needle into carcass under drumsticks; draw through.
6 Tie the two thread ends firmly at side.

To truss with a skewer:
Push skewer through bird below thigh bone, turn onto its breast. Catch in the wing pinions, pass string under ends of skewer and cross pinions over its back. Turn bird over, bring up string to secure drumsticks and tie around pope's nose.

1

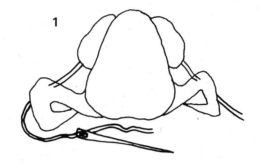

2

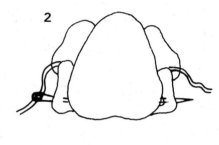

3

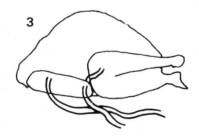

4

5

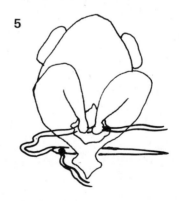

6

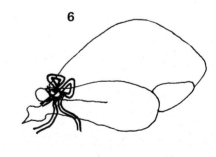

CHICKEN
carving a cooked

1 Hold bird firmly with carving fork down through back. Cut skin around leg, place knife between leg and carcass and press gently outwards to break thigh joint. Cut through, slipping the knife point under back to release the oyster (choice meat lying on each side of the backbone) with thigh.

2 With knife at top end of breastbone opposite where breast and wishbone meet, cut down parallel to one side of wishbone to include a good slice of breast with wing. Sever wing joint.

3 and **4** Carve similar pieces from other side of bird, then remove wishbone by slicing behind it, down front of carcass. Carve remaining breast into 2–4 even slices, depending on size of bird. With a large chicken, divide leg in two through joint, leaving a good portion of thigh meat with drumstick. Trim protruding bones using half-hole in scissors or poultry shears.

1

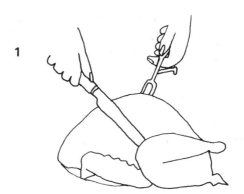

2

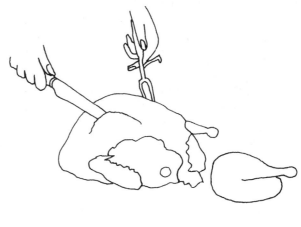

3

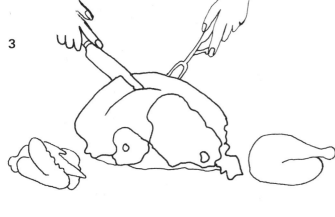

4

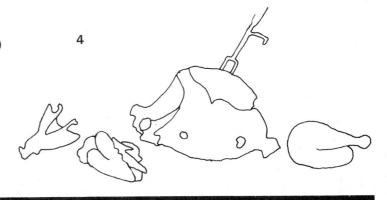

Tomato chartreuse

Gâteau au chocolat

Cinnamon is a warm aromatic spice used ground as a flavoring for cakes, cookies and breads. It comes from the bark of the cinnamon tree and is also available in sticks. In Middle Eastern countries cinnamon is used as a flavoring for meat dishes and it is very popular in Indian rice and curries.

Civet is a stew made from furred game cooked with red wine. The most well known is civet de lièvre (jugged hare).

Clamart refers to a dish garnished with peas, often piled onto artichoke bottoms. Clamart is a suburb of Paris where peas used to be grown.

To clarify 1 To remove impurities by melting used fat, such as beef drippings, with one-third quantity of water, then boiling, straining and cooling the mixture. When set, scrape any sediment from the base of the solidified fat. 2 To clarify butter by heating gently until foaming, skimming well, then leaving to set to a solid cake. The sediment (milk solids) at the bottom is discarded. 3 To clear cold stock with egg whites by whisking while bringing to a boil, then cooling and straining.

Clotted cream is a speciality of the west of England and made by heating whole unhomogenized milk for about 7 hours. The milk is left to cool, then the thick yellow sweet cream is skimmed off the top and served with fruit pies or instead of butter.

Cloves are the flowers of the clove tree that are picked in the bud and dried in the sun to form the characteristic nail shape. Either whole or ground, they flavor both sweet and savory dishes and often a few stuck in an onion are added to stocks, soups, stews and some sauces.

Coat means to completely cover sliced meat, fish, poultry, vegetables or eggs with a sauce, glaze, mayonnaise, aspic or dressing. To coat, hold the stem of a large metal spoon close to the bowl and dip it into the liquid. Then carefully spoon the sauce onto the food by tipping the long edge nearest you and pulling the spoon away from you so the sauce coats the piece of food. *Coat a spoon* is the term used to describe sauces or custards that are just thick enough to coat the back of a spoon.

Cocido is a Spanish stew of pork, beef, chorizo sausages, chicken, chick-peas, root vegetables, and a ham bone, all cooked together so no single flavor predominates the broth. The broth is served with noodles, then the vegetables are served as a separate course, flavored by the meats and chicken.

Cocottes are small round heatproof porcelain dishes with handles, usually used for making individual egg dishes.

Cointreau: See Curaçao.

Colby is an American Cheddar cheese that is softer and more open in texture than a hard Cheddar.

Collards, part of the cabbage family, are leafy green vegetables that grow in tufts. They closely resemble spinach, cabbage or kale, and are prepared in the same way.

Cole slaw is a salad usually made from shredded green cabbage mixed with mayonnaise or vinaigrette dressing. It is generally considered an American recipe but it takes its name from the first Dutch settlers who took over Manhattan Island; in Dutch, *kool* means cabbage and *sla* salad.

Compote is the term for fresh or dried fruit poached (whole or in quarters), in a thick syrup of sugar and water to which flavorings may be added.

Concasser means to chop roughly or shred coarsely. The term is usually applied to tomatoes that have been peeled, quartered, seeded, then coarsely chopped.

Condé is the title of an old French family and the name given to a molded rice cream.

Condiment is a seasoning, usually a spice like pepper, a highly flavored sauce, or a relish.

Consistency is the degree of thinness or thickness of a mixture, especially important in batters, cakemaking and pastry.

Conserve: See Jams.

Consommé is clear soup made from clarifying well-flavored meat stock. It can be served hot or chilled and garnished with strips of vegetables (julienne), diced vegetables (brunoise), diced tomatoes (tomatoes), or pasta. See Clarify 3.

Coriander is a member of the parsley family whose lacy leaves are used in mixed pickling spice; the ground seeds are used in curry powder, and often for flavoring wild game and sausages.

Cornstarch is very fine flour made from corn, used largely as a thickening agent. To thicken a sauce, first make it into a paste with a little water then stir the paste into boiling liquid and cook until it thickens.

Coulis is French for a purée of tomatoes, or any liquid pulp, used to flavor stews and ragoûts. The term may also be given to the strained juice of meat, fish or poultry, thickened with bread, flour or cornstarch.

Coupe means goblet and as a dessert the term means a combination of ice cream and fruit, garnished with cream, candied fruit or flowers, or chopped nuts, and served in a glass or silver cup.

Couronne means crown and refers to a dish that is molded or arranged in a circular shape. 'En couronne' is to arrange in a semi-circle around a dish.

Court bouillon is stock made from water, root vegetables, white wine or vinegar, herbs and seasoning, that is simmered, then strained and used to poach fish or veal.

Couscous is a coarse-grained semolina made from coarsely ground wheat. It is a popular North African dish; the couscous is often steamed over stock with vegetables and meat, fish or poultry, then served with this mixture.

Crayfish resemble small lobsters and are found in some rivers here and particularly around New Orleans and in Wisconsin.

Cream, how to whip: chill the bowl, beater, and cream thoroughly, then gradually beat the cream until it starts to thicken. It can curdle easily at this point; keep beating and if the cream turns yellow, stop at once. If a recipe says to whip cream 'until it holds a soft shape', whip only until the cream is slightly thickened and holds its shape; if it says 'stiff peaks' whip until the cream forms a stiff peak when the beater is lifted, but do not overbeat. On a hot day, or if the kitchen is very warm, whip cream over ice to prevent curdling.

Cream of tartar is juice from grapes that is pressed out after fermentation, then refined to powder. It is used as a leavening agent, to keep egg whites firm and to cut the grain of sugar syrup and prevent it from crystalizing.

Crécy refers to a dish characterized by carrots. Crécy is in Picardy, in northern France, and is known for its carrots.

Crêpe is a very thin French pancake that can be sweet or savory, filled or rolled without stuffing; sometimes crêpes are coated with a sauce.

Cressonnière refers to a dish garnished or made with watercress.

Croissants are French pastries that are made into the shape of crescents. The recipe is said to have originated in Budapest in 1686 when the city was being besieged by Turks, who tunneled under walls in an attempt to break the siege. They were overheard by bakers working at night who raised the alarm. The city was saved and the bakers were granted the privilege of making a special pastry, shaped into crescents like the crescent moon on the Turkish flag.

Croustade is a case made from pastry or bread that is filled with a savory mixture. To make a croustade from bread, stamp out large rounds with a cookie cutter, bake them in the oven, or fry them in deep fat, then carefully scoop out the centers to form cases. The whole loaf can be used as a croustade if it is scooped out and the outside is decorated with the point of a knife.

Crudités are raw vegetables such as shredded red cabbage, carrots, and celery that are arranged on a platter and usually served as an appetizer.

Crumpets (from England) look like our 'English muffins' but they have a spongy texture and are full of porous holes.

Cubat usually refers to a dish characterized by mushrooms and a mornay sauce. Pierre Cubat was a very successful and wealthy chef to Alexander II, Emperor of Russia. No matter how large the attendance at the Emperor's meals, Cubat was paid according to the number of guests.

Cuisine maigre is the name given to the foods permitted during the fast days ordained by the Church, as opposed to 'cuisine gras' that is forbidden during this period. Cuisine maigre basically consists of simple recipes that rely heavily on fish, using little or no milk products and no meat.

Cuisson is the cooking liquid from meat, fish, poultry or vegetables.

Cumin is a strongly aromatic spice that is an essential ingredient of chili powder and curry powder. It is sometimes used to flavor cheeses, breads or liqueurs.

Curaçao is a liqueur made from the rind of oranges; it was originally made on the Dutch island of Curaçao. Since it became popular, many companies have produced similar liqueurs such as Grand Marnier, Cointreau and Triple Sec.

Curdle means that a smooth mixture has separated into solid and liquid parts. Curdling usually occurs because of overheating or the addition of an acid.

Currants are small fresh acidic berries that are often made into a jam or jelly. They can be red, green, black or white, but red are the most commonly used. Dried currants are completely different — they are tiny seedless dried grapes that have a sharper flavor than raisins.

Curry is a term for a blend of many spices including ginger, chili, coriander, cinnamon, fenugreek, turmeric, mustard, pepper and cloves. Depending on the amount of chili, the blend varies in strength and proportion. In India and the Far East people grind and mix their own blends.

Custard is a cooked mixture of eggs and milk, usually sweetened.

Plum compote

Chicken curry

D

Darne means slice or slab in French and refers to the center cut of a large fish, usually salmon, cod or haddock.

En daube means to braise meat slowly for a long time so it is tender enough to cut with a spoon. A daube is traditionally Provençal but it has become popular all over France and there are many versions.

To deglaze means to dissolve congealed juices from the bottom of a pan. First the food is removed, and excess fat is discarded, then the remaining sediments are heated with stock and wine to make a gravy or sauce.

Dégorger means to remove impurities and strong flavors before cooking. For example, ham should be soaked in cold water for a specified length of time. Vegetables such as eggplant or cucumber should be sprinkled with salt, covered with a heavy plate and left up to 1 hour. Then the salt is washed away and the vegetables are dried with paper towels.

Demi deuil literally means 'half-mourning' and refers to white meats such as poultry or veal that are larded with slices of black truffle. For poultry the truffles are thinly sliced and inserted between the skin and breast meat.

Dépouiller: See Skim.

To devil means to marinate or apply a highly seasoned or spiced paste to food before broiling or frying, often in breadcrumbs.

To dice means to cut food into small squares.

Diable (à la) means deviled and refers to dishes flavored with spices and prepared sauces such as Worcestershire or Tabasco.

Dieppoise (à la) refers to food prepared in the style of Dieppe, a French port on the northern coast, known for its shrimps and mussels that are usually combined with sliced mushrooms and white wine.

Dijonnaise (à la) refers to a dish characterized by Dijon-style mustard. Dijon-style mustard is made from white and black powdered mustard seeds that are mixed with verjuice (the acid juice from large unripened grapes) in place of vinegar, sometimes with the addition of a few herbs.

Dill is an aromatic herb with a delicate flavor that combines well with fish and fresh cucumber and is a main ingredient in the making of pickles.

Diplomat pudding is a baked pudding made with candied fruits, vanilla-flavored Bavarian cream, and sponge ladyfingers soaked in liqueur.

To dissolve means to melt a solid substance, sometimes over heat, usually by mixing with a liquid.

Doria (à la) usually refers to a dish garnished with cucumber.

Dressing is the term given to a liquid that is served on salads. Well-known dressings include vinaigrette and mayonnaise. See Stuffing.

Dubarry (à la) refers to cauliflower. As a garnish it is often cooked in sprigs, then reshaped into miniature cauliflowers and coated with a mornay sauce.

Duchesse potatoes are boiled potatoes that are drained, dried well over heat, then mashed or sieved. Hot milk, butter, seasoning and egg yolks are added, then they are often piped from a pastry bag fitted with a star tube to make a border around cooked dishes.

Dugléré refers to a dish characterized by a velouté sauce with tomatoes and parsley.

Duxelles is a finely chopped mixture of mushrooms, shallots and herbs, cooked in butter and used to flavor soups, sauces and stuffings. The name probably originated in the 17th century with La Varenne, a famous chef, who was an official member of the household of the Marquis d'Uxelles.

E

Egg glaze is a mixture of beaten egg and salt that is brushed over pastry before baking so it will become golden brown and shiny when cooked.

Emmenthal is a Swiss cheese, similar to Gruyère, that is firm, with large 'eyes' and a nut-like flavor; it is both a cooking and table cheese.

Enchiladas are tortillas that are dipped in sauce before frying, then rolled around a filling and covered with sauce before being baked in the oven.

Entrée is the main course of a meal, but in France the entré (entry) is the appetizer.

Entremet means 'between dishes' and used to refer to all vegetables and salads served as the second course, except for the meat. Now, the term entremet is used to refer to any dessert (served after the cheese in France).

Escalope is a very thin slice of meat or chicken that is pounded to make it flat.

Escoffier, Auguste (1847–1935) was known as the 'King of Chefs and the Chef of Kings'. French-born Escoffier was the first chef to break away from elaborately adorned food and inedible garnishes. Originally developed by Carême, these garnishes had become a way to camouflage food of inferior quality. Among the many dishes he created are Peach Melba, for opera singer Dame Nellie Melba, and Strawberries Sarah Bernhardt, for the actress. His cookbooks include 'Le Guide Culinaire' and 'Ma Cuisine'.

Espagnole is the basic brown sauce on which all other brown sauces are based. It is made from root vegetables, a bouquet garni, seasonings, flavorings, and brown bone stock. See Sauces.

Eventail means 'fan' and refers to the arrangements of food in a fan shape on a platter.

F

Farce: See Stuffings.

Fécule (starch) is a very fine potato flour or arrowroot used for thickening soups and sauces.

Fennel is a bulbous white root that looks a little like a fat celery heart, and has a pleasant flavor of anise. Herb fennel is a perennial plant with a very strong taste that goes well with fish.

Fenugreek is a spice with a slightly bitter taste not unlike burnt sugar. Its principle use is for flavoring imitation maple syrup and it is added to curry powder and chutneys.

Feta is a white cheese traditionally made by the shepherds in the mountains near Athens from goats' or ewes' milk. Slightly astringent and salty, it is used in Greek cheese pastries and is also good in salads.

Financière (à la) literally means 'banker's style' and refers to a rich garnish of kidneys, sweetbreads, mushrooms and quenelles.

Fines herbes are a classic blend of herbs that includes chervil, tarragon and chives, all chopped and mixed together. Parsley is not correctly a fine herbe although it is often included. Fines herbes are used to flavor omelets, salads and broiled meats.

Flake means to pull food apart into its natural divisions or to shred into thin pieces.

Flamande (à la) means in the Flemish style and as a garnish for meat usually refers to braised root vegetables.

Flamber (to flame) means to add flavor to food in a pan by pouring warmed spirits, brandy or sherry over the food, igniting and continuing to cook, while burning off the alcohol content; this flame also helps burn off excess fat.

DUCK OR GOOSE
how to carve

1 Set the bird on a board and cut off the legs, remembering that, unlike a chicken, the joints are set under the back. Cut legs in half through the thigh joint or slice meat from the bone.

2 Slip a knife between breastbone and breast to loosen meat. Remove knife. Sever wing joint, angling the knife so that a good piece of the breast meat is left attached to each wing.

3 To slice the breast, make the first cut along the breastbone, then make parallel cuts to it down the breast, always slanting the knife well towards the inside of the bird as you slice.

4 To loosen the slices from the breast of the bird, return the knife along the first cut, then cut firmly up towards the breastbone. This will give good-looking, long slices of meat.

1

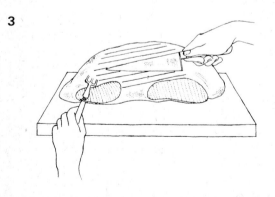

2

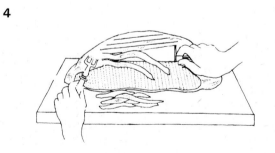

3

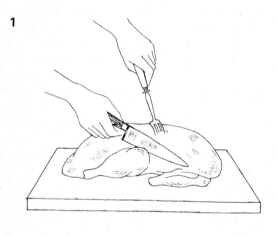

4

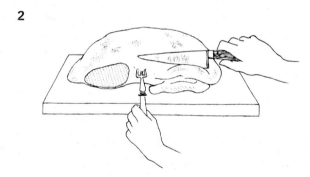

cutting up a small duck/goose

1 *Set the bird on a board; cut along the breastbone. With shears cut through breastbone and each side of backbone, then discard the backbone.*

2 *Lay each half on board and cut diagonally between wing and leg to separate them. This will give four portions each with some breast. Trim away any bone.*

1

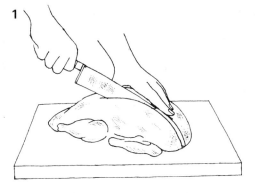

2

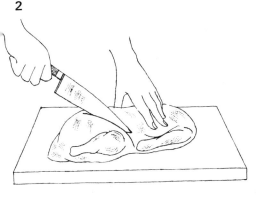

Braised duck

Roast lamb Doria

Fillet of beef with Espagnole sauce

FISH

cleaning and skinning round fish

1 *With a sharp knife, cut down the back with the blade on top of the backbone. Lift off the top fillet*

2 *Slip knife under backbone. Keep close to bone and work down to tail with short strokes to free other fillet*

filleting round fish

1 *After slitting the skin below the head, scrape out the intestine and discard*

2 *Lift tail end to slip knife between flesh and skin and cut flesh away*

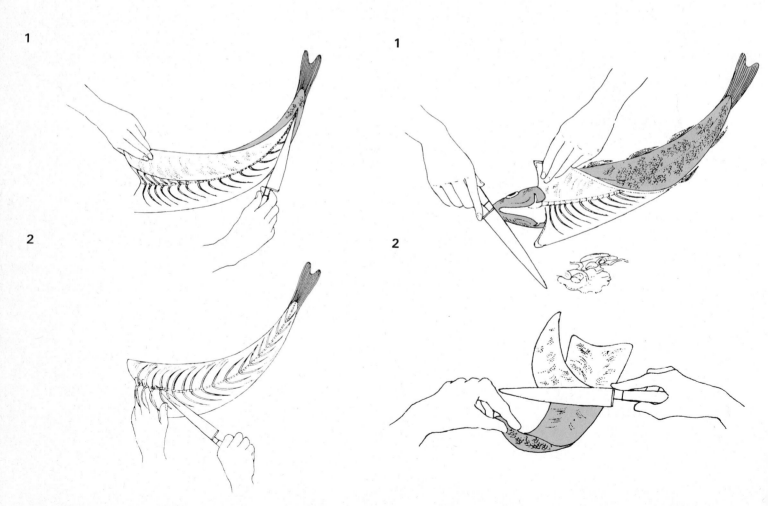

skinning flat fish

Cut off fins, slip thumb about 1 inch under black skin at cut where the fish was cleaned.

Run thumb around fish, keeping it under the skin. Grasp tail end firmly, rip off skin. Repeat on the other side

filleting flat fish

1 Run knife down backbone from center of head out and down to tail to lift off first half of fillet

2 To remove other half fillet on same side, turn fish around and start from tail end

1

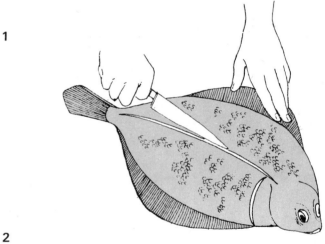

2

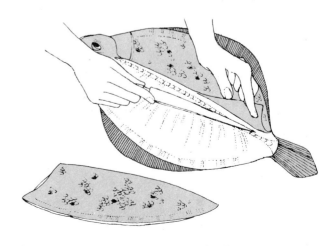

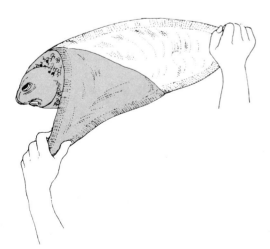

Flan is the favorite dessert of Portugal and Spain. It is a lemon and cinnamon-flavored custard that is baked in a caramel-lined dish, then turned out for serving. The French version of this dish is called crème caramel.

Flans are open pies made with pastry that is lined in a special metal ring laid on a baking sheet. A flan can be filled with a sweet or savory mixture, or with fruit.

Fleurons are small crescents of cooked puff pastry that are used as a garnish.

Florentine (à la) always refers to a dish characterized by spinach; the name comes from the city of Florence, Italy.

Foie gras, a great delicacy, is the liver of a goose that has been specially fattened. It is usually cooked in a pâté flavored with truffles. When used as garnish or flavoring in a hot dish, it does not disintegrate as other liver pâtés are inclined to do. In France any canned pâté made with fattened goose liver can legally be labeled 'pâté de foie gras' but the best known comes from Strasbourg.

To fold is the process of mixing a very light substance with a heavier one without losing any lightness. The heavy mixture is lifted from beneath, usually with a large metal spoon and folded over the light one, but never stirred in a circle.

Fondant is a mixture of sugar and water that is boiled to the soft ball stage ($240°F$ on a sugar thermometer) then worked on a marble slab with a sugar scraper. Fondant is the basis of most chocolate-covered creams and bonbons and is also used for icing gâteaux.

Fondue (literally melted) is a hot cheese mixture made with Gruyère or Emmenthal cheese, white wine and kirsch, that is served at the table in a flameproof casserole set over a burner. Using special long forks, cubes of bread are dipped into the hot mixture. Fondue also refers to any concentrated mixture of vegetable cooked in butter or stock until thick. For example,

Tomato fondue, is a concentrated mixture of tomatoes that have been cooked in butter or oil until thick. It is often seasoned with onion and garlic and is used to flavor or garnish eggs, meat, poultry and fish dishes.

Fondue Bourguignonne is raw beef steak cubes that are dipped into a deep pan of smoking hot oil, then into a selection of spiced sauces in separate dishes.

Fool is a fruit purée mixed with thick, whipped cream.

Frangipane is an almond, sugar and butter mixture that can be used either as part of a pastry or gâteau or on its own as a cake. It is thought to have been invented by an Italian perfumer named Frangipani who had a very sweet tooth. He lived in Paris during the reign of Louis XIII.

Frappés are iced desserts similar to ices. They are frozen in ice trays and often small pieces of fruit are added to the basic mixture of sugar, water and flavorings. Frappés are usually served in sherbet glasses, often topped with whipped cream.

Freeze is to chill food below the freezing point of water ($32°F$). Freezers for storing food should be kept at $0°F$. Refrigerator freezing compartments are often warmer.

Fricadëller (or fricadelles) are balls of raw or cooked meat that may be fried or cooked in a sauce.

Fricandeau (de) is a braised veal dish traditionally served with a purée of sorrel and spinach, or leaf or puréed spinach.

Fricassée is a stew of white meat, poultry, fish, or vegetables usually made with a white or velouté sauce. It can also mean reheated, cooked chicken in a white sauce.

Fritot is a kind of fritter made with small pieces of meat, poultry or variety meats. It is a popular way of serving brains.

Fritters are made from cooked meat, raw or cooked vegetables, or fresh fruit that is dipped in a batter, then fried in deep fat. The word fritters comes from the Celtic word for swelling.

Fritto misto (literally 'mixed fry') is an Italian dish that includes meat, variety meats, fish, poultry and vegetables that are either shallow or deep fried, with or without a coating of egg and breadcrumbs.

Fry 1 Dry: to cook steaks or chops over high heat in fat barely covering the base of a heavy frying pan. 2 Shallow: to cook eggs, fish or breaded chops briskly without burning, in $\frac{1}{4}-\frac{1}{2}$ inch layer of fat. 3 Deep: to immerse and fry food that is coated with batter, breadcrumbs or flour in fat or oil.

Fumet is well reduced fish stock or the essence from cooking fish, meat or game.

G

Galantine is a dish made with a boned chicken, turkey, duck or game bird, or with a boned breast of veal that is spread with stuffing, then rolled and sewn or tied and poached in stock. When cool, it is either sliced or left whole and coated with aspic.

Galette can refer to any sweet or savory mixture that is shaped in a flat round.

Garam masala (Hindustani for 'mixed spice') is a combination of cinnamon, cloves, cardamons, black cumin seeds, nutmeg and mace, ground together and used in Indian dishes.

Garibaldi (à la) usually refers to a dish with Marsala wine. In the nineteenth century, Garibaldi launched the campaign from Marsala (in Sicily) that led to the uniting of Italy under one flag.

To garnish means to decorate a dish either before or after it is cooked. Often a dish takes its name from the garnish.

Gâteau is the French word for cake and usually refers to the classic French cakes with Génoise base.

Gâtinaise usually means a dish containing honey that comes from the Gâtinais area of France, near Orleans.

Gazpacho is a popular Spanish soup that is flavored with garlic and served iced. It contains tomatoes, cucumber, green pepper and breadcrumbs for thickening.

Gefilte fish are dumplings made from pounded fish; they are served on Jewish holidays or on the Sabbath.

Gelatin is a substance used to set molds, aspics and creams. It comes in the form of a white powder or translucent strips that must be softened in water or fruit juice, then dissolved over hot water. Gelatin is made by cooking beef bones, cartilage and tendons together. The word gelatin also refers to a sweet or savory set mold.

Génoise is a rich sponge cake made from beaten eggs and sugar, with the addition of flour and softened butter. Sometimes called Genoese sponge cakes, they are richer and closer textured than sponge cakes, which are made in the same way but contain no fat.

Georgette often refers to dishes characterized by baked potato.

Germiny refers to dishes — usually soups or omelets — that contain sorrel.
See Sorrel

Ghee is made from butter that is cooked over low heat for a long time to clarify it. It is the principle fat used in India for frying.

Ginger is a hot, sweet, clean-flavored spice that gives zest to meat. It comes in root form, fresh preserved in syrup or crystallized as a sweet candy. Ginger is also dried and sold in pieces or ground to a powder. The powder is used in cakes, cookies, and breads.

Glacé is a sugar icing for cakes, candied fruits or cookies. It is made from confectioners' sugar and sugar syrup or water, and can be flavored with chocolate, coffee or vanilla.

Glasse, Hannah is the author of 'The Art of Cookery Made Plain and Easy, By a Lady'. First published in England in 1747, editions of the books continued to be published for 105 years. The wife of an attorney, Hannah Glasse is the first well-known woman cook.

To glaze means to make shiny with egg, water and sugar, or milk. Jam or fruit glaze is used for coating desserts and cakes. Meat glaze is reduced bone stock that is added to sauces. See Meat Glaze.

Gloucester (single and double) is an orange-colored hard Cheddar cheese from England.

Gluten is an elastic substance present in flour that makes a dough hold together. During breadmaking, kneading develops the gluten in the flour. Special semolina flour with a high gluten content is best for pasta.

Gnocchi are Italian pasta made from flour, corn meal or semolina, that are shaped into dumplings, then poached or baked and sprinkled with cheese and butter. Gnocchi can also be made from potatoes.

Fondue bourguignonne

Galantine

Galantine, to prepare

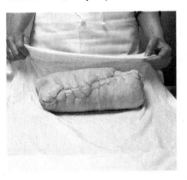

Wrap the sewn-up boned, stuffed veal in a dish towel Fasten dish towel securely with string and a safety pin

Gazpacho

Gorgonzola is a blue veined cheese that comes from a town near Milan, Italy; it is streaked with mold and has a yellowish color. See Blue-veined Cheeses.

Gougère is savory choux pastry mixed with cheese, then baked plain or filled with a savory mixture such as tomatoes, chicken livers and onions. Gougère originated in Burgundy, France, but is now served in many parts of the country.

Goulash (or gulyàs) is a Hungarian stew that is usually seasoned and made with onions and sweet paprika. Gulyàs literally means 'herdsmen's stew' and probably originated from the nomadic herdsmen's habit of cooking in a single pot over a campfire.

Grand Marnier. See Curaçao.

Grand'mère refers to home-style dishes made with ingredients like potatoes, onions and bacon.

Granités are iced desserts that are frozen in ice trays and not stirred during freezing so the consistency is very coarse, almost like rock salt.

To grate means to scrape into small pieces by rubbing hard food, such as cheese or raw vegetables, on a metal or plastic grater.

Gratin (au) means to cook food covered in crumbs, butter, sauce or grated cheese in the oven. The term gratiner means to brown cooked food under the broiler.

To grease means to coat with a thin layer of butter, margarine or shortening.

Grecque (à la) refers to dishes cooked in Greek style, often with olive oil and herbs.

Grenadin is a small piece of veal, resembling a tournedos steak, cut $\frac{1}{2}-\frac{3}{4}$ inch thick and usually taken from the round. Two weigh about $\frac{1}{3}$ lb and serve one person.

Gribiche is a cold sauce made with hard-cooked egg yolks, oil, vinegar, capers, gherkins, herbs and strips of egg white. It is served with fish and cold veal.

Griestorte comes from two German words — 'gries' meaning semolina, and 'torte' a round cake or pie. A griestorte, a round cake made from semolina flour, has an unusual chewy texture.

To grind means to reduce to tiny pieces by working through a food grinder.

Grits are hulled ground corn, rye, oats, rice or buckwheat. Farmers have been eating grits for centuries in Europe, but today, only hominy grits are eaten in the South. Groats, more coarsely ground than grits, are made from corn, barley, buckwheat and oats. Buckwheat groats are also called 'kasha'.
See Hominy.

Gruyères is a valley in the Swiss canton of Fribourg where the original Gruyère was made. A similar cheese, also called Gruyère, is made in the Dauphiné region of France and large quantities of domestic Gruyère are made in this country. True Swiss Gruyère has only a few tiny holes but the French and domestic types have the large holes that are often regarded as characteristic of the cheese. It is ideal for cooking as the texture is dry and it has a rich, nutty flavor, especially when well aged.

Guacamole, a Mexican dish, is a purée of avocados flavored with chili. It can be used as a sauce for raw vegetables or as a dip.

Gumbo is a Creole dish that is a cross between a soup and a stew. It may be made with a variety of ingredients including ham, chicken, shrimps, oysters, crabs, garlic and vegetables. It is always thickened with okra or with filé powder, ground from sassafras leaves. Both thickeners give the characteristic, slightly sticky consistency to the gumbo. The word is a corruption of the Choctaw word for sassafras — 'konbo'.

Hachis (hash) is a finely chopped mixture of cooked meat, fish or poultry. It can have a white or brown sauce added.

Hazelnuts, to brown and grind: bake in a moderately hot oven (375°F) for 8–10 minutes or until browned. Rub the hazelnuts in a rough cloth, then grind in a rotary cheese grater or in a blender.

Hearts of palm are the small hearts of a tropical palm tree — the whole tree must be chopped down to extract them. They can be used raw in salads or cooked with a sauce.

Hollandaise is the basic butter sauce on which many others are based; it is made with egg yolks and butter. See Sauces.

Hominy is corn without the hull and germ. Popular in the South, hominy is usually fried or it may be ground to make hominy grits. See Grits.

Homogenized refers to an emulsified liquid such as homogenized milk, in which the fat particles have been broken up and dispersed.

Hongroise refers to a dish characterized by Hungarian paprika in a sour cream sauce.

Hors d'oeuvre (meaning 'outside the work') are hot or cold finger foods served before a meal or as a first course.

Horseradish is a perennial plant of the mustard family with a hot flavor. Its most important use is as a table relish with roast beef, oysters and tongue.

Hymettus refers to dishes that use honey. The word originates from Mount Hymethus, near Athens, Greece, which is renowned for its fine-tasting honey.

Ices resemble sherbet; both are made from similar mixtures and frozen by the same methods but ices contain no stabilizer. Lack of stabilizer gives an ice a firmer, coarser consistency than a sherbet.

Indienne (a l'), literally in Indian style, usually refers to dishes that contain either curry or chutney or both, accompanied by boiled rice.

To infuse means to steep flavorings in warm, not necessarily boiling, liquid. The flavorings are usually strained out before the liquid is used.

Jams comprise regular jam and conserves. Regular jam is sugar and fresh fruit that is boiled together until thick. Conserves are whole or sliced fruit preserved in heavy syrup — they are usually more syrupy than regular jam but sweeter and richer in flavor.

Japonais is a meringue mixture of ground almonds folded with sugar into stiffly whipped egg whites. For a white Japonais, the almonds are blanched and ground, or they can be toasted, then ground and added to the whites. Japonais is used as a base for gâteaux or as a part of a pastry.

Jardinière (meaning 'garden-style') is a platter or garnish of small carrots, peas, string beans, button onions and small potatoes. It can also be a vegetable soup.

Jelly bag is a cone-shaped bag made of close-textured cotton or linen. Jelly bags are essential when making fruit jellies which cloud easily.

Judic usually refers to a garnish of braised lettuce and scallions. Anna Judic was a celebrated actress in the 19th century who had several dishes created for her by Escoffier.

Julglögg is a Scandinavian hot punch made from aquavit and red Bordeaux wine with flavorings of cardamon, cloves, orange peel and cinnamon stick.

Julienne are fine matchstick strips of meat or vegetables. A julienne strip is usually about $\frac{1}{8}$ inch thick by $1\frac{1}{2}-2$ inches long. The term julienne can also mean a clear vegetable soup (consommé julienne) to which a mixture of finely shredded cooked vegetables has been added. See Consommé.

Juniper berries are the dried fruit of an evergreen tree or bush and they have a bittersweet taste. They are most commonly associated with sauerkraut, game, marinades and gin.

Jus (au) is the term used for meat served in its own natural juices from cooking.

Asparagus with Hollandaise sauce

Fruits for jam making

To knead is the process of pushing dough away with the heel of the hand then bringing it forward with fingers, so all the ingredients become thoroughly combined. When making yeast doughs, kneading distributes the yeast and develops the gluten in the flour.

Kneaded butter (beurre manié). See Butter.

Kosher is the term used for Jewish food prepared in accordance with certain dietary laws.

Kromeski is the name given to small pieces of cooked, creamed chicken, veal or game mixture wrapped in thin strips of bacon before being dipped in batter and fried.

Kugelhopf is the name of a German coffeecake that is made with a rich yeast dough and filled with currants and slivered almonds. The tube pan with a rounded base and fluted sides in which the coffeecake is traditionally made is called a kugelhopf pan.

Kulich is a spiced Russian Easter bread shaped like an Orthodox priest's hat. It is usually decorated with paper roses and cut into rounds for serving with paskha. See Paskha.

Kumquat is a small citrus fruit shaped like an oval orange. The bushes are often used for decoration and the fruits are available preserved.

Kale, a member of the cabbage family, is usually green with large open leaves. The color varies to reddish-brown and tinges of purple and the leaves are either smooth, curled or slightly wavy. The flavor is slightly peppery.

Kasha is made with medium or coarse cracked buckwheat cooked in water or stock and served instead of rice, potatoes or as a stuffing. See Grits.

Kedgeree, the British version of an Indian rice dish 'kitchri', is made from cooked salmon. or smoked haddock, hard-cooked eggs, and boiled rice.

Kirsch is a liqueur made from fermented juice of wild cherries. It is a specialty of the Black Forest region of Germany, and used in many sweet dishes.

Langues de chats or cats' tongues cookies are so called because of their shape — thin, flat and narrow like a cat's tongue. They are served with sparkling wines and iced desserts and are also used as an ingredient in various desserts.

Lard is rendered pork fat, used for frying or as shortening in some pastries.

Larding means the insertion of small strips of fresh pork fat or bacon (called lardons) into the flesh of meat that has very little natural fat. To add flavor, other ingredients, such as anchovy fillets, are used for larding. This prevents meats such as fillet of beef, veal and venison from drying out when roasted. Larding is done by threading lardons through a larding needle and pulling them across the grain of the meat.

Larding needle is used to pull strips of fat (lardons) through meat and game birds that lack natural marbling. Larding needles either have a channel at one end to enclose the fat or a spring at the end to catch the fat so it can be pulled through the meat. They are usually 8–9 inches long.

Lardons are $\frac{1}{4}$-inch thick strips of fat salt pork or bacon ($1\frac{1}{2}$ inches wide) that are used for larding (see Larding). The fat should be chilled before being cut into strips. Lardons can also be added to casseroles and garnishes for flavor; they are cut in $\frac{3}{4}$ X $\frac{1}{4}$ X $\frac{1}{4}$-inch pieces and blanched before using. 'Lard' in French means bacon.

Leavening agents are substances such as yeast, baking soda, baking powder, and cream of tartar, that release a gas when heated and make the bread, cake or biscuit in which they are used expand and rise. Other means of leavening include air, which can be beaten into egg whites, and steam, which is generated when water is heated to a high temperature, as in choux pastry and Yorkshire pudding.

Leicester is a bright orange English Cheddar-type cheese with a creamy texture and a tangy after-taste.

Liaison is a mixture of egg yolk and cream, cornstarch, arrowroot, or kneaded butter (beurre manié) that is used to thicken a sauce or soup at the end of cooking. Another liaison, flour and butter roux, is added at the beginning of cooking. Cornstarch is generally used for fruit and cream pies, arrowroot and kneaded butter for sauces and gravy; egg yolk and cream enriches as well as thickens sauces and soups. See individual names.

Loganberries are red fruits that look like a blackberry and taste like tart raspberries. Grown on the West Coast, they are used for pies, jams and jellies, as they are usually too tart for eating out of hand.

Longhorn is an American Cheddar cheese that is softer in texture than other Cheddars.

Luting paste is a flour and water mixture used to seal terrines and pâtés for cooking. To make it, stir 6–7 tablespoons water into 1 cup flour with a teaspoon or your forefinger to form a paste. Do not stir too much or the paste will become elastic and shrink during cooking.

Lyonnaise (à la) refers to dishes characterized by an onion and potato garnish. It refers to the province of Lyonnais, France.

Mace is akin to nutmeg and can be bought whole as 'blades of mace' or in ground form. Mace is the lacy outer coating of the nutmeg kernel and the two spices can be used interchangeably, most often to flavor fish sauces, soups and gravies.

Macédoine is either a mixture of diced or sliced cooked vegetables that are served in a dressing, or cooked or uncooked fruits in a syrup or liqueur.

To macerate means to soak or infuse (usually fruit) in liqueur or syrup.

Mâconnaise (à la) refers to meat or fish dishes flavored with red wine (a Burgundy, but not necessarily from Mâcon).

Madeira is a fortified wine from the island of Madeira. It is used as a flavoring in sauce for meat, particularly veal and kidneys, and shellfish.

Madeleines are shell-shaped light sponge cakes that are often flavored with orange flower water or grated lemon rind. They are made in special madeleine pans that give the characteristic shape.

Mandoline is a rectangular piece of wood or metal fitted with a plain or fluted sharp blade that can be adjusted to regulate the thickness of slices. It is used for slicing firm vegetables, such as potatoes and turnips, into thin, even rounds.

Mange-tout is the French name for a variety of peas (similar to Chinese peas) that are eaten whole in the pod.

Mangoes are oval red, green or yellow fruits with juicy flesh and a large pit. They are native to Asia. Mangoes are used in many chutneys, pickles, jams and jellies or they can be eaten out of hand.

Maraschino is a liqueur made from cherries. Maraschino cherries are sweet cherries that are pitted, colored with red food coloring, and bottled in a sugar syrup.

Marengo is the name of a chicken dish hastily composed by Napoleon's chef on the night of June 14, 1800, when the Austrians were defeated at the Battle of Marengo. All that was available for the celebration was a small hen, eggs, tomatoes, crayfish and garlic — but the result has become a classic dish.

Macédoine of fresh fruits

To marinate is the process of soaking raw meat, game, fish or poultry in cooked or uncooked spiced mixture (marinade) of wine, oil, herbs and vegetables for a few hours or days. This marinade not only adds flavor but also softens the fibers and tenderizes tough meat or game.

Marjoram is a spicy aromatic herb that is used in stuffing and as a flavoring for lamb. Dried wild marjoram (called oregano) is good when mixed with thyme and savory.

Marmalade is a preserve made from citrus fruits; marmalades generally contain pieces or slices of fruit suspended in a clear jelly.

Marmelade is fruit, usually apple, that is stewed and reduced to a thick, almost solid purée or butter. It is used as a pie or flan filling.

Marmite is a stockpot of copper, earthenware or iron. It was originally the name of the French pot used for making pot-au-feu. Petite marmite is a clear soup made in a marmite pot.

Marrow is the fatty substance found inside beef bones. It is prized for its rich delicate taste. Marrow can be served on its own, sliced and fried, poached in stock, or made into soup with root vegetables.

Marzipan (almond paste) is made from sugar, egg white and ground almonds. It can be rolled and used to cover a cake or tinted with food coloring, then molded into the shapes of fruit and vegetables.

Masa harina is flour made from corn and it is used extensively in Mexican cooking.

Matelote (or sailor-style) is the French name for a fish stew made with wine. The same name is also sometimes given to dishes made with veal and poultry.

Mayonnaise is a cold sauce made from egg yolks and oil. The many variations include Sauce Remoulade, Sauce Tartare, and Sauce Gribiche. See Sauces.

Meat glaze (glace de viande) is made from strained brown bone stock that is boiled for a fairly long time until it is a thick, glossy, brown syrup. The finished glaze will set to a firm jellied consistency and can be stored for several months in a covered container in the refrigerator. It is used to flavor sauces and sometimes cut into small shapes to garnish a platter of meat. At one time in France the chef who made the meat glaze was permitted to sell any extra to earn pocket money.

Ménagère (à la) means housewife and refers in cooking to plainly prepared dishes like mashed potatoes with diced onion and ham, or meat garnished with carrots, turnips and potatoes.

Meringue is a light and airy mixture of beaten egg whites and sugar. It is thought to have been invented in the early 18th century by a Swiss pastrycook called Gasparini. He worked in the town of Mehrinyghen, from which the name 'meringue' is said to be derived. The three types of meringue are Suisse, Italienne and cuite. Suisse is made by beating the whites until stiff, then folding in the sugar. To make meringue Italienne the whites are beaten until stiff, then sugar syrup boiled to the soft ball stage is beaten into the whites. For meringue cuite, (meaning cooked), the egg whites and confectioners' sugar are combined in a bowl over hot water and beaten together.

Meunière is the term used to describe the method of frying small whole fish or fish fillets in butter, then finishing them with meunière butter — butter cooked to a nut-brown color, then flavored with lemon juice and fresh herbs and poured, foaming, over the fish.

Milanaise (à la), in the style of Milan, usually refers to dishes with macaroni, cheese, tomato and ham.

Mimosa refers to dishes garnished with sieved hard-cooked egg yolk and egg white — the egg yolk resembles the flowers of the mimosa tree.

Mincemeat is a mixture of candied citrus peels, raisins, currants, spices, chopped apples and nuts, suet, and rum or brandy. Originally cooked chopped meat was an ingredient and the fruits and spices acted as a preservative in the days before refrigeration. It is a traditional Thanksgiving and Christmas dish when filled into a pastry shell.

Mint comes in many species — heart-mint, apple mint, orange mint, horsemint and lambmint; peppermint and spearmint are the most popular. Mint is used in sauces, vinegars, salads, candies, teas and often to flavor small new potatoes.

Mirepoix is the mixture of diced or sliced vegetables used for flavoring braises and sauces. A mirepoix is sweated (cooked gently for a few minutes in butter) to draw out the flavor. Diced ham or bacon and bay leaf are sometimes included and the mirepoix is always strained out of the final sauce.

Monosodium glutamate is a natural product made from glutamic acid and is used to heighten the flavor of a dish. Usually called MSG, it is used extensively in Japanese and Chinese cooking.

Montmorency, the most popular European variety of tart cherry, has given its name to sweet and savory dishes with a cherry garnish.

Morels (morilles in French) are dark wrinkled mushrooms with a very rich aromatic flavor. They grow wild in many areas of the U.S. but are very hard to find, so they are expensive. Morels are available dried or in cans.

Moscovite is a molded cream dessert usually either filled with fruit or garnished with fruit after being turned out. Moscovites are also the name given to small canapés covered with aspic.

Moule à manqué is a French cake pan with sloping sides, often used for gelatin molds because they are less likely to collapse while unmolding. The moule à manqué is said to have been named by a Paris patissier who criticized a cake mixture made by his chief baker. The baker, who did not like his cake called a failure (un manqué), added butter, covered the cake with praline, and sold it to a customer, who came back for more. It was christened 'un manqué' and a special mold was designed for it.

Moussaka is a Middle Eastern dish made from ground lamb and eggplant cooked together in layers in a baking dish, with a topping of white sauce.

Mousse is a sweet smooth mixture, airy, but rich, made from eggs, sugar, cream and flavorings such as coffee, chocolate or fruit. Savory mousses, set with gelatin, can be made from salmon, lobster, veal, chicken or ham, and are usually served chilled.

Mousseline is a mixture resembling a mousse — it is lightly spongy and particularly delicate in flavor and is usually served hot. It can be made with fish, chicken, rabbit or veal that is ground, then pounded in a mortar and pestle while gradually working in egg whites, cream and seasoning. The most famous mousseline is made into fish dumplings called quenelles. See Quenelles.

Mulligatawny is a soup made from lamb, root vegetables and apples, flavored with curry powder. It is one of the dishes created by the British in India.

Mustard seed is a spice often added to pickles and salad dressings. When ground to a powder, it is used to make mustard sauce, to flavor mayonnaise and salad dressings, and many cheese dishes.

Nantua (à la) is the name given to dishes that include a shrimp or crayfish garnish or purée.

Naturel (au) is the French term that means uncooked or plainly boiled.

Navarin is the name of a lamb stew cooked with root vegetables. The word comes from the Greek town of Navarino where the decisive battle for Greek independence was fought in 1827. The French chef Carême, who liked to name his recipes for battles, wrote a recipe for a navarin in 1830.

Nesselrode pudding is made with chestnut purée, egg custard and cream, flavored with candied fruits, raisins and maraschini liqueur, then frozen in a bombe mold. The pudding is named for Count Nesselrode, a famous Russian statesman.

Niçoise (à la) usually refers to a dish characterized by tomatoes, anchovies, tuna fish, garlic and black olives. It is the term used for dishes that originated around Nice, in Provence, France.

Nivernaise (à la) refers to a dish characterized by carrots; the name comes from the Nivernais region in France.

Noisette 1 A small 'nut' of lamb made from boned loin or rack that is rolled, tied and cut in neat 1–1½ inch slices. 2 Flavored with hazelnuts. 3 Butter cooked to a nut-brown color.

Normande (à la) usually refers to braised fish dishes coated with a cream sauce (sauce Normande). When the sauce is added to cuts of meat or chicken, it includes cider and sometimes Calvados (a strong apple brandy) that is made in Normandy. Normandy is also known for its apples and pears, butter and cream, any of which can make a dish à la normande.

Nutmeg is a sweet, nutty spice that is popular in cakes, cookies and custards and is used in white sauces. Nutmeg is about the size of a large acorn and, although available ground, it is at its best only when freshly grated at home.

Nut milk is made by infusing dried flaked coconut or ground almonds in boiling water for 1 hour. It is often used in Indian cooking.

Meringues

Moussaka

O

Orloff refers to a way of preparing veal by cooking a roast of veal, then carving it, spreading each slice with mornay or soubise sauce and reassembling the whole roast. The name is said to have come from an 18th century Russian nobleman, Count Orloff.

Orly usually means fish or meat that is coated with a rich batter, then fried in deep fat until crisp.

Osso buco is an Italian dish made with slices of veal shank cooked in a tomato sauce.

Oysters Rockefeller originated in 1889 at Antoine's, the celebrated restaurant founded in New Orleans by M. Antoine Alciatore. The original recipe has never been disclosed but a reasonable facsimile includes oysters on the half shell topped with a mixture of finely chopped spinach, celery and scallion, mixed with butter, Tabasco and Pernod. According to legend, the recipe was named when one of the customers tasted it and said 'Why this recipe is as rich as Rockefeller'.

P Q

Paella is a saffron-flavored Spanish rice dish that includes mussels, chicken, pork or ham, peppers, and garlic. All the ingredients are cooked together in a special shallow two-handled pan.

Panada is a binding agent of choux pastry, thick béchamel sauce or breadcrumbs that is used to thicken fish, meat or vegetable cream molds and mousselines.

Papaya is a round fruit resembling a melon that has a sweet musky flavor; its juice is used to tenderize meat.

Papillote (en) is the French word for 'cocoon' and means to wrap meat, fish or poultry in a buttered paper case, then cook and serve it in the case. This conserves juices and aromas, especially of delicate foods.

Paprika is the ground red powder of the pepper plant and the Hungarian name for sweet pepper. It varies in strength from hot to sweet and mild, but always has a definite flavor.

Parboil means to begin the cooking process by boiling until half-cooked, as with potatoes before roasting.

Pare means to remove a very thin layer from the surface of fruits or vegetables with a knife or vegetable peeler.

Parfaits are rich iced desserts made with an egg mousse base and lightly flavored whipped cream. They are often layered with meringues or ladyfingers and frozen in individual clear glasses so the layers can be seen. The consistency should be just firm enough to hold its shape, not stiff like ice cream.

Parisienne (à la) usually refers to a garnish of tiny white button mushrooms called 'champignons de Paris' in French. They are left whole and, before cooking, the stems are trimmed level with the caps so the mushrooms keep their shape.

Parmentier was an 18th-century Frenchman who introduced the potato to France. Parmentier refers to a dish garnished with potatoes.

Parmesan is a close-grained Italian cheese whose dry texture and subtle but pervasive flavor make it perfect for cooking.

Parsley is the most common herb and is used widely as a garnish, fried with fish, or freshly chopped as a flavoring. The bright green sprigs often garnish platters of cold meats and a little chopped with dried herbs brings out the flavor of the dried herb.

Paskha is the traditional sweetened cheesecake served during the Russian orthodox Easter. It is shaped in a special wooden pyramid which marks the letters XB on one side, standing for 'Christ is Risen'. Paskha is always served with kulich. See Kulich.

Pasta is a flour and water paste, usually with eggs added, that is cut into different shapes such as spaghetti, macaroni and vermicelli. Pasta is said to have been invented in China, but it has been adopted by the Italians and is now almost always associated with Italian dishes.

Pasteurize means to heat milk or other liquids to a temperature between 130—180°F to kill some of the bacteria and prevent fermentation.

Pastry is a basic mixture of flour, fat and water with milk, sugar, egg or cream added, depending on the kind. Basic pastries include pie, rich pie, French flan (pâte sucrée), rough puff, puff (pâte feuilletée) and choux (pâte a choux).

Pastry & Tartlets. See page 111.

Pâté is a savory mixture usually made from ground chicken, calves' or pigs' liver with the addition of other meat, poultry or game. It is always highly seasoned and varies from smooth and velvety to coarse in texture.

Pâtisserie is the French word for a pastry, small cake or gâteau.

Paupiette is a strip of meat, poultry or fish that is filled with a stuffing, then rolled into a small cylinder and cooked.

Pavlova is a meringue cake filled with whipped cream and fresh fruit. Both Australia and New Zealand claim the honor of having created the dessert for the famous Russian ballerina, Anna Pavlova (1885—1931).

Paysanne means peasant fashion and refers to homey dishes.

Peach Melba is a dessert of freshly poached peaches set on a bed of vanilla ice cream and topped with a spoonful of raspberry purée. It was created by Escoffier for the famous soprano Dame Nellie Melba. When first served, the peach and ice cream lacked the raspberry purée and sat on a swan carved from a block of ice, but Escoffier added the purée a few years later.

Pectin is a natural, gum-like substance which acts as a setting agent for preserves so they will jell. It is present to some extent in most fruit, but if fruit with a very low pectin content is used for preserving, commercially prepared pectin can be added. Apples, blackberries, cranberries, red currants, gooseberries, grapefruit, lemons, oranges and plums are generally rich in pectin.

Peppers, fresh, how to peel: broil the pepper or hold it over a flame until the skin is charred all over. Using a knife, peel off the skin and rinse the pepper under running water, if necessary.

Peppercorns are the dried berries of the plant Piper nigrum. Black peppercorns have the outer husk removed and they should be bought in small quantities and ground at home in a peppermill as ground pepper is less pungent and aromatic. White peppercorns are used to season foods when specks of black pepper would spoil the appearance of the finished dish.

Pepperoni is a kind of salami made from coarsely ground pork and beef, flavored with ground red pepper and spices.

Peppers, bell, are a seeded red or green fruit of the Capsicum family. They are often referred to as 'sweet peppers' to distinguish them from the hotter chili peppers, and are eaten raw in salads and cooked as a vegetable or garnish for many meat and poultry dishes.
See Chilies.

Perigourdine (à la) refers to dishes characterized by truffles.

Pestle and mortar consist of a thick bowl of marble or stone (mortar) and a thick short instrument (pestle) for pounding spices or other ingredients into a smooth powder or paste.

Petits fours are tiny pastries that are easy to eat in one mouthful. They take their name from the small ovens in which they were originally baked. The ovens were developed in the mid-17th century when La Varenne, the famous French pâtissier, recommended that cooks use them for baking small quantities of pastries. Petits fours are served in paper cases, either for dessert after a large dinner, or with coffee.

Phyllo is a pastry in sheets as thin as tissue paper that is used widely in the Middle East for making sweet and savory dishes.

Pickle is the brine used in preserving or salting meats. Pickles are also vegetables (usually soaked in brine first) that are preserved in vinegar.

Pickling salt is a fine-grained, pure salt with no additives. It is particularly good for pickles because it leaves no cloudy residue when dissolved.

Pickling-spice is a mixture of whole spices (peppercorns, allspice, mace, etc.) used for pickling.

Pilaf (or pilau in Indian) is a rice dish made from long grain rice sautéed in fat with onion, then cooked in stock. It is popular throughout India, Persia and the Middle East.

Pimientos are heart-shaped red peppers with a sweet flavor that almost always come canned as they spoil rapidly.
See Chilies.

PASTRY FINISHES

1 When using only one layer of pastry, **forking** the edge is adequate. Press the back of the fork prongs into the pastry edge.

2 When using two layers, **seal** edges by placing the side of the left forefinger on top of the pastry edge and, with the back of a broad-bladed knife, make indentations in double edges to seal. This prevents layers splitting when baked.

3 To **scallop**, indent by pressing the left thumb on top of the outer edge. Draw the back of the knife towards the center for $\frac{1}{2}$ inch, repeating all the way around. Leave $\frac{3}{4}$ inch between cuts for savory pies, $\frac{1}{4}$ inch for sweet ones.

4 **Crimp** by pinching the pastry edge between thumb and forefinger of each hand, twisting slightly in opposite directions.

5 **Flute** by placing a forefinger on the pastry edge, then pinching pastry with the forefinger and thumb of the other hand. Repeat all around the pie at $\frac{1}{2}$ inch intervals.

1

2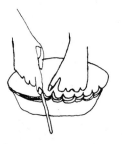

3

4

5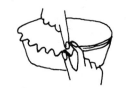

PASTRY BOATS & TARTLET SHELLS
how to make

To line small molds with dough, arrange molds close together near the pastry board. Roll out the dough on the board until just under $\frac{1}{4}$ inch thick. Lift onto the rolling pin and lay gently on top of the molds. Take a small piece of dough and dip it in flour. Use this to work the dough down into each boat or tartlet mold. Take the rolling pin and roll it over the tops of the little molds. This neatly cuts the pastry off the top of each one. Lift up each tin mold and pat the pastry down with your thumb dipped in flour. Put a small piece of wax paper or foil, crumpled, and a few grains of rice into each mold. Paper and rice hold the pastry in position while it bakes. Bake blind in a moderately hot oven (375°F) for about 8 minutes or until pastry is lightly browned. Remove paper and rice and leave pastry shells until nearly cold before removing them from molds.

 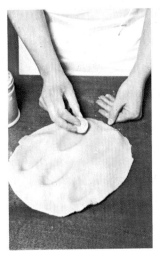 

Apple pie

OMELET
how to make

To make an omelet: stir eggs with a fork

Start to turn omelet over with a palette knife

Fold over, with pan tilted

Tip omelet onto a plate

P *continued*

Fresh pineapple, to peel and cut: slice off bottom of pineapple with serrated-edge knife. Hold pineapple firmly and with a sharp stainless steel knife cut down between 'eyes' at a 45° angle. The pineapple eyes should come out easily in strips. Remove plume, slice flesh thinly and cut out core with a grapefruit corer. This method of peeling and coring disposes of 'eyes' but avoids waste.

To pipe means to shape a mixture using a pastry bag fitted with a tube. Whipped cream, butter cream frosting and royal icing are piped in rosettes, flowers and patterns to decorate sweet dishes. Almost any savory mixture of the same consistency such as mashed potatoes, butter or cream cheese can also be piped. Mixtures such as meringue and choux pastry may also be piped into neat shapes before baking. See page 117.

Piquante means a sharp or stimulating flavor which gives its name to a brown sauce flavored with capers, shallots, gherkins and white sauce.

Piroshki are savory Russian pastries filled with a fish, meat or cabbage mixture and served with borscht.

Pistachio nuts are valued in cooking for their sweet delicate flavor and for their bright green color. Some have a red skin (those with red shells have been dyed) and others have beige skins and shells.

To Pit means to remove stones or seeds from fruit.

Pita is an Arab bread baked in large flat rounds that puff around the edge and become slightly hollow in the center.

Pith is the white part of citrus fruits between the peel and the flesh. It can taste very bitter so should always be removed when fruit is peeled.

Pizza is made with rounds of bread dough baked with a variety of toppings such as sausage, anchovy, cheese, tomato, mushroom and onion. Pizza originated in the area around Naples, Italy.

Plantains are very similar to bananas; they are green in color and must be boiled or baked before eating.

To poach means to cook gently in trembling (not boiling) liquid. Fish, poultry, fruit, pasta and eggs can all be poached. See Simmer.

Poêler means to cook meat or poultry with a vegetable garnish in a partially covered casserole. The word literally means 'to cook in a frying pan'.

Poivrade refers to the addition of pepper; sauce poivrade is a piquant sauce made with white wine, vinegar, stock and peppercorns.

Pont l'Evêque is a soft cheese similar to Camembert but with a stronger flavor and a square shape; it comes from Calvados, in the Normandy region of France.

Poppy seeds have a nutty but subtle flavor that gives an interesting taste and texture to pastries and desserts. They are also used to top breads.

Port is a fortified dessert wine from Portugal that is used in making sauces.

Port-salut is a semi-soft ripened cheese from France. The inside is creamy yellow and the outside is dark orange.

Portugaise (à la) usually means a tomato fondue (a concentrated purée of fresh tomatoes) made with oil and butter and flavored with onion, garlic and parsley. The term can also refer to any garnish prepared in the style of Portugal.

Potato starch is often used for thickening sauces and soups at the end of cooking. It thickens as soon as it comes to a boil, but if boiling is continued, it tends to thin again. Potato starch will leave a sauce or syrup almost clear.

To pot roast means to cook a cut of meat or poultry (after browning) by simmering or steaming it slowly, usually in the oven. The meat may be roasted in a covered casserole in its own juices with a little liquid. The lid must be tight-fitting.

Poultry shears are specially designed to cut the bones of birds. At the base of one of the saw-edged blades is a semi-circle for cracking bones.

To pound means to reduce to a powder or smooth paste. Pounding is usually done in a mortar and pestle, but a heavy bowl and the end of a rolling pin will do instead.

Praline is a mixture of caramelized sugar and almonds which is ground or crushed before being used as a flavoring for sweet dishes. The word praline dates from the time of Louis XIII, when The Duc de Choiseul-Praslin offered his favorite mistress a new confection, which was such a success that a confectionery shop was opened to sell it.

Preserve means to cure, smoke, can or freeze meats, fish, poultry or vegetables. It is also the name given to fruit cooked with sugar to form a jam or conserve.

Princesse (à la) usually refers to dishes characterized by a garnish of asparagus tips.

Printanièr (à la) refers to a garnish of fresh spring vegetables cut into various shapes, cooked separately, then arranged on a platter.

Provençale (à la) refers to dishes using oil, tomatoes, peppers, eggplants, garlic, olives and other specialties of the Provence region of southern France.

Puchere is a Spanish stew made from beans, meat, sausage, and poultry. The broth is usually served separately as a soup, followed by the meat and poultry.

Puff Pastry (pâte feuilletée) is a crisp airy pastry that rises in the oven 3–4 times the height of the original dough. The dough is wrapped around a cake of butter, then rolled and folded 6 times to make the innumerable layers. The best known puff pastry dishes are bouchées (mouthsful), vol-au-vent (puff of wind) and mille feuilles (thousand layers), but in French cuisine the dough is used in many other ways.

Purée is a mixture of fruit, vegetables or meat that is sieved or blended to a thick cream. The ingredients are usually precooked before puréeing.

Quatre épices (four spices) is a French spice mixture consisting of white pepper, ginger, nutmeg and cloves.

Quenelles are oval dumplings made from fish, chicken, rabbit or veal. They are made from a mousseline mixture (pounded fish, chicken, rabbit or veal with the addition of egg white, seasoning and cream) that is poached in simmering salted water, then served with a sauce.

Quiche is a savory egg custard flavored with cheese, ham or fish and baked in a pie shell. The most famous version is quiche Lorraine, made with cheese, ham or bacon and sometimes onion, which is named after the district of France bordering on Germany. The word is derived from the dialect spoken in Lorraine and can be traced back to küchen, the German word for cake.

Ragoût is usually a brown stew made of pieces of meat or fish that are cooked slowly without thickening. A ragoût can also be white, for example Irish stew which is not browned before cooking.

Ramekins are small heatproof dishes shaped like miniature soufflé dishes. They are used for making individual egg dishes, custards or pâtés.

Rare means meat that is roasted or broiled until deep pink. See Saignant.

Rechauffée literally means reheated and refers to a mixture of cooked meat, fish, game or poultry that is made into a new dish and reheated.

To reduce means to boil down a sauce or liquid to concentrate the flavor and, sometimes, to thicken the consistency.

To refresh means to pour cold water over previously cooked or blanched and drained food. This 'sets' the color of vegetables and stops the cooking. Variety meats are refreshed to clean them and wash away any scum.

To refrigerate is to store food at about 40°F so the bacteria that cause spoilage are relatively inactive.

Reine (à la) traditionally refers to puréed white meat of chicken with a sauce suprême (a velouté sauce enriched with egg yolks and cream).

Rémoulade is a cold sauce made from mayonnaise with the addition of capers, gherkins, herbs, mustard and anchovy. However, celeri remoulade is celeriac (root celery) cut into strips and tossed with an eggless mayonnaise made from mustard, seasonings, vinegar and oil beaten in drop by drop.

To render means to melt down fat gently into liquid, then strain, or boil with a little water and strain when clear.

Ravenir means to fry lightly without really cooking.

Ribbon is the term used to describe the degree to which eggs and sugar are beaten when making a whisked sponge cake, génoise or egg mousse. When the beater is lifted, the mixture should make a trail on itself that stays for 10 seconds.

Ricotta is a bland, fresh cheese resembling unsalted cottage cheese. It is used extensively in Italian cooking in both sweet and savory dishes.

A PIPING CONE
how to make

1 *Fold a 10 inch square of wax or silicone paper; cut into two triangles. With center point up, fold one long edge to meet right-angled point.*

2 *Take the other long edge and bring it over and around to back until all the points of paper triangle meet at center back to form a cone or bag*

3 *Fold over the area where all three points of cone meet. Firmly crease this flap with a fingernail so as to prevent cone from unfolding.*

4 *Snip a little bit off point of cone; drop in decorating tube to see if it fits. If necessary, carefully cut more off tip so tube fits tightly*

5 *To start piping, drop decorating tube into the bottom of the paper cone and fill it with icing. Before using, fold over the top of the cone so that it presses on the icing.*

PIPING DECORATION

1 *Before starting any decoration, practice the shapes. If you want to decorate a cake with flowers, practice making the centers of flowers by building up a number of small circles, one on top of another.*

2 *Make a fresh piping cone; this time cut a small 'v' at the point. Practice making petals (without a tube) by pushing icing through cone onto a firm surface; quickly draw cone away to make sharp point.*

3 *For finished flowers: pipe onto silicone paper first petals for outside of each flower, then pipe second row petals inside. (With experience, flowers can be piped directly onto the cake.)*

4 *Pipe centers and leave the completed flowers on the paper until they are dry. Carefully lift flowers off paper with the tip of a knife. Attach to cake with a dab of icing on the bottom of each flower*

1

2

3

4
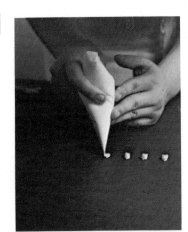

Pizzas

Puff pastry

Rijstafel is an Indonesian specialty based on rice with a large selection of accompaniments. The dishes, often served buffet-style, include such things as poached chicken with rice, barbecued pork kebabs (satés), shrimp and corn fritters, and a selection of fruit and vegetable salads.

Rillettes are a type of pork pâté made from unsmoked pork belly and goose, rabbit, chicken or turkey; they are usually packed into small brown crocks. The best rillettes are made around Tours, on the Loire river in France.

Rissoler means to brown slowly in fat.

Rissoles are made from mixtures of cooked meat, poultry or finely chopped hardcooked eggs bound with a thick sauce. They are usually covered with pastry and formed into crescent-shaped turnovers, before being fried in deep fat.

To roast means to cook by direct heat in an oven. Meat, poultry, game and fish can all be roasted. Roasting was originally done on a spit over an open fire. The outside of the meat browned evenly and was continually basted by its juices as it turned.

Rosemary is one of the most fragrant herbs and comes from an evergreen shrub. It goes well with lamb and pork and was once used as a magic charm against witches. Rosemary adds flavor to stuffings, soups and salad dressings.

Roquefort is a blue-veined cheese with a yellowish tinge; it is made from curds of ewe's milk mixed with fine breadcrumbs. True Roquefort comes from the place of the same name in the Aveyron district of France, where the cheeses mature in cool natural caves to acquire their characteristic green mold. See Blue-veined Cheeses.

Rossini usually refers to a dish made with small cuts of meat, foie gras and truffles coated with a Madeira sauce. Rossini was an 18th century Italian composer.

Roulade means roll. It refers either to a piece of meat, usually pork or veal, that is spread with stuffing, then rolled and often braised or poached, or to a sweet or savory soufflé mixture that is baked in a jelly roll pan or paper case, then filled with a contrasting filling and rolled.

Rutabaga (also known as Swedish turnip or swede) is a yellow or white root vegetable somewhat resembling a turnip; it should be cooked in the same way.

Roux is a liaison of a fat and flour mixture that is used to thicken many sauces. There are three types of roux — white (blanc), blond (blond) and brown (brun). A white roux is not cooked after the flour is added, a blond roux is cooked until straw-colored and a brown roux is cooked until it is a deep brown color.

Sablé (sandy) means very delicate rich pastry, with a short crumbly texture. Sablé pastry is always made with a high proportion of butter to flour and can be sweet (when an equal amount of sugar is added) or savory. The dough is often shaped into cookies that are sandwiched together with jam or with a creamy savory mixture.

Safflower is a plant with leaves like thistles and red or orange flowers. It is native to India and the Middle East and is used for a dye and to make oil.

Saffron the most expensive spice, comes from the dried stigmas of the autumn crocus and each stigma is picked by hand. Saffron has an affinity for rice and is essential to such dishes as paella and bouillabaisse.

Sage is a perennial herb with an affinity for turkey, pork and veal; it is often used in stuffings.

Saignant ('bleeding') is the term used for extremely rare meat or game that has been roasted or broiled. When the meat is cut, the blood runs.

St. Hubert is the patron saint of hunters. He was converted to Christianity when he was hunting on a Good Friday and saw a vision of the Crucifix between the horns of the stag he was about to kill. The name is often given to game dishes.

Sake is a rice wine that is heated in the bottle, poured into a tiny jug and served as an accompaniment to Japanese meals.

Salé means 'salty' in French and is often used to describe savory dishes. It is also the name of a savory cheese pie. Pré salé refers to lamb raised on salt marshes in France.

Salmis a form of ragoût, is a stew made from feathered game or poultry that is first lightly roasted, then cut up and gently simmered for a short time in a rich brown sauce.

Salpicon is the name given to a mixture of ingredients that have been cut into shreds or strips. It may be served as a garnish, or used as a filling for pastry cases. Salpicons are often bound with a rich white or brown sauce.

Satés are spicy little Indonesian kebabs made from beef, pork or chicken. They are often part of the rijstafel table. See Rijstafel.

Sauces (savory) fall into three categories: white, brown and butter. The basic 'mere' (or mother) white sauces, made with a butter and flour roux and milk or stock, include white sauce (made with milk), béchamel (made with milk infused with seasonings) and velouté (made with stock and often enriched with egg yolk and cream). Other white sauces based on these 'mother' sauces are: mushroom (chopped mushrooms with white or béchamel sauce); mornay (white sauce with cheese); soubise (white or béchamel sauce with puréed onions); caper (white or béchamel sauce with capers); parsley (velouté sauce with puréed parsley); suprême (velouté sauce with the addition of egg yolks, cream and sometimes butter); and aurore (white sauce with tomato purée).

Brown sauces are also made with a butter and flour roux, but cooked to a dark brown with stock added. Espagnole is the 'mother' brown sauce, made with brown stock, root vegetables and seasonings. Other brown sauces based on espagnole include demi-glace (with the addition of sherry and butter); bigarade (made with the juice of a bitter or Seville orange); Bordelaise (red Bordeaux wine); chasseur (sliced mushrooms); Madère (Madeira); Perigueux (truffles); Robert (white wine vinegar and gherkin pickles).

Butter sauces are based on egg yolks and vinegar or lemon juice to which butter is added. The 'mother' butter sauce is hollandaise, and other butter sauces include bearnaise (flavored with vinegar, chopped herbs and meat glaze); maltaise (made with the juice from blood oranges); mousseline (the addition of whipped cream); and choron (flavored with tomato paste). Sauce blanche au beurre is also a butter sauce, but made from a butter and flour roux to which boiling water and butter are added. Among the variations are caper sauce, mustard sauce, and sauce Vénitienne (made with the addition of puréed spinach and fresh herbs.)

Sauces (sweet) are not based on a standard recipe, but they can be divided into categories: chocolate sauces, fruit sauces, hard sauces, and sauces based on eggs. The most famous egg sauce is vanilla custard, made with egg yolks, sugar and milk. Other egg sauces such as sabayon and mousseline are made with eggs beaten with sugar and flavoring until light. Hard sauces are all based on a mixture of equal amounts of sugar and unsalted butter beaten with a flavoring such as rum, lemon or brandy. Popular fruit sauces include pineapple sauce, orange cream sauce and Melba sauce made from raspberry purée.

Sauerbraten (literally sour roast' in German) is beef that is marinated in vinegar and wine to give a characteristic sharp flavor, then braised with vegetables and served with a rich sauce.

Sauerkraut literally means sour or fermented cabbage and is made by shredding firm white cabbage, then leaving it for 4–6 weeks in brine to ferment.

Sauter means 'to jump' and is the term used to describe brisk cooking in a small quantity of butter or oil. In the old French kitchens, shallow straight-sided pans with a long handle were used for sautéing, and the food was turned by tossing it in the air.

Savarin is the rich liqueur-soaked yeast cake that is traditionally baked in a ring mold, often called a savarin mold. It is a variation of kugelhopf and babas.

Savory is the term used to describe any dish without sugar. It is also the name of an aromatic herb similar to marjoram; the herb savory has an affinity for peas and lentils, for dishes including tomato, and stuffings for meat or poultry.

Savoy cabbage has dark-green curly rough leaves and a very mild flavor.

Savouries are highly-seasoned small dishes such as herring roes on toast that are traditionally served at the end of a British dinner. Originally they were served to clean the palate before the port was passed after the meal.

To scald means to heat a liquid such as milk to just under boiling point. Tomatoes and peaches are scalded to facilitate peeling.

Scallops are small white shellfish that are found in large shells. There are two kinds: bay scallops, which are scarce and cherished because of their sweet nut-like flavor and sea scallops, which have a robust taste and are more widely available.

To score means to mark with a series of shallow, even cuts.

To sear means to brown food over fierce heat for a few minutes to seal in natural juices. This often precedes stewing.

Seasoned flour is flour mixed with salt and pepper; it is used for coating foods before they are fried.

Seasoning always means salt and pepper in the Grand Diplôme Cooking Course, but in general it is used to refer to all flavorings. To 'correct' seasoning is to taste towards the end of cooking to see if more salt, pepper or other flavors are needed, then to adjust accordingly.

Semolina is the hard portion of wheat that remains after the flour, bran and chaff have been removed. There are two types of semolina — one is made from regular wheat and used for desserts, and the other comes from hard durum wheat and is used for all good quality homemade or commercial pasta.

Fish roulade

Savarin chantilly

S *continued*

Sesame seeds, one of the sources of polyunsaturated fats, give an interesting taste and texture to breads, candies, cookies and cakes. They are a popular ingredient in Asian cooking and are used to make tahina paste, a standard Middle Eastern condiment.

Shallots are part of the onion family and grow like garlic in a cluster on a common vine. Their mild flavor is a good addition to soups, sauces and stews, and they are often added to dishes containing onion to enhance the flavor.

Shashlik are Russian and Middle Eastern kebabs containing cubes of lamb and pieces of onion; they may be broiled or grilled.

Shortening is solid vegetable or animal fat that gives a 'short' crisp quality to pastry and cakes. Fats with the least liquid have the greatest shortening power.

Shoya is Japanese soy sauce and is less salty than the Chinese variety. It is a pungent brown liquid flavoring made principally from soybeans and roasted corn.

To shred means to cut or break into uneven strips.

To sieve means to work food through a strainer or food mill to make a purée.

To sift is to shake a dry, powdered substance through a sieve or sifter to remove any lumps and give lightness.

To simmer means to cook in liquid at about 195°F or just below boiling point so that bubbles occasionally break through the surface.

Simmons, Amelia was the author of the first wholly American cookbook. Dated 1796, 'American Cookery' includes recipes for applesauce pie, Indian slapjack, pickled watermelon rind and American cookies.

To skim (dépouiller) means to remove fat or scum from the surface of sauces, soups or stocks. This is done by bringing the liquid to the boil very slowly, taking the pan from the heat and skimming it.

Smetana is the Russian word for 'sour cream' and when used in a rich sauce it often gives its name to the dish.

Smørrebrød is the Danish name for an array of many different open sandwiches, made with eggs, smoked fish, cheese, pâté and cold meats; they are called smörgåsbord in Sweden. Correctly, the ones containing fish are eaten first, then the meat sandwiches, followed by the vegetables, like a meal in miniature.

Socle means base in French and is the name given to a mound of rice or other edible food that forms a platform on a serving dish.

Sorrel is a tart, dark green-leaved vegetable that is occasionally avilable in the spring in specialty markets; Arugla is a good substitute.

Soubise refers to a garnish or flavoring of puréed or finely sliced onions, usually mixed with rice, seasonings, butter and cream.

Soufflés are made with stiffly beaten egg whites that are folded into a flavored base mixture. When cooked, a soufflé expands and puffs above the edge of the soufflé dish and should be served immediately. The basic mixture can be sweet or savory. A cold soufflé can be made by molding a gelatin mixture in a soufflé dish with a collar, so that, when set, the high mixture resembles a hot soufflé in appearance.

Soufflé dish is a circular with straight sides so that soufflé mixture can rise straight up. The deeper the dish, the higher the mixture rises as it puffs. The classic soufflé dish is made of white ovenproof porcelain with ribbed sides but dishes also come decorated with flowers or fruit and vegetable patterns.

To souse means to cover food in wine vinegar or wine and spices and cook slowly; the food is cooled in the same liquid. Sousing gives food a pickled flavor.

Soyer, Alexis (1809–1858) was the chef of the Reform Club in London. French born, he was a clever, eccentric and theatrical man who enjoyed inventing cooking equipment and recipes. During the Crimean War he developed a type of military stove that was still in use in the early 1900s. Once, he sold the recipe for a bottled sauce to two men named Crosse and Blackwell. His books include 'The Modern Housewife' and 'Soyer's Shilling Cookery'.

Soy sauce is a liquid made from naturally fermented soybeans and wheat that varies from light to very dark and strong. It is widely used in Chinese and Japanese cooking either for dipping or to combine with other condiments to flavor a dish.

Spatchcock means to split a small bird down the backbone and flatten it for broiling.

Spätzle are a type of German noodle that are poached in water, then fried in butter with seasoning.

Sponge cakes are the lightest of all cakes, based on eggs and sugar, which are beaten until light and fluffy and then combined with a small portion of flour.

Springerle are anise-flavored German Christmas cookies that are pressed into wooden molds or shaped with special wooden rolling pins.

To steam is to cook food by moist heat on a rack in a closed container. The food must not touch the water.

Sterilize means to heat to a temperature high enough to kill any microorganisms. The easiest method of sterilization is boiling, but dry heat is also used sometimes. Sterilization by radiation, in which the foods can be sterilized in their packages, is becoming more popular.

To stew means to cook meat, vegetables, fish or poultry slowly in liquid in a covered pan. There are 5 types of stew: fricassée, ragoût, salmis, blanquette and navarin. See individual names.

Stilton is an English blue-veined cheese that goes well with port. See Blue-veined Cheeses.

Stock is liquid made by simmering meat bones, poultry, vegetables or fish for several hours. It is the base for many classic sauces and soups and is used in stews and to make gravy.

Stroganoff, the name of a 19th century Russian count, usually refers to a beef, veal or game dish made with sour cream.

Strudel is made of a paper thin layer of pastry that is spread with a sweet or savory mixture, then rolled and baked.

Stuffing (dressing or farce) is a mixture of savory ingredients used to fill cavities in fish, poultry, meat or game. Stuffings can include ground meat with breadcrumbs, rice, vegetables, nuts, spices and often eggs, milk or a sauce to bind; they should be highly seasoned.

Suchet is the term used to describe a dish characterized by carrots. The name comes from Louis Suchet, one of Napoleon's most brilliant generals.

Suédoise is usually a sweet fruit purée set with gelatin and then molded. It is served with cream or custard.

Suet is finely ground beef fat without membrane, usually taken from around the kidney.

Sukiyaki is a popular Japanese pan-cooked dish in which all the raw ingredients — beef, mushrooms, noodles, snow peas, cabbage, spinach and bamboo shoots — are prepared in a heavy skillet at the table.

Suprême is all the white meat on the chicken from the breast down to the wing bone. It should be removed in one piece from the bones on each side. Suprême is also the name of a rich sauce with a velouté base. See Sauces.

Suzette refers to orange-flavored crêpes flamed with orange liqueur. Suzette is said to have been the Parisian dancer for whom the dish was created.

Sweat means to cook diced or sliced vegetables very gently in a little melted butter until soft (not brown) in a covered pan; this extracts the most flavor.

Syllabub is a traditional English dessert made by beating cream with wine or fruit juice until thick.

Syrup is a mixture of sugar and water boiled together to a specific temperature. Syrup can also be derived from other sources of sugar such as corn and maple trees. Stock syrup is a mixture of sugar and water that is used for mixing with drinks or with icing to give a glossy appearance.

T

Tacos are small tortillas used in Mexico to make a type of sandwich. See Tortilla.

Tammy strainer is made of very fine double mesh wire. When a sauce is worked through a tammy strainer it emulsifies and becomes smooth and glossy.

Tammy cloth is a rough textured material like coarse flannel used for tammying sauces.

To tammy means to work a sauce through a tammy strainer or tammy cloth. This removes impurities, binds the fat and flour together, and gives the sauce a particularly smooth glossy finish.

Lemon soufflé

T *continued*

Tapioca is a starch that comes from the root of the cassava tree. It is processed in many forms, but the two most widely available, quick-cooking and pearl tapioca, are used for thickening soups and puddings.

Taramasalata is a Greek fish paste made from the smoked roe of carp.

Tarragon is a fragrant herb that complements chicken, fish and egg dishes. It is used to make an aromatic vinegar and to flavor béarnaise sauce, to make decorations under aspic, and often combined with chervil and chives to add to salad.

Tarte is an open pastry shell filled with a variety of sweet or savory mixtures.

Tempura, a Japanese dish, consists of pieces of fish, meat, poultry or vegetables that are dipped in a batter and lightly fried; individual bowls of a soy-flavored sauce are served for dipping.

To tenderize means to break down tough fibers in meat by heating, marinating or beating it with a mallet.

Terrine is a mixture of seasoned meat similar to that used for a pâté but usually of coarser texture.

Terrine molds are made of ovenproof china or earthenware and are usually oval. The lid must fit well and should have a hole for steam to escape and to allow for testing with a skewer.

Thickening agents See Liaisons.

Thyme is a warm, aromatic, pleasant herb that forms part of a bouquet garni. It is used as a flavoring for soups, vegetables, stews, poultry, game and often mixed with marjoram.

Timbale (from the Arab word 'Thabal' meaning drum) is a term used to describe dishes cooked or served in a high pie crust or sponge cake container. The term may also be used to describe different types of metal, china or earthenware pans for cooking.

Tomatoes, to peel: pour boiling water over the tomatoes, let stand 10 seconds, then drain. Or, spear them through the core with a fork and hold over a gas flame for 15–20 seconds, turning until the skin chars slightly all over and peels away easily.

Tomato fondue, is a concentrated mixture of tomatoes that have been cooked in butter or oil until thick. It is often seasoned with onion and garlic and is used to flavor or garnish eggs, meat, poultry and fish dishes.

Tortillas are thin, flat Mexican pancakes made with masa harina (corn flour). See Masa Harina.

Tournedos are steaks cut from the beef fillet. They can be as thick as 2 inches and should be completely trimmed of fat; they are tied with string so they keep their shape during cooking.

Tourtière, often called a tourte, is a round deep double crust pie that is usually filled with a savory rather than a sweet mixture. Tourtière also refers to the traditional round earthenware mold in which a tourte should be cooked.

Trifle, an English dessert, is a combination of cream, custard, fruit and cake, often flavored with sherry and served in a large glass bowl.

Trout, how to bone. See page 130

Tube is the metal cone-shaped tip that is fitted into a pastry bag and used for piping. The shape of the tip governs the design. See To Pipe.

Truffles are coal black fungi, sometimes as large as apples, that grow underground attached to the roots of stunted oak trees. Their aroma and flavor adds richness to sauces and pâtés, but the limited supply make them very expensive. The best truffles come from the Perigord region of France. They are sold here in small cans, either whole or in pieces. White truffles, with a slightly peppery flavor, are found in Piedmont, Italy.

To truss means to secure the legs and wings of poultry or game with string or skewers to give the birds a good shape and make carving easier.

Turkey, how to stuff and carve. See page 132.

Turmetic is the spice made from the dried root of a tropical plant closely related to the ginger family. It gives a gold color and distinctive flavor to curry and is used in pickles and relishes.

UV

Ugli fruit is a very thick-skinned type of grapefruit that is eaten fresh.

Vacherin is a meringue and nut mixture that is usually baked in two or more pieces, then sandwiched or filled with whipped cream and fruit.

Vanilla bean is a long pod-like bean from the vanilla plant – small white crystals on the bean indicate freshness. The flavor of vanilla is particularly good in custards, creams and ice creams. The seeds inside the beans hold most of the flavor, so the bean should be split and the tiny black seeds scraped out. Rinse in warm water and dry to use several times. Vanilla extract is made by pulverizing the bean and combining it with an alcohol solution.

Vanilla sugar is made by leaving a vanilla bean in a jar of sugar for several days. The result can be used instead of vanilla extract and plain sugar.

Vatel, François (1631–1671) was one of the earliest of the great French chefs who has passed into history because he stabbed himself to death at a royal banquet after confusing orders.

Velouté is one of the basic French sauces made with a butter and flour roux, and stock; it is enriched with an egg yolk and cream liaison. Velouté is also the name of a soup made with stock and finished in the same way as the sauce.

Véronique usually refers to a dish containing green grapes, but Potage Véronique is a tomato-based soup.

Vert pré ('green meadow') usually means a green garnish – maître d'hôtel butter, watercress or parsley.

Villeroy (or Villeroi) refers to a rich velouté sauce with finely chopped pieces of ham, tongue or mushrooms.

Vinaigrette dressing is an oil and vinegar dressing that can be flavored with herbs. The same dressing without herbs is also called French dressing.

Vichy is a term that is used to describe a dish characterized by carrots. The French health spa, Vichy, is well-known for its mineral water and for its carrots that are said to be good for the liver.

Vol-au-vent is a round case of puff pastry filled with small pieces of cooked meat, poultry, or shellfish in a thick sauce. See Puff Pastry.

WXYZ

Water bath (bain marie) is a method of cooking delicate mixtures by setting the dish in a roasting pan of water in the oven. To keep sauces warm in a bain marie, a saucepan is placed in a larger pan of hot water (a water bath), giving the same result as a double boiler.

Wensleydale is a white English Cheddar-type cheese with a tangy taste.

Whisk means to beat fast with a circular motion so that a mixture is made lighter by incorporating air. This can be done with an electric mixer, a rotary beater or a balloon whisk.

Wok is the all-purpose Chinese pan designed for stir-frying and also used for steaming, stewing, boiling and deep fat frying. It looks like a large stainless steel salad bowl with two handles and usually has a lid; home size woks measure about 14 inches in diameter.

Xérès is the ancient name for Jerez in Spain, the home of sherry. It is used for dishes containing sherry.

Yeast is a living plant that needs warmth and moisture to grow. It is the raising agent used for breads and some cakes. Yeast comes in dried and compressed form and is usually dissolved in luke-warm liquid before being added to the other ingredients.

Yorkshire pudding is the traditional British accompaniment to roast beef. It is made from a batter of eggs, milk, flour and beef drippings that is put into a baking dish or muffin tins and cooked in a very hot oven until puffed (like popovers) and golden.

Zabaglione is a rich Italian wine custard made from egg yolks, sugar and Marsala that is beaten over heat until thick, then served warm in stemmed glasses or as an accompanying sauce. The French version is called sabayon.

Zakouski is the Russian word for hors d'œuvre – a collection of hot and cold canapés that can include pickled mushrooms, radishes in sour cream, salted and pickled herring and stuffed peppers. The most famous zakouska is blini with caviar.

Zest is the rind of a lemon or orange that is removed without any of the underlying pith, which can be very bitter.

Zuppa Inglese is an Italian dessert that literally means 'English soup'. It is made with ladyfingers, candied fruits and almonds layered in a bowl with chocolate-flavored whipped cream, and often Marsala. It is said that the dish originated when British tourists started visiting Italy and asking for the English dessert, trifle. See Trifle.

TROUT
how to bone

Trout can be boned before or after cooking.

To bone a raw trout: snip off the fins with scissors and 'vandyke' the tail by cutting it into a 'V'. Cut off the head with a sharp knife and slit down the back, keeping the knife on top of and touching the backbone; open up the fish until it lies flat on the board. Insert the knife under the backbone at the head end and cut the bone away from the flesh, working towards the tail with short strokes of the knife; discard backbone.

To bone a cooked trout: carefully remove and discard the skin (this is easiest when the trout is warm), then insert a knife along the back and gently detach the flesh from the bone. Snip the backbone at the head – this is usually left on cooked trout – and tail with scissors and pull out the bone sideways, starting at the tail.

Above: slit down back of raw trout and open up fish flat. Below: remove skin of cooked trout; detach flesh from backbone before pulling out

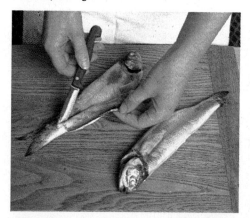

Trout à la Genevoise

TURKEY, to stuff

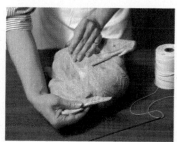

Above: first stuff body cavity of the bird through the vent end (be sure stuffing is cool). Then (below): draw thighs close to the body and tie string around knuckle joints and pope's nose

Above: to stuff neck end, fill breast cavity; fold skin over stuffing; tuck under wing tips. Then (below): sew up neck end of bird to keep stuffing in place or fasten securely with a skewer

TURKEY, to carve

Set bird on a carving board or platter with breast towards you. Insert fork into carcass between leg and breast, then slice skin between leg and carcass; bend leg out. Carve breast in slanting slices, parallel to rib cage, starting at wing end and working towards the pope's nose. Include some of the stuffing with each slice. Cut drumstick from thigh and on a large turkey cut thin slices of dark meat, parallel to the bone, from both drumstick and thigh. If turkey is small, simply cut legs in half at the joint. When one side of bird is carved, turn it around and carve the other side

Roast turkey

MEASURING & MEASUREMENTS

The recipe quantities in the Course are measured in standard level teaspoons, tablespoons and cups and their equivalents are shown below. Any liquid pints and quarts also refer to U.S. standard measures.

When measuring dry ingredients, fill the cup or spoon to overflowing without packing down and level the top with a knife. All the dry ingredients, including flour, should be measured before sifting, although sifting may be called for later in the instructions.

Butter and margarine usually come in measured sticks (1 stick equals $\frac{1}{2}$ cup) and other bulk fats can be measured by displacement. For $\frac{1}{3}$ cup fat, fill the measuring cup $\frac{2}{3}$ full of water. Add fat until the water reaches the 1 cup mark. Drain the cup of water and the fat remaining equals $\frac{1}{3}$ cup.

For liquids, fill the measure to the brim, or to the calibration line.

Often quantities of seasonings cannot be stated exactly, for ingredients vary in the amount they require. The instructions 'add to taste' are literal, for it is impossible to achieve just the right balance of flavors in many dishes without tasting them.

Liquid measure	Volume equivalent
3 teaspoons	1 tablespoon
2 tablespoons	1 fluid oz
4 tablespoons	$\frac{1}{4}$ cup
16 tablespoons	1 cup or 8 fluid oz
2 cups	1 pint
2 pints	1 quart
4 quarts	1 gallon

OVEN TEMPERATURES

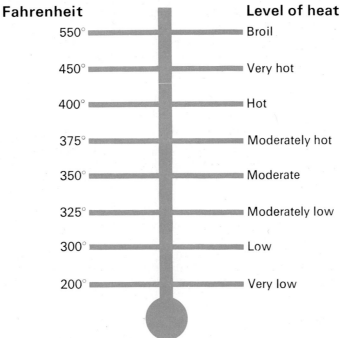

Fahrenheit		Level of heat
550°		Broil
450°		Very hot
400°		Hot
375°		Moderately hot
350°		Moderate
325°		Moderately low
300°		Low
200°		Very low

OVEN TEMPERATURES AND SHELF POSITIONS

Throughout the Cooking Course, oven temperatures are stated in degrees Fahrenheit and in generally agreed levels of heat such as 'high' and 'moderate'. The equivalents are shown on the table above.

However, exact temperature varies in different parts of an oven and the thermostat reading refers to the heat in the middle. As the oven temperature at top and bottom can vary as much as 25°F from this setting, the positioning of shelves is very important. In general, heat rises, so the hottest part of the oven is at the top, but consult the manufacturer's handbook about your individual model.

Pans and dishes of food should be placed parallel with burners or elements to avoid scorched edges.

When baking cakes, there must be room for the heat to circulate in the oven around baking sheets and cake pans; otherwise the underside of the cakes will burn. If baking more than one cake in an oven that has back burners or elements, arrange the cakes side by side. If the oven has side burners, arrange cakes back and front.

Oven thermostats are often inaccurate and are unreliable at extremely high or low temperatures. If you do a great deal of baking or question the accuracy of your oven, use a separate oven thermometer as a check on the thermostat.

NOTES

Notes

Notes